In the Hot Seat with Hel

Helio means Sun.

The skeptics have a favorite lampoon. "You astrologers," they say, "act as if the Earth sits in the center of the solar system." And the conclusion they draw? "Since that's not true, astrology is bunk."

Even Love, that great irrational institution of cooperation in intimacy, fashions a more sophisticated logic than that. This book calls the skeptics' bluff. What will they do with a work the very title of which is *The Sun at the Center*?

Still, though love defies reason, it's natural. We can tell ourselves that the Sun is at the center of the solar system, but the natural thing is to talk about its rising and setting. You may feel the "earth move under your feet," but you see the Sun move across the sky.

Even astrologers bicker about which is the true astrology, heliocentric or geocentric. Finally here is a book that transcends the fray and deals with heliocentric exactly for what it is, a *new and different system of discovery*.

Are you completely satisfied with your present system? If not—and who is?—this book deserves your attention. Learn that there is no need to abandon your geocentric astrology. *The Sun at the Center* is a call to integration, a new way to look at the *big* picture.

Unreasonable mystique and pompous hype have veiled heliocentric values for too long. Yes, there is a new jargon here, and you do have to start looking inside from the outside instead of self-centeredly outside from the inside. But the reward is great: expansion of spirit. Here is a one volume how-to manual for dropping a spiritual suit of asbestos over your chilly, earth-bound soul.

Have you ever caught yourself scoffing at the "beach rotisserie"—that devoted group of sun-baskers tanning their bodies? Sure, there's a reason they call it tanning. Ask any cow. But do you also wonder how close these folks might be to absorbing the solar flares of spiritual transformation? With *The Sun at the Center* put *your spirit* on the beach. Grow before you wither!

Bring this new Apollo-power into your lives.

About the Author

Philip Sedgwick began his study of astrology in 1969. He started astrological counseling in 1975, becoming a full time professional in 1980. He has lectured internationally and has conducted classes and seminars in many major conferences and conventions. His areas of expertise include metaphysics and parapsychology.

Co-founder and President of Delta Dynamics—an Astrological Consulting and Research Company, Philip has used astrology with business clients ranging from sole proprietors to Fortune 500 corporations. He is currently working with the entertainment industry as well as with programs to increase commercial aviation safety.

Together with some astrological giants, he pioneered the realm of Galactic Astrology, which includes Galactic effects such as black holes, quasars, the Galactic center and Halley's Comet. He is exploring research correlating planetary phenomena with solar disturbances.

To Write to the Author

We cannot guarantee that every letter written to the author will be answered, but all will be forwarded. Both the author and the publisher appreciate hearing from readers, learning of your enjoyment and benefit from this book. Llewellyn also publishes a bi-monthly news magazine with news and reviews of practical esoteric studies and articles helpful to the student, and some readers' questions and comments to the author may be answered through this magazine's columns if permission to do so is included in the original letter. The author sometimes participates in seminars and workshops, and dates and places are announced in *The Llewellyn New Times*. To write to the author, or to ask a question, write to:

Philip Sedgwick
c/o THE LLEWELLYN NEW TIMES
P.O. Box 64383-738, St. Paul, MN 55164-0383, U.S.A.

Please enclose a self-addressed, stamped envelope for reply, or $1.00 to cover costs.

Llewellyn's Modern Astrology Library

The Sun at the Center

A Primer on Heliocentric Astrology

by Philip Sedgwick

1990
Llewellyn Publications, Inc.
St. Paul, Minnesota 55164-0383, U.S.A.

FIRST EDITION

International Standard Book Number: 0-87542-738-3
Library of Congress Catalog Number: 90-62430

Library of Congress-in-Publication Data:
  Sedgwick, Philip,
    The sun at the center : a primer on heliocentric astrology / by Philip Sedgwick.
      p. cm. — (Llewellyn modern astrology library)
    Includes bibliographical references.
    ISBN 0-87542-738-3
    1. Heliocentric astrology. I. Title. II. Series.
  BF1717.3.S43   1990   90-62430
  133.5'3—dc20   CIP

Cover Design: Terry Buske

90 91 92 93   10 9 8 7 6 5 4 3 2

Llewellyn Publications
A division of Llewellyn Worldwide, Ltd.
P.O. Box 64383, St. Paul, MN 55164-0383

The Llewellyn Modern Astrology Library

Books for the *Leading Edge* of practical and applied astrology as we move toward the culmination of the 20th century.

This is not speculative astrology, nor astrology so esoteric as to have little practical application in meeting the needs of people in these critical times. Yet, these books go far beyond the meaning of "practicality" as seen prior to the 1980s. Our needs are spiritual as well as mundane, planetary as well as particular, evolutionary as well as progressive. Astrology grows with the times, and our times make heavy demands upon Intelligence and Wisdom.

The authors are all professional astrologers drawing from their own practice and knowledge of historical persons and events, demonstrating proof of their conclusions with the horoscopes of real people in real situations.

Modern Astrology relates the individual person in the Universe in which he or she lives, not as a passive victim of alien forces, but as an active participant in an environment expanded to the breadth *and* *depth* of the Cosmos. We are not alone, and our responsibilities are infinite.

The horoscope is both a measure and a guide to personal movement—seeing every act undertaken, every decision made, every event, as *time dynamic*, with effects that move through the many dimensions of space and levels of consciousness in fulfillment of Will and Purpose. Every act becomes an act of Will, for we extend our awareness to consequences reaching to the ends of time and space.

This is astrology supremely important to this unique period in human history, when Pluto transits through Scorpio, and Neptune through Capricorn. The books in this series are intended to provide insight into the critical needs and the critical decisions that must be made.

These books, too, are "active agents," bringing to the reader knowledge which will liberate the higher forces inside each person to the end that we may fulfill that for which we were intended.

—Carl Llewellyn Weschcke

Other books by the author:

The Astrology of Transcendence
    Seek-it Publications
The Astrology of Deep Space
    Seek-it Publications

Contributor to:

Llewellyn's New Worlds Astrology Series
    Ed. Joan McEvers
    Spiritual, Metaphysical & New Trends in Modern Astrology

Llewellyn's Sun Sign Book
    1991, 1989, 1988, 1986

Acknowledgments

Whenever one undertakes a massive project such as the writing of a major book, tremendous amounts of support, receptivity and encouragement are required to see the thing through. This manuscript was initially written in 1983, the ideas for it having percolated some time before that. Now, almost 1991, it sees the light of publication. At various points thorugh the writing and "fixing" of this work, frustration took its toll.

My thanks go to Tom Bridges of Llewellyn for recognizing the potential and value of this work. When he approached me at the July, 1989 United Astrologers Congress in New Orleans I was still feeling disenchanted about this book. Despite his enthusiasm I considered not going through the steps necessary to rekindle the solar flames of the passion I had once felt. It turns out Tom came in at just the right time, as things often go.

Upon returning from the UAC I had a series of conversations with my friend Patti Peregrine, a writer in her own right. Patti began a relentless campaign of encouragement and ultimately gave this book a thorough editing herself. Her understanding of writing, her love of words and her belief in my efforts made all the difference. With deep appreciation and thanks for her loving support I acknowledge the energy.

Thanks to Michael Erlewine and his crew at Matrix Software for customizing the heliocnetric chart form that appears for the first time anywhere in this book. Erlewine's early work in heliocentric set an open stage for many of us.

And finally, on the subject of pioneers, I would like to thank the late Neil Michelsen, programmer and publisher of the fine heliocentric ephemeris which eased my work in this system and will now ease yours. Neil's support of and interest in my works over the years were merely a reflection of his generous contributions to the entire field of astrology.

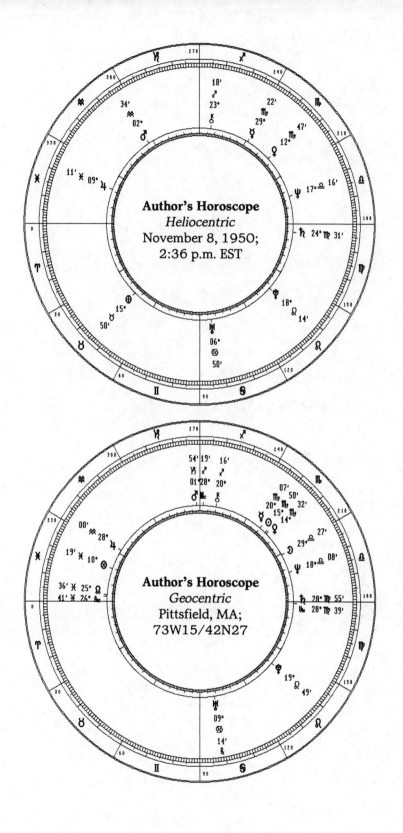

Table of Contents

Introduction

Philip Sedgwick's *The Sun at the Center* is a passionate work about one of the babies in astrology's cradle of techniques, heliocentric. How this subject, through this book, outgrew its diapers for me bears telling.

Sedgwick writes of the growing pains associated with adopting any new system of knowledge. My first reading of this work was accompanied by mental fatigue. Could I ever hope to wrestle heliocentric concepts into my geocentric worldview? But my consternation must have been a spiritual form of sleep; I am at rest with the concepts now.

The scene was the 1990 American Federation of Astrologers Convention in Orlando, Florida. I had packed the final galleys of this book in my suitcase, thinking a new location, away from the "factory," would infuse a final vision into the work.

Call me psychic. But the riddle is that the book, in substance, did not change (beyond the usual blazons of red ink and fussy editorial remarks).

It was July 4, Independence Day, and after a busy morning of workshops and author recruitment I retired with the others for an afternoon of whatever-you-may. But the thought of queueing up for half a day to get into Universal Studios raised that old retreat impulse, and I took the afternoon to myself. I wanted to regroup for the three non-stop-people days ahead.

Hardly a half hour later I came across these lines from this book (page 52):

> The aphelion of Earth in the normally perceived cool sign of Capricorn suggests a principle of a converse nature. It takes place each year between July 2 and July 4. The Earth's aphelion indicates a point of retreat in which one must contemplate potential and restore energy for redirection in a quality manner of kinetic release later and not now. . . . It is recommended that the aphelion of Earth be treated as a point of physical solitude and spiritual healing of the physical body. Refuge must be taken before reintegration back into the collective.

July 4th? Wait a minute. Retreat? This was one of those times you could hardly believe what you were reading *when* you were reading it. Sedgwick's words modeled my preconceived notions *exactly*.

That's when the book was born for me, during the aphelion of Earth, our planet's furthest reach from the Sun, its own mode of retreat. Surprising images of creaton filled my mind. A womb, I thought, was aphelion for the human-to-be, the strange proximity with creative force that only distance unveils.

I've talked to Philip Sedgwick many times over the phone, but meeting him in person is what brought his passion and conviction home to me. And what is soul but passion and conviction? Heliocentric, in Philip's hands, becomes a soul elixer.

When you get to the part of this book where Philip discusses paradigm shifts, reflect how often a "simple" change of perspective has transmuted your worries into wisdom. Before astronomers developed telescopes, *light* was a sacred substance not to be inquired into. Acting as if sources of light ourselves, we literally could not be illuminated. Now we understand reflection and our give and take with an outside source of light.

That's heliocentric astrology. Familiar archetypes, but a different angle. In fact, *new* angles, such as Mercury opposite Venus.

The experience I had with this book during Earth's aphelion was intensely human, and so I think similar experiences await you.

—Tom Bridges

Onward and Upward

Actually this part of a book should be called a foreword. However, because this astrological treatise discusses a reasonably new realm of astrology for which the guidelines and rules are yet a bit unclear, I believe that the foreword can have an unusual title. The use of "Onward and Upward" implies the expansion of mind which embracing heliocentric thought requires.

The major portion of this manuscript was written in November of 1983 in Massapequa Park, New York. At that time Pluto transited my natal Moon in Libra, part of the feminine support system of life. The book lay dormant for some time and became a literary frustration. Publishers threw up their hands: "Who would be interested in such a thing?" "Is it viable?" "I don't agree with your premise." All are ways of publishers saying "No thanks!"

While rewriting a portion of the book, updating information, editing and improving my style, Pluto crossed over my natal Venus for the last of its passes—again a part of the feminine support system.

Personally, I have always felt this book to be feminine in nature. It pleases me that the feminine element is now recognized and that the potency of what was conceived in 1980 and written five years ago now enters its creative power—a publication puberty of sorts.

This work is intended to expand your horizons. You do not have to agree with all of my conclusions. I certainly do not expect you to use all of them. In fact I would be concerned if you did. These ideas are part of a new sense of identity. Such a new identity must flex, stretch and reach out to find its effective parameters of life. Consider this effort in heliocentric astrology to be psychic aerobics, inducing an awareness of a part of your psyche previously latent but now gaining strength.

To your creativity and fertility of thought . . .

Philip Sedgwick
Burbank, California
September 21, 1989

"All right—now who's going to tell the Pope?"

Chapter One

A New Model

The use of heliocentric astrology represents a new, progressive and exciting model of astrological application. Gone are the days of rising signs, retrogrades and controversies over house system superiorities. The traditional model of astrology, geocentric or Earth centered astrology, stems back into the deep roots of astrology when the astronomers and astrologers were one and the same. Our predecessors worked with the optimum instruments and theories of their time when conducting astronomical observations and performing calculations. Despite their efforts, the tools available often did not perform the job in an accurate manner. Inaccuracies were often perpetrated due to strong egos in eccentric personalities, fear of punishment and/or religious banishment as well as political ramifications. Unfortunately, modern astrology is still experiencing the residual effects of all of these situations.

Documented geocentric astrology goes back to the days of Claudius Ptolemy, a Greco-Roman scholar living in the second century in Alexandria, Egypt. Ptolemy proposed in his famous treatise, *The Almagest*, that the Earth was the middle of the heavens—exactly what one sees on any clear night.

Ironically, another astronomer from Alexandria and one of Ptolemy's forerunners, Aristarchus of Samos (310-230 B.C.) was the first to develop a heliocentric solar system which included all things visible.

The proposed heliocentric model initiated by Aristarchus was influenced by the work of Heraclides of Pontus. Heraclides (388-

315 or 310 B.C.) offered two discoveries which supported a heliocentric theory. First, he noted the daily rotation of the Earth about its axis. Second, he stated that the "inferior" planets, Mercury and Venus, revolve in space about the Sun at the center.[1]

Upon Heraclides' death Aristarchus proposed heliocentric views with the theories which he advanced as a mathematician. Nicolaus Copernicus, many years later, quoted Aristarchus from *The Placita,* eliminating all doubt as to the origin of the model. A student of Aristarchus, Archimedes (of "Eureka!" fame), first bore witness to the heliocentric theories and abstractions of Aristarchus. Archimedes wrote,

> His hypotheses are that the fixed stars and the sun remain unmoved, that the earth revolves about the sun in the circumference of a circle, the sun lying in the middle of the orbit . . .[2]

Plutarch, a Greek astronomer, later mentions the work of Aristarchus in *De facie in orbe luna* by stating,

> Only do not, my good fellow, enter an action against me for impiety in the style of Cleanthes, who thought it was the duty of the Greeks to indict Aristarchus of Samos on the charge of impiety for putting in motion the Hearth of the Universe, this being the effect of his attempt to save the phenomena by supposing the heaven to remain at rest and the earth to remain at revolve in an oblique circle, while it rotates, at the same time, about its own axis.[3]

Selucus of Seleucia lived about a century after Aristarchus and is said to have confirmed the heliocentric theory to be true. However, a contemporary of Seleuceus, Hipparchus, renounced the heliocentric theories and biased thinking in favor of the geocentric model. Hipparchus, a man established as a great authority of thought, sealed the fate of the heliocentric theory as if in a hermetic vacuum for centuries to come.[4]

Nicolaus Copernicus (1473-1543) was next to propose a heliocentric model of the solar system. This view was not at all popular in his day. The preface in the 1543 publication of Copernicus' *De Revolutionibus,* written by Osiander, a Lutheran minister, stated that the

---

[1] Heath, Sir Thomas, *Aristarchus of Samos,* p. 254-255.

[2] Heath, Sir Thomas, *Op Cit.,* p. 302.

[3] *Ibid,* p. 304.

[3] *Ibid,* p. 308.

heliocentric perception came from mathematical abstractions convenient only for the purpose of calculations. Danish astronomer, Tycho Brahe (1546-1601), despite his astronomical and observational abilities, did not agree with the suggestions of Copernicus, primarily because he failed to recognize the Earth as a planet in motion. Galileo Galilei (1564-1642), an Italian contemporary of Johannes Kepler, adopted the Copernican heliocentric theory sometime in the 1590s. The Catholic Church, in pure inquisitional fashion, opposed this theory and forced Galileo to renounce the Copernican concept of a Sun-centered solar system. The church issued a decree in 1616 proclaiming the Copernican doctrine as "false and absurd." The Catholic Church later attempted to pardon Galileo from any wrong doing in promulgating the theories of Copernicus. This proposed absolution took place in 1979! However, in 1988 the Catholic hierarchy noted that absolving Galileo implied the fallibility of the Pope and rescinded the pardon. Thus, Galileo still stands as a heretic. And now one can only wonder what fate exists for Catholics supporting heliocentric concepts.

Johannes Kepler (1571-1630) was an early convert to the heliocentric system, defending it amongst his colleagues. Kepler is credited with substantiating the validity of a Sun based solar system. He avoided the religious and political rejections experienced by other heliocentric proponents primarily by living in a Protestant country. A comforting sidelight in Kepler's life was an active involvement in the occult. His mystical tendencies presumably inspired him to compose his *Harmony of the Worlds*, a musical score representing the singing of the planets.

Sir Isaac Newton's formulas for gravitational constants finally confirmed the heliocentric theories. Now with only minor pockets of dogmatic resistance, the heliocentric model of the solar system stands as accepted.

Perhaps it is human nature to resist converting astrology from the standard geocentric system to the unfamiliar heliocentric mode, considering all of the past social rejection associated with proposing a heliocentric point of view. Changes frequently are not easy and at best remain uncomfortable in transition. Making major systemic alterations to astrological methodologies which work exceptionally well may appear insane. It appears, however, that the seeds of heliocentric astrology quietly germinate in the collective consciousness of all astrologers right now.

This work is not intended to arrogantly state that a total conversion to the precepts of heliocentric astrology must occur. It is understood that many may not choose to pursue the realm of this relatively new astrological technique. Astrologers know that geocentric astrology retains the same validity it held when passed down through the preceding generations. If an astrologer is comfortable and proficient with geocentric astrology, whether tropical or sidereal, then that system of astrology continues to serve purposes of facilitation for many. An astrologer seeking something more or a new dimension of astrology may well wish to pursue the precepts of heliocentric astrology established in this primer.

It is submitted that the mechanisms of astrology must change to coincide with the apparent burst of consciousness and humanitarianism which is due to manifest with the influx of the touted Age of Aquarius. Heliocentric astrology may be the vehicle to transport astrologers to exactly the place they need to be in this new time of human history. Many changes in behavior patterns originating within the consciousness of individuals must preset the complete evolution into the New Age.

One of the more important transitions requires that individuals free themselves from the bondage of egos and develop the unadulterated confidence of their souls. This transition receives perfect definition from the transition of geocentric astrology into heliocentric astrological practice. The time for heliocentric astrology is ripe and fertile.

Many astrologers today purport that in geocentric astrology the Sun sign is not so much a matter of who or what an individual is as what he or she is becoming. The individual is seen as astrologically developing the personality ego/soul considerations of the Sun in the natal map. What would happen if the individual in a horoscope totally manifested the Sun within the contextual configurations of the nativity? Simple, the individual would then ideally relate to the heliocentric chart. This process evolves out of an alignment with and a centering upon the attributes of the natal Sun, totally synthesizing those qualities and being of the dynamic will implied by the natal Sun. The individual is now ready to use the Sun as the plane of reference of being and to examine the solar system of residence in a new light, the light of the Sun.

The existing ephemerides of heliocentric astrology should be mentioned so that the reader has a resource from which to obtain appropriate references for this new dimension of research. Two planetary catalogs now exist. First, is *The Astro-Graphics Heliocentric Ephemeris 1981-1990* (Astro-Graphics Services, Inc., Box 28, Orleans, Massachusetts 02653, 1981). A more complete reference is *The American Heliocentric Ephemeris of the 20th Century*, compiled by Neil F. Michelsen (published by Astro Computing Services, P.O. Box 16430, San Diego, California 92116, 1982). The latter of these references not only encompasses more time, but also includes heliocentric nodes, perihelia points (closest point of approach to the Sun), aphelia (farthest point from the Sun) and planetary aspects. (See Appendix C for a sample page and Robert Hand's introduction, printed courtesy of ACS Publications.)

Shifting to a heliocentric horoscope requires that an individual give up a good deal of tightly tied personality points, namely the ego. Astrologers shifting to the heliocentric method of astrological interpretation must likewise give up a series of items of intimate familiarity. First, the houses disappear, along with the midheaven and rising sign. A quadrant emphasis replaces the houses, based upon the Vernal Equinox (0° Aries). Secondly, retrogrades are relinquished. The solar observation of *true motion* of the planets replaces the Earth based *apparent motion*. The Earth and its Moon become virtually indistinguishable within the zodiac. This merger represents an integraton of the Earth and its satellite, the Moon. Lastly, the Sun disappears—or so it seems. This is not true either; the Sun merely becomes the point of reference (view).

The sacrifices of the shift to heliocentric astrology are uncomfortable indeed, much like giving up the typical ego reactions employed for entire sequences of lifetimes. The subsequent enlightenment and purity of being to be reclaimed make it all worthwhile. Each of the astrological considerations lost is replaced by a new premise, perhaps of true proportions. Truly, no loss exists.

The movement to heliocentric astrology creates additional space in which the individual or event of consummation obtains more operating room. This diminishes the probability of the individual tripping in the very process of motion. The mundane influences of life begin to evaporate just because there is no room for the influences to occupy. This can create great difficulty for individuals seeing no benefit in a life without inherent difficulties. Life becomes simpler and it remains imperative that the new space created be filled with issues and evolution outside the individual. This dynamic defines the nature of pursuing life from within to without. Life without resistance evolves. The essence of the August, 1987 Harmonic Convergence blends awareness and action.

Heliocentric horoscopes initially appear to be suspended in space with very little to stand upon, which of course is not true. In fact the entire mass of the Sun may now be used as a basis. The Sun contains 99.8% of all the physical matter in the solar system! This creates a large, energized platform for the baseline of one's existence. More pressure and push results within the heliocentric chart. This pressure is self-generated and self-contained, arising from the agreement of the soul to truly evolve. The transition to heliocentric astrology symbolically represents a greater commitment on the part of the soul to utilize its incarnation upon the planet Earth with maximum application.

The first experience of a heliocentric map may be one of, "So what do I do with it now?!?" The reader is encouraged to recall the first view ever held of a geocentric nativity. Remember the perplexity of trying to understand all of the astrological dynamics that everybody else except you knew so well? Remember the overwhelming sensation of being mentally overloaded? Remember the sense of never being able to learn it all? Welcome to round two of astrological perceptual disorders.

The disorder of first heliocentric experiences result from insufficient background information. Even some basic theory would dispel much of the discomfort. The initial reaction to the heliocentric chart is much like having the ego defense mechanisms and facades in life stripped away. Everyone understands you at the soul level. This is frightening. This is capable of producing paranoia, fear and over-reaction to rejection. Then an interesting phenomenon results. Those people do not seem to care about your personality. They recognize you at the soul level and view the greatness contained by the soul housed by the organism known as a human body. Relief results and the negative reactive emotions melt in the heat of the solar mass. Heliocentric astrology is like always running on solar power!

New aspects of the self emerge based upon parts of the soul never considered and perceptions which require that an individual be removed from physical situations to clearly perceive them. These new considerations result from contingencies offered in heliocentric astrology which do not appear in geocentric systems. Shifts in astrological priorities yield shifts in consciousness describing the essence of the individual. Once one lets go of the astrological premises relevant only in geocentric astrology one encounters the new phenomena: heliocentric planetary nodes, occultations (essentially eclipses) of all planets, aphelion (farthest planetary point from the Sun in orbital revolution) and perihelion (closest solar contact point within the orbital geometry).

Astrologers will also experience relief from individuals not knowing accurate times of birth. Time is a much less critical consideration since no angles or rapid lunar placements are calculated. The greatest error in a heliocentric horoscope with an inaccurate birth time will occur for the planet Mercury.

New aspect patterns arise (for instance, Mercury opposed Venus). This offers new insight into traditional methods. Consider the Mercury/Venus opposition: a clear individual recognition of one's needs through direct communication. The need to communicate is dramatically exposed heliocentrically where in geocentric astrology it would never be noted. It is true that some other geocentric aspect may have suggested this need, but not with the direct perspective of the heliocentric point of view.

There will be growing pains in heliocentric astrology. It is to the advantage of the heliocentrically inquisitive astrologer to notice the areas of discomfort. Later on in the study of heliocentric astrology, correlate these initial discomforts to the resultant awareness. Chances are that reduction of ego and development of soul occur in the process.

It is recommended that all astrologers, especially those working on a professional level, either calculate a heliocentric horoscope or have one generated by a computer service for themselves.

Professional astrologers may be perceived by others (including peers) as either arrogant or extremely self-centered. This seems to be a natural occupational characteristic. It appears that to be able to work with others in such a concise and facilitating manner as astrology provides requires the confidence of a well developed soul. Notice that no where in the last sentence did the word ego appear. A heliocentric map stands to facilitate each astrologer in dealing with the power and responsibility which exists in the realm of astrology. It is a journey of the inner cosmos of the soul.

The concepts of heliocentric astrology require that the astrologer first give up a series of notions. These are:

Relinquished Precepts
a. retrograde planets
b. angles and houses
c. Moon signs
d. fictitious model of the solar system
e. loss of relative (apparent) bias

Obtained Concepts
a. true motion of planets
b. quadrant system referenced to 0° Aries
c. integration of Earth and Moon
d. solar basis of activities and views
e. accurate (true) model of the solar system
f. gain of objectivity
g. heliocentric planetary emphasis
h. perihelia interpretation
i. aphelia interpretation
j. new aspect possibilities

The motion from geocentric astrology to heliocentric astrology contains within it all of the makings of a paradigm shift. A paradigm shift, a term coined by Thomas Kuhn, suggests that some accepted examples of actual scientific practice—examples which include law, theory, application and instrumentation together—provide models from which spring particular coherent traditions of scientific research.[5] Kuhn suggests further that such a shift in scientific consciousness merely opens the doors for redefinition of an existing grouping. Such a paradigm shift took place initially when Aristarchus of Samos proposed the heliocentric model of the solar system. Copernicus created the same type of scientific scandal and subsequent furvor with his postulate of heliocentricism during the Middle Ages. It remains essential to bear in mind that a paradigm shift does not establish a context of falsehood for the preceding model; the shift merely notes the incompleteness of the old model and the perimeter at which the outdated system fails to function. Heliocentric astrology now creates a paradigm shift with respect to geocentric astrology.

Such shifts are not met with collective ease of adjustment. Plutarch suggested, in his quote of Aristarchus, that he did not seek

---

[5] Kuhn, Thomas S., *The Structure of Scientific Revolutions*, p. 10.

rejection or persecution as a result of his support of the heliocentric thinking. It has been noted that in the Middle Ages great duress and hardship was endured by those bold enough to think contrary to tradition.

Even Copernicus was aware of the problems of establishing the leading edge of a new movement in thought and consciousness. In *De Revolutionibus* he noted that the astronomical traditions he received from his ancestors had created a monster. The 16th century astronomers realized that the astronomical paradigm in existence failed with respect to traditional problems of application. This awareness established the psychological dynamic which preset the Copernican rejection of the proposals of the Ptolemaic paradigm.

Kuhn points out that if the Greek system of science in the third century had not been so dogmatic and deductive, that heliocentric astronomy may have prevailed in thought eighteen centuries previous to its accepted manifestation.[6] Kuhn further notes that at the time of Aristarchus no perceived need existed for the use of the heliocentric model and no reason existed for taking the mathematician seriously.[7] The Ptolemaic paradigm resulted, received acclaim and subsequently broke down centuries after Aristarchus walked the planet.

What good is a new system of any dimension of science or thought if it only conjures up a series of speculations to establish or disestablish? What good is a system which only creates confusion and induces a crisis to respond to the new awareness? Quite simply, the time and space for major change in consciousness exists.

Kuhn again fulfills our rhetorical needs as he summarizes both Copernicus and Einstein, both leaders in respective paradigms:

> Copernicus complained that in his day astronomers were so inconsistent in these (astronomical) investigations that they cannot even explain or observe the constant length of the seasonal year. 'With them, it is as though an artist were to gather the hands, feet, head and other members for his images from diverse models, each part excellently drawn, but not related to a single body, and since they in no way match each other, the result would be monster rather than man.' Einstein wrote only, 'It was as if the ground had been pulled out from under one, with no firm foundation to be seen anywhere upon which one could have built.'[8]

---

[6] Kuhn, Thomas S., *Op Cit.*, p. 69.

[7] *Ibid*, pg. 75.

[8] Kuhn, Thomas S., *Op Cit.*, p. 83.

Given the general acceptance of Earth as a fixed position, that which cannot be moved, a good deal of predictable resistance to the theories and suppositions of Aristarchus and his students and Copernicus and his proponent came from the mere violation, semantically, of the system in which they believed. Faith in the Divine Order had been interrupted and, as Einstein suggested, such a removal of the ground defies all perceptions of abstract, deductive and conceptual belief. What is left?

What is left is the need to create a new model and system of belief without dogmatic attachment. Astrology, with its strong scientific parallels, must now work with an accurate point of view of the solar system to survive and evolve within the paradigm shifts of modern day sciences. The antiquated must be discarded as we observe the lack of applicaton of the used systems of astrology. As the interpretations fail to sustain the needs of clients and as delineations fall short of creating the necessary insight to accommodate personal and spiritual change, the format of applied astrology must also submit to a paradigm shift.

The paradigm shift in astrology is as inevitable as the paradigm shifts in every other sphere of consciousness or thought. The need for newness must be met, embraced and supported. New perceptions of astrological parameters are in order. Purpose must be kept in mind and consciousness. An astrological revolution has begun and is in progress. It will continue until the consensus aligns with the principle. It is not intended to be a maverick or disruptive revolution. It may be that the need for change is not yet perceived; however, that perception is near, very near. The transition from geocentric astrology to heliocentric astrology is the next natural revolution of the wheel of perceived space.

Chapter Two

Sunscreen

An amazing level of astrological neutrality begins with the heliocentric horoscope. In the standard version of geocentric astrology, one flaunts, acts, models and flashes the qualities of the Sun sign. Suddenly, in heliocentric astrology, the Sun is the center of reference and is presumably integrated into fullness of being, actualization or "having one's gig together."

It is offered for consideration that one is not the Sun sign, but one is becoming the Sun sign. Modern astrologers claim this thought form as new and part of the new age astrological humanism. However, Xenophanes of Colophon (570-478 B.C.) noted many centuries before the popularization of Sun signs that the Sun "is useful with reference to the coming into being and the ordering of the earth and of living things in it . . . "[1] Each individual upon the planet strives to cultivate his or her basic solar identity or ego under the ambient conditions of the environment. Yet the current mechanisms of astrology, society and astrologers strive to hold down an individual well along the path to self-illumination. Realize that it may appear that the individual is exploiting the basic dynamics of the Sun sign. But then, how will the individual come to know the extremes of cold and hot that can be generated by the amount of natal Sunshine utilized? The extremes must be understood and the virtues of extremes must be fully explored or integration into a closed system will never occur. The ego transfers into true solar confidence when the process of solar identity is complete.

---

[1] Heath, Sir Thomas, *Aristarchus of Samos*, p. 56.

This reality shows up frequently when astrologers tell their clients how not to be their Sun sign. It is like telling a Taurus not to be materialistic. How else will the Taurean learn what is truly of value? Or telling a Libra not to relate with others. How can a Libra be expected to define the self without interaction? In this line of typical astrological absurdities, try telling a Scorpio not to engage in sexual endeavors. The Scorpionic nature may then revert to patterns of celibacy and sexual denial. Then the individual may proclaim the transformation of the sexual libido. Not so! The individual merely repressed the innate creative forces into oblivion in the interest of being good, or more tragically may lose touch with his or her own internal power.

Each individual living life through the geocentric horoscope strives to develop the qualities inherent in the Sun sign, thereby completing the process of becoming. As this concludes, a natural gravitation to the heliocentric horoscope draws the individual into a unique level of consciousness.

This new level recognizes that through an inherent uniqueness one may realize that all beings are created (not born) equal. Each being is a soul manifested in a physical body struggling to reclaim the essence of the soul and to live out the warmth of the heart center chakra. The process of so(u)lar development is not as easy as it would appear and creates considerable tension for the individual in transition.

One strives in solar consciousness to define individuality and uniqueness. Comparisons and contrasts begin to take place, further increasing the frustration, especially when some comparisons elevate the ego and others ruthlessly tear the ego apart. The heart center offers a solution. Project from the heart's memory and project a quality of love throughout your essence. It sounds simple but the procedure remains difficult to implement spontaneously. Significant alterations in one's solar output must occur first.

The ego is like a Sun in varying degrees of emanation and manifestation from day to day, often from minute to minute. Sometimes the ego over-projects and extends solar flares outward into one's environment in which all persons, places and things subject to the ego feel the effects. Bear in mind that each individual has a series of subjected persons, places and things and that congestion of personal space creates much overlap. Everyone is subject to everyone else. This is the point when the solar matrices become confused and the egos begin to one-up everyone else's projections.

As the ego over projects, those subject to it back off to create distance from the discomfort of the intense ego projection. The projector may interpret that the vibrations radiated were not intense enough to complete the transaction. The vibrations are then increased in total intensity, inducing the subjects to retreat further. This double-binding mechanism continues until the projector observes what is truly happening with those subject to the projections. The projector turns down the personality emanations, allowing the receiving subject to return to a more comfortable level of subjectivity.

The reduction of intensity may develop another double-bind as the projecting individual realizes the pattern of projection. Should concern develop for de-intensifying the vibrations transmitted, many times a withdrawal of the energies results. This allows the projector to appear cool, aloof and impersonal. Ego attachments will be made by the recipients in this circumstance.

The thrust of the transmission dilemma allows one to run the range of basic solar identity and to understand at a soul level the distinction between ego and confidence. Then a new level of memory begins; a mode of operation follows and the individual develops uniqueness, sameness, involvement and space—all at once! Now the heliocentric horoscope can be explored to cultivate the new dimensions of the individual.

The new memory of the soul allows an unconscious recall of understandings and information once accessed without the conscious need to hold the data in conscious memory. Confidence in one's knowing ability derives its basis from this procedure. The solar based Egyptians established the phrase, "to learn by heart" in typification of the soul memory procedure.

The implementation of the heliocentric horoscope assumes that the individual under investigation stands upon a well founded sense of self. It is a soul-knowing vibration which allows for the effective and comfortable transmission of love to others in the environment (or those subject to the sphere of influence). The stronger the soul urge becomes, the more gravitational effect the individual exerts in the environment. Often this is referred to one's "influence." Unfortunately, influence can be connoted through an energy of ego rather than the emanation of the soul. The natural and brilliant confidence demonstrated by the heliocentric individual refers strongly to a sense of direction and purpose for effort, energy and vibratory transmismission. One begins to live through an energy of loving understanding and comprehends the polarity which often exists with the transception of such vibrations. The past effect synchronizes to the present and the soul recognizes its ongoing changeability and lack of fixation at any point in space and time. Fear is replaced by interest and rejection is overpowered by a sense of acceptance on the soul level.

The heliocentrically based person functions from a mode of knowing and a conducting purpose. Their geocentric counterparts may or may not sense this purpose. Regardless, the geocentrically bound individuals struggle for meaning, validation, confidence and spend most of their time soliciting strokes to become acceptable at a very primal level.

A valid question which may arise at this time is "Alright, fine, I understand about people; now I want to know about events and mundane heliocentric charts." The basic essence of heliocentric astrology penetrates the mundane event dimension as well. Heliocentric horoscopes can be erected for relationships, disasters, business transactions, weddings or the birth of a pet. No limits exist. The key resides in the subtle essence of each of the nativities. The underlying purpose, in a Universal sense, understates the heliocentric horoscope. More subtle issues may prevail in the delineation of the heliocentric chart. Witness for example, the November, 1982 conjunction of Saturn and Pluto through geocentric observations. We could expect this to bring the physical manifestations to the planet Earth related to the archetypes of the alignment. The December 24, 1982 heliocentric conjunction stands to alter awareness with distinctions realized and applied as a result of the preceding event. It will be much more subtle in nature. The consciousness of an event or non-human (how geocentrically arrogant) map still stems from the basic solar consciousness. From the event, the collective derives personalized influence and reaction designed to cultivate a stronger sense of soul-self. The push of the heliocentric chart seeks to generate a heart vibration to collectively permeate the planet. Further, the memory of the heliocentric event map intends to be learned by heart.

The use of the heliocentric horoscope puts the person right on the hot seat of the Sun! It is expected that productive use of unique heliocentric considerations will occur. Pressure and intensity exist in the heliocentric interpretations that escape the geocentric parallel of space and time. It is a new way of viewing the persuasions of the other planets, a new point of view originating from the core of a vitalized self.

Chapter Three

Planetary Persuasions

The planets in heliocentric astrology, as with any system of astrological mapping, form the content of the horoscope. The planets occupy and stimulate influences to which an individual reacts. Individuals' choice of reaction to the impelling astrological forces develops their attitude toward occurrences which appear to be external circumstances. None of this changes in heliocentric astrology.

Many new considerations revolving about the planets do arise in the heliocentric system. Configurations such as heliocentric nodes of the planets, perihelion and aphelion must now be integrated. New aspect configurations arise. New concern for planetary orbital dynamics (which could be ignored before) must now surface into the conscious awareness of the heliocentric astrologer. Such awareness allows the planets to create a new series of dimensions of astrological influence or persuasion. Appendix A lists relevant data for the planets.

Heliocentric aspect configurations require a new level of flexibility within astrological thought. First and foremost comes the notation that the aspects are, of course, solar based. Each aspect represents the angular relationship between the planets involved as measured to the solar center. Realize again that the Earth based aspect may not, although it may, appear as the same aspect alignment.

Planetary conjunctions as viewed from the Sun bear strong implications. A planetary cycle develops from the conjunction of any two planets, establishing a trend in solar consciousness evolution. These conjunctions occur as a function of the mean orbital periods of the planets involved. The periodicity of the conjunction occurs at an interval longer than the period of the faster planet and shorter than the period of the slower planet. Appendix B provides lists of the conjunction cycles of the planets. These calculations come from the mean orbital period for each planet (which result from the mean angular velocity in the planetary orbit about the Sun). Accurate conjunction dates cannot be derived from this table due to the mean motion. The actual duration between conjunctions, however, remains very close to the intervals listed.

These conjunctions obtain added influence if the planets align in latitude as well as zodiacal longitude. These effects are known as occultations and are essentially an eclipse of a planet or star by another object. Occultations occur at varying intervals depending upon the total alignment of the solar system. All planetary eclipses maintain significant astrological meanings and, like lunar eclipses, occur when the planet resides in proximity to the nodal axis of the planet. The occultations result from the geometric perfection of the orbits of the planets involved with respect to the relative positions of the planets' orbital planes (inclination to one another), all with respect to the Sun.

The basic astrological supposition arising from an occulation states that the planets are in a position to contribute to each other. Should the occultation form with respect to the planetary north node, the occultation bears a conscious awareness of the energies. Individuals in these circumstances cognitively respond to the energies and become more focused upon their conscious intention to utilize the planet in the heliocentric format. An occultation residing in a planet's south node's neighborhood stimulates subconscious reactions to the manifestation of the planetary energies. Persons involved in such a conjunction tend to initiate the active dynamics of the planets involved without thought preceding action.

Such occultations are not that common. Mercury, for instance, last made an occultation with the Earth on November 13, 1986. This was preceded by Mercury/Earth occultations on November 7, 1960 (the day before the presidential election in the United States); May 5, 1957; November 14, 1953 and November 10, 1973. Occultations between these two terrestrials will occur on November 6, 1993 and November 15, 1999.

The occultation of the Earth by Venus is even more infrequent. Venus strode precisely between the Sun and the Earth in 1761 and 1769, in the heartbeat of political revolution, then in 1874 and 1882 within the pulse of industrial and labor revolution. The next scheduled Venusian eclipse of the Earth is due on June 8, 2004. Not one of these occultations manifests within the time frame of the 20th Century.

The planetary nodal axis figures prominently in the occulations of any two planets. Heliocentric planetary nodes, unlike their geocentric planetary counterparts, are always in opposition (geocentric *lunar* nodes are always in opposition). The nodes do not precess but move forward in motion at a rate of one degree in approximately one hundred years.

Heliocentric Planetary North Node Placements

	1-1-1901	1-1-1950	1-1-2000
☿	17 ♉ 10	17 ♉ 44	18 ♉ 20
♀	15 ♊ 48	16 ♊ 14	16 ♊ 40
♂	18 ♉ 48	19 ♉ 10	19 ♉ 33
♃	9 ♋ 27	9 ♋ 58	10 ♋ 29
♄	22 ♋ 49	23 ♋ 15	23 ♋ 38
♅	13 ♊ 34	13 ♊ 46	13 ♊ 59
♆	10 ♌ 43	11 ♌ 17	11 ♌ 47
♇	18 ♋ 52	19 ♋ 41	20 ♋ 17

Previous statistical studies in heliocentric astrology point to the nodal placements as highly sensitized points focusing the dynamic reflex action of the planet. A *karma/dharma* relationship exists within the planetary nodes. The south node obtains the *karmic* alignment (cause) and the north node relates to the current *dharma* in life (effect). It is imperative to stress that neither node suggests anything of good or bad with respect to the planet it represents. The nodal implications remain inert with regard to good and evil, right and wrong and other judgments. The reaction to the nodes of the planets must be immunized by the individual occupying the horoscope for the nodal reflexes to occur in a natural evolutionary process.

The planetary north node suggests an approach to the present life circumstances which enables the individual to glean the most from subsequent actions in reflexive motion. The individual must clearly pursue the north node to avoid repetition of past patterns and to ensure that the natal energy of the associated planet be fulfilled. The north node of a planet resembles a beam of laser light, straight and direct, which the individual may use to fine-tune directional guidance.

The south node of a planet represents causations of the planetary energy of past time frames. It is important to isolate the south planetary node from the types of innuendos often tied to the lunar south node in geocentric astrology. First, the *karmic* implication of a planetary south node does not have to maintain any relevance to past incarnations lived upon the Earth. Such suggestions should be discouraged. Secondly, past in terms of time may be confusing. Past means five seconds ago, not necessarily some great life time in Atlantis or Egypt. Past is measured in the soul's evolution whether in an incarnation or not. The considerations of time's relationship to space advanced by Albert Einstein and contemporaries suggest that the past is now. Regardless, with respect to the heliocentric south node of any planet, past connotes something done or completed. Experiences still in progress align the individual with the *dharma* of the north planetary node.

The points in a planet's orbit known as aphelion and perihelion enter upon the heliocentric platform as potent points to ponder. Astronomically, perihelion is the closest point that an object in orbit with the Sun makes to the star in the orbital path. Aphelion is a point reached by the object in solar orbit retreating as far from the Sun as it will within the opposite reaches of the solar system.

The letters q and Q refer to the distance a planet occupies from the Sun at perihelion and aphelion, respectively. A lower case letter q is used for the closest point of approach. The upper case Q represents the longest distance of aphelion.

The direction of planetary travel (from perihelion to aphelion or from aphelion to perihelion) is astrologically significant. The best analogy for this effect comes from the lunation cycle. The aphelion point resembles the new Moon, a point of maximum darkness. The planet moves towards perihelion, receiving more intensity of solar light as it approaches culmination, which is akin to the full Moon. The planet then recedes towards aphelion to duplicate the cycle.

Heliocentric Planetary Perihelion (q)/Aphelion (Q) Positions*
1-1-1901　　　　1-1-1950　　　　1-1-2000

	q	Q	q	Q	q	Q
☿	15 ♊ 52	15 ♐ 52	17 ♊ 25	17 ♐ 25	17 ♊ 26	17 ♐ 26
♀	10 ♌ 23	10 ♒ 23	11 ♌ 02	11 ♒ 02	11 ♌ 11	11 ♒ 11
⊕	11 ♋ 14	11 ♑ 14	12 ♋ 05	12 ♑ 05	12 ♋ 56	12 ♑ 56
♂	4 ♓ 18	4 ♍ 18	5 ♓ 10	5 ♍ 10	6 ♓ 05	6 ♍ 05
♃	12 ♈ 16	12 ♎ 16	13 ♈ 40	13 ♎ 40	15 ♈ 32	15 ♎ 32
♄	1 ♋ 33	1 ♑ 33	0 ♋ 19	0 ♑ 19	29 ♊ 38	29 ♐ 38
♅	26 ♍ 18	26 ♓ 18	21 ♍ 26	21 ♓ 26	20 ♍ 33	20 ♓ 33
♆	13 ♈ 7	13 ♎ 7	3 ♉ 57	3 ♏ 57	7 ♉ 06	7 ♏ 06
♇	13 ♏ 30	13 ♉ 30	13 ♏ 58	13 ♉ 58	14 ♏ 03	14 ♉ 03

The points of aphelion and perihelion result from the non-circular pattern of orbital rotation held by the planets. The planetary spheres' rotation pattern about the Sun resembles a slightly squashed or oblong circle. This orbital trajectory, called an ellipse (see Figure 1), maintains two focal points in its geometry. The Sun presides at one of the foci. The speed of the planet varies with respect to its position in the elliptical orbit. The planet accelerates to maximum speed at perihelion and upon reaching the closest point of solar approach begins to put on the brakes. The slowing of the planet continues until the planet is at aphelion, where the acceleration begins again. Thus, the planet moves fastest and has the greatest distance value at perihelion. The planet will spend less time in the sign of the perihelion than any other sign. Aphelion produces the slowest planetary motion, less distance traveled per unit time. A planet occupies more time in the signs of aphelion.

* You will notice that perihelia positions for each particular planet remain relatively static, varying at most only six degrees of zodiacal longitude—with the glaring exception of Neptune. Due to a radically eccentric orbit and a higher axis of inclination, Neptune's perihelion/aphelion axis varies widely. The following listing, by decade, of Neptune's perihelia points will give you an idea of the change. Neil Michelsen's ephemeris gives you all positions for January 1 of the stated year—1901: 13 Aries 7; 1910: 3 Gemini 36; 1920: 21 Gemini 39; 1930: 25 Taurus 46; 1940: 01 Taurus 48; 1950: 03 Taurus 57; 1960: 27 Aries 02; 1970: 16 Taurus 08; 1980: 00 Gemini 52; 1990: 24 Taurus 55; 2000: 07 Taurus 06. As you can see, the position moves forward and backward. Also see Appendix D on page 209.

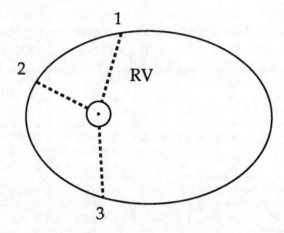

Figure 1. An Elliptical Orbit

A few planetary oddities exist within the dynamics of the perihelion and aphelion. Mercury reaches perihelion in Gemini, a sign with which it is associated. Mercury ends up spending less time in its own sign and races through the dualistic zodiacal window in record time. Saturn, on the other hand, approaches and achieves aphelion in Capricorn, its zodiacal counterpart. Saturn moves most slowly in the vicinity of its characteristic sign. Pluto achieves perihelion in Scorpio. Pluto has its closest solar contact in the sign it presumably rules and spends a minimal amount of time in residence at home.

A planet at its perihelion has an added intensity due to its proximity to the object of reference, the Sun. More light is shed upon the planet at its perihelion and an individual's conscious effort to remain functional, alert and undistracted within the purpose of the planetary energy (defined by the planet's nodal axis) must prevail. Urgency of effort is required to utilize the more rapid motion of the planet and economy of effort must also result to procure optimum results. The time when the planet nears, reaches and departs from its closest point of approach to the Sun describes a time when the individual may understand the pure, unimpeded flow of the planet's energy. The flow may require a redirection of effort implied by the turning of the energy as the planet culminates at perihelion. A mode of involvement prevails with the planet coming up to perihelion and a manner of selective retreat and discrimination sets the theme for the motion in the direction of aphelion.

At aphelion, a planet resides in the coldest place in its orbit (maximum distance from solar light and warmth). A level of detachment develops often considered to be the process of introspection. As the planet retreats into the depths of space constituted by its aphelion, the individual cultivates a sense of detachment and senses an urge to begin to re-integrate towards the collective purpose or illumination. The time surrounding approach to aphelion suggests a time in which deliberate removal from accustomed environment occurs. Conversely, upon aphelion, the need or urge to proceed back into the real world becomes evident. These suggestions do not presume that the directions of the will correspond with the natural flow of the planet. One may commonly feel an overwhelming urge to invalidate the planetary direction and go off on one's own course. Soon circumstance and other self-generated causal forces dictate the need to revert back to the natural path and to follow the planet's dance through space and time. Events surrounding the planetary aphelion may seem to drag out indefinitely due to the time involved in rotating about the distant gravitational pivot in the solar system. Issues, events and circumstance can also contribute to slowing individual action.

These perihelion and aphelion effects may exist natally and result collectively as the transits of the planets approach their respective turning points in space. The pivots at aphelion and perihelion may indeed resemble the energy of a stationary period of a planet's retrogradation in geocentric astrology. The planet at either of these points submits to an intensive gravitational attraction or repulsion, which induces a change in direction and perspective. The process of passing by a perihelion or aphelion point is a natural change in the acceleration of the orbital speed resulting in a major reorientation.

The set of polarized squares to aphelion and perihelion also contain a certain sensitivity in the heliocentric realm. These squares appear at the midpoints of aphelion and perihelion and represent the balance of the innate extremes of the planet. Introspection upon these points may allow the individual to gain understanding of the natural fluctuations of effort and action which occur within the nature of any planetary essence.

Moderation appears to be a key factor of the perihelion/aphelion midpoint. The near and far, high and low ranges of any planetary essence can be derived from examining it. An individual may encounter a dilemma in the resolution of these extremes and may seek solutions at the midpoint. The perihelion/aphelion midpoint, also noted as q/Q, generates a working awareness of high and low planetary tides. This awareness obtains a discrimination of viability within modulation. Planetary modulation works by making the high points a slight bit lower and the low points a trifle higher. This effect induces less fluctuation of planetary development, enabling the person to maintain a sense of greater equilibrium in the evolution of any given planet's natural energy. Sometimes the energy may just seem too intense. The solution for de-intensifying experience resides in the q/Q midpoint as a point of remedy.

Heliocentric astrology creates a need to review the planetary considerations held in geocentric astrology. It would be worthwhile to understand the planets' meaning in general as well as consider the points of heliocentric origin specifically applied to each planet.

The first group of planets to be discussed are terrestrial. The term terrestrial suggests resembling the terra or Earth. These planets include Mercury, Venus, Earth and Mars. This collective grouping arises astronomically due to the similar sizes and densities of the planets.

Mercury

Mercury maintains the closest orbit to the Sun. It cruises through the zodiac once every 88 days, rotating very slowly upon its axis. Mercury must travel about the Sun three times for both sides of its surface to be exposed to solar light, establishing a three to two revolution to rotation ratio. Mercury carries with it two excessive motions in the planetary system. Except for the distant Pluto, Mercury bears the greatest ranges in latitude, extending as far as seven degrees north or south of the ecliptic. The second great motion of Mercury results from the rapid movement of the tiny planet about the Sun. Mercury, being the closest planet to the solar center, subsequently becomes the most rapid in solar revolution. Based upon mean orbital motion, Mercury transits four degrees and six minutes daily and is the greatest diurnal longitude factor in heliocentric astrology.

Both the ranges in latitude and the quick zodiacal transits provide the most inner planet with two characteristics which support the mythological association of the fleet-footed messenger, perhaps even more so than in geocentric realms. The motion of Mercury in latitude suggests that more operability can be derived from application of the north and south ranges. The solution to utilizing these fluc-tuations towards polar opposites requires that one not decline to express needs. The tendency, especially as Mercury crosses another planet through parallel or contraparallel, is to naturally express the desired communication but usually non-verbally or through reac-tions to received communications from others. The tendency may be to attempt to have others conduct the communication desired, enabling the naturally disposed transmitter of communication to function as the receiver. Mercury's latitude aspects note that direct communication without disguises of any type paves the way for optimum interaction. Such a mode of conscious, direct communica-tion eliminates many of the rapid up and down fluctuations of com-munication so often seen in relationships.

Covertness often results from indirect communication. It would appear that mental or perhaps psychic communication results from Mercury's latitude in transmitting impressions designed to penetrate the sensitivities of another. The parallel (two planets at the same northern or southern degree of celestial latitude) involving Mercury usually indicates more conscious awareness of any covertness in communication. This parallel effect may induce the individual to be more conscious and overt, basing the interaction on honesty and openness of heart. Conversely, the contraparallel (two planets at the same degree of celestial latitude on opposite sides of the plane of reference) with Mercury requires that the individual consciously explore subconscious mental processes with honesty. Such con-scious exploration prevents deceit and trickery.

Mercury achieves its rapid whirl through all of the signs of the zodiac in just below three months. Daily distance references of Mer-cury observe mean movement of four degrees, six minutes. Diurnal Mercurial motions under the mean amount indicate slow a Mercury and above the mean value constitute a fast Mercury.

The relationship of fast and slow Mercury placements within horoscopes of individuals does not present an obvious or direct meaning. In true Mercurial fashion, the message is encoded. One might anticipate that a fast Mercury indicates fast processing, speak-ing and listening ability and a slow Mercury relates to slow thinkers, speakers and receivers. This, however, is not true.

The base keywords are impulse, a fast Mercury, and delibera-tion, for a slow Mercurial motion. Patience levels also correspond to the relative Mercury. Greater levels of patience are intrinsic in the slower Mercurial placements. Less tolerance of time and space develop with the faster motions of the planet.

Slow Mercury individuals bear the qualities of methodical and intuitive learners. These individuals often take time to contemplate or digest a new statement, thought or concept before acting. These individuals, regardless of the speed of internal mental processing, generally think before speaking. The slow Mercury placement sets up the capacity for good listening abilities and an empathetic ear. These individuals are concerned about the level of completion in any given communication interaction. They often ask if the question is understood or that answers beclarified.

The slow Mercury person bears a great level of innate patience within communication. This makes the individual more naturally disposed for research or in-depth investigation. A naturally inquisitive mind resides in the brain and the individual demonstrates less gullibility and naivete.

Fast Mercury individuals are inclined to be more assumptive than their slow Mercury peers. Conclusions develop faster in this Mercury type kind and may require more revision depending upon the individual's objectivity. The fast Mercury tends to be more precognitive and less objective overall. As the fast Mercury listens, conclusions and new conclusions constantly are being formed based on the influx of information. These individuals want to get on with it, at times acting impulsively on thoughts. Less talk and more action sets the stage of the faster Mercurial dynamics.

Naturally predisposed subjectivity provides the fast Mercury individual with a reject filter regarding communication. Highly discriminating by nature, a fast Mercury is inclined to offer critical reviews of information. Some difficulties in relationships may occur either due to assumptiveness or speaking without thinking. The fast Mercury bears less mental compassion than the slower Mercurial type.

Strong analogies to support both Mercury types may be derived by comparing the formats computers use to process information. One computer system updates information constantly, maintaining an overall average or mean of information. This correlates to the fast Mercury. Other computers process more slowly, with accumulative updates and greater accuracy. This computer system relates well to the slower Mercurial motion. The qualities of slow and fast Mercuries are not hermetically sealed motions, isolated from the total context of the horoscope. Should a fast Mercury, for instance, be squared by natal Saturn, the person would be utilizing the rapid essence of the planet with more pragmatism and conservatism similar to the dynamics of the slower Mercury. A slow Mercury conjunct Jupiter or Uranus may explode communicatively, defying the natural qualities of deliberate contemplation which are inherent in the slow placement and thus resembling a fast Mercury.

The three to two ratio established by the rotation of Mercury upon its axis with respect to solar orbit creates another interesting activity of the fast planet's nature. Mercury, traditionally corresponds to (rules) the signs Gemini and Virgo. Both signs are mutable and tie in with the strong mental considerations offered by the ruling planet. This ratio, it should be noted, relates to the manner in which both sides of the Mercury's topography have an opportunity to face the Sun. This process actually takes 263.91 days (based upon mean motion). Three years of Mercury bring a totally balanced solar view of the planetary surface.

This ratio of light psychodynamically refers to the cognitive ability of the human mind. The essence of Mercury in the heliocentric format is to communicate the expanded will of the individual as a foundation. The nature of the three to two ratio states that for any given thought or stream of consciousness three considerations of the issue will bring all views to light. It would be very tidy if that was the end of the thought process but that's usually not the case.

The heliocentric Mercury understands more clearly that one side of its nature is not exposed to the light, despite the fact that total objectivity is sought within the ratio. The duration of the Mercury day indicates that the extent and range of the darkness contains a mental grey scale in which some shadow areas reside even within the cognitive process. These shadows take the form of logic loops, where one gets stuck in thought. It is the dilemma of knowing and not being able to escape. This loop creates the ability to deceive the self.

The last of these considerations is the most complex. It is quite conceivable that the individual is aware of the mental games inside the head. The mental manipulations induce a system of justification to explain behavior patterns. One may realize that the mental magic in the mind weaves a spell of self-deceit but indulges in it anyway. Mercury, the master of trickery, works best on home territory— within the mind of the thinker.

The individual now functioning from the mode of self-obscuration sets out to convince the world that his or her behavior patterns are quite logical, all things considered. These things considered do not include those issues which remain without solar attention on the dark, cold side of the planet. The coolness of the dark side of Mercury correlates to the cool, calm and collected syndrome purported to be ideal behavior in a society afraid to feel. The end result becomes interaction between individuals in which the souls shake their etheric heads in dismay as the egos frantically try to be honest and open. The ironic truth is that the individuals know all the while that these processes of unclear communication exist and predominate the typical interactions occurring upon the planet Earth.

Heliocentric astrology ultimately brings the point of undeniable Mercurial understanding to the attention of the individual. This point of understanding establishes a view through which the individual can see the previous uses of Mercury to be correct, knowing that the mental dilemmas they created have established the possibility for the knowledge now in the mind. This point of conscious perception marks the moment when the contemplator will never again be able to return to the mode of self-deceit. Nor will the individual ever again use a system of justifications or logic manipulations to explain away life. Something in the mind shifts and the individual realizes the futility of pretentious communication.

The occultation of an inferior planet (one in an orbit closer to the Sun) to a superior planet is astrologically significant. The term eclipse is not an exacting description as the size of Mercury is too small to obscure the Earth's light from the Sun. The configuration is such that Mercury crosses the solar disk (as it is said astronomically). This alignment takes place when Mercury, the Sun and Earth form a straight line in both zodiacal longitude and latitude.

The Earth's occultation of Mercury represents a formative time in the communication cycle. It is imperative at these times to prohibit semantical discrepancies from impeding the exchange of information. These alignments represent times when mundane activities must support the overall purpose and thrust of Mercury's nature. This need is seen due to the nearness of conjunction to the Mercurial nodes. The occultation of Mercury/Earth represents a critical time in which new levels of spontaneity can be developed out of an actual breakdown of communication. A form of interactive regeneration requires that new formats of communication, negotiation and exchange take place. The occultation re-defines the need to share in two-way communication. Both sides must transmit and receive. The barriers attributed to not speaking the same language, connotations and denotations must all be eliminated. These conjunctions offer strong persuasive ability to conduct such upgrades in exchange. Direct communication with the source is also dictated. Rumor, hearsay and third party information must be excluded from the process of information gathering, interpretation and action. To say exactly what was meant resolves conflict and subsequent misunderstandings. The words used need to be as universal as possible to minimize distortion. Finally, ears must remain receptive and open.

Mercury's North Node rested at 18 Taurus 06 as of January 1, 1980, placing the South Mercurial Node at 18 Scorpio 06. The nodal theme creates the need to communicate about people, places and things. The communication should be done in a worthwhile way, bearing information of substance and redeeming value, rather than indulging in abusive communications, idle thought running the mental motors. This process requires letting go of any Scorpionic memories, which tend to last forever, and relinquishing the urges to equalize any outstanding intrapersonal debts of any form. This release allows for an instantaneous regeneration of the qualities of a relationship by transforming words and thoughts into communications designed to focus, support and stimulate mutual growth patterns (or any involved in the communication loop). The Taurus North Node states that human or soul resource becomes known as the most valuable commodity on the planet. Its essence is recognized for the intangibility that it insists upon maintaining to avert corruption.

Mercury's perihelion falls in one of the signs that Mercury traditionally rules, Gemini. Minimum time is spent in this sign. Mercury dwells the longest in the sign of Sagittarius, when it is at its slowest point in orbit around the Sun. Mercury's proximity to perihelion speeds up mental, verbal and listening processes. A sense of urgency surrounds the perihelion, which may breed impulsiveness and generate communications which fall short of the mark. Assumptions tend to prevail. Efforts should be made to avoid interrupting the thoughts, dialogues and Mercurial processes of others. It may appear that deceit and false projection predominate the perihelion interval. Actually, the Mercury point of view indicates that the pretense came from the conscious inability to remain focused long enough to complete thoughts, listen in entirety or formulate opinions before speaking. It is possible that later, near aphelion, the misdirection may require revision, sorting and reiteration of communication. Focused attention provides a sound remedy for Mercury at perihelion time of orbit.

Aphelion for Mercury comes in the usually "go-for-it" sign of Sagittarius. The motion of the fleet-footed messenger slows down, allowing a lazy stroll through the Sagittarius sector in the sky. The implication arising reveals that direction in thought form, word form and listening form develops as a result of deliberate contemplation, not the usual flitting about associated with the Mercury mental process. The essence of Sagittarius strives to obtain and produce truth. The pitfall of the truths of Sagittarius occur when truth and dogma become a system of justification for a form of Mercurial activity. This effect extends through all communications, trickery of a deliberate nature and those things known as practical jokes.

The perihelion/aphelion polarity of Mercury will remain in Gemini/Sagittarius, respectively, for quite some time. The perihelion of Mercury precesses through the zodiac very slowly, requiring 225,784 years for one complete passage through the signs. It is interesting to note that this nodal precession assisted Einstein with his calculations of gravitational warping in his model of relativity. With more immediate repercussions, people will continue to process the activities of Mercury and its purpose throughout the polarity of duality and singularity (ranging back and forth between extremes roughly every 44 days).

Venus

Venus exists next on the planetary agenda. The geocentric implications of Venus include a desire to substantiate and obtain needs and desires. That all remains the same with the heliocentric interpretation of the second planet from the Sun.

However, heliocentric supposition regarding Venus relates to more subtle levels of need, want and desire. It also suggests that conscious responsibility for the effects of causal desires presides in the conscience of the seeker. Venus defines a new level of needs created as one fulfills the mundane needs and psychological desires and encounters a void feeling in the pit of the stomach.

The implication of the void felt at such a deep emotional level informs the individual that the priorities once established can no longer be fulfilling at any level. A new level of need must be organized to ensure a feeling of contentment. These new desires stem from soul level needs as opposed to ego level needs. The tendency which occurs in a baser-urged Venus is to identify with the needs to a point when identity loss disappears. For instance, many times a person perceives self-identity upon the basis of material gain and acquisition or through a relationship. Both of these Venusian issues do not compose the integral needs of the individual; those needs remain external to the self and allow for vacancy at the gut level where needs are felt.

The need and value of growth presets the heliocentric Venus. One must invoke a responsible commitment to personal growth to cultivate the essence of Venus. The process of heliocentric need fulfillment begins with a definition of true need. A system of consistent priorities must occur wherein the individual clearly recognizes the relationship of one's needs for importance. The final step requires that the individual set action into motion regarding newly perceived responsibilities to the self. Should the individual determine that no action can or will be taken in the interest of need procurement, then a question of lack of responsibility regarding the quality of need arises. The individual would benefit by reviewing a personal list of need priorities in order to ascertain what action could or should be taken.

A statement of self-orientation, self-worth and self-validation—all heliocentric Venus considerations—arises. The statement requires that the individual explore self-acceptance and self-worth to decide if sense of worth leads to fulfillment of needs. Should an awareness of worth exist, the next step would be to confront the rejection which may result as one strives to have a need fulfilled, especially if another individual becomes involved. This sense of potential rejection may inhibit one's initial assertion or causal force of need manifestation. This promotes the understanding of one's own happiness. No one else can make a person happy. This comes to be known through the heliocentric Venus placement. One accepts the responsibility for internally generating a sense of self-contentment and projects fulfillment which already surrounded the individual. None of this was realized prior to self-actualization.

The Venus process requires that the individual realize the needs of the soul in the interest of ongoing *karmic* evolution. This by no means suggests that all fun and enjoyment must disappear from life. The opposite is quite true, in fact. When the individual tunes into the pure needs of evolution, the needs of the personality, ego and the physical plane begin to develop and are met in a prosperous manner.

Evolving one's soul does not require that a person enter a vow of poverty on the planet Earth. The survival/poverty mechanism often associated with spirituality may only repress one's need to experience involvement in the physical plane in the interest of transcending materialism. A lack of involvement does not necessarily promote transcendence; many times it merely promotes anxiety and fear of confronting the world of matter.

The Venusian nodal forces and the orbital pivots of perihelion and aphelion also make their contributions respective statements to this discussion. The Geminian North Node of Venus promotes objectively relating the need level inherent in the soul. The needs must be extended without assumption that the person or thing to whom the need has been extended must be the commodity to fill the need. This allows for meeting needs in an unencumbered way. The statement defines the need, presents the need and awaits the response to the need. The Venus South Node in Sagittarius lets the individual hear responses knowing that there is more than one path to a personalized Promised Land. Many roads, events and people may occupy the path. To assume rejection on the basis of only one experience becomes ridiculous. Worst case reactions to Venusian needs include a sense of rejection and the cultivation of a belief system which assume that past actions and interactions will continue to occur in the present and the future.

Venus encounters perihelion in the likely sign of Leo. This means that Venus will spend less time in the vibration of Leo, striving to reduce self-indulgence and yet at the same time scrambling to attain emotional completion. The aphelion point of Aquarius in the Venus trek about the Sun allows for the self-sustained and fulfilled individual to share with others, in a non-involved acceptibly aloof manner. The reason that the non-involvement must exist is to free the person from being objectified by others as a source of fulfillment. A natural tendency to attempt to capture the intangible joy and contentment of those self-sustained ones occurs on the part of the unfulfilled majority. The unfulfilled must realize that fulfillment comes from within themselves, not from others. The need-actualized spirit also recognizes the need to be unattached and unpossessed. The individual recognizes that participation without attachment and involvement can and must result. Although the nodal and proximity points of Venus appear to offer a contradiction in development, it is the only way that the innately frail human ego can play the game and not be swept away by the process. Ultimately, what seemed to be a one way path becomes the loving two-way exchange it truly is.

No occultations of Venus to the Earth will manifest in the 20th Century. The theme of previous Venus/Earth orientations would be expected to prevail through the turn of the century. This induces a repetition of previous patterns of morality, allowing the conscience of society to fluctuate widely. These are divergent periods of self-indulgence and lack of indulgences, eras in which lack of indulgence was "moral" and everyone indulged secretly. The hypocrisy and paradoxical standards of the past two centuries stand to be decimated by the upcoming Venus/Earth alignment on June 8, 2004. Complicating these contradictory matters further, Venus exhibits a retrograde rotation, implying greater need for internalization.

The conjunction in the year 2004 must work to offset a round-about or backwards approach to attainment of need. The interval must be marked by an acceptance of individuals as they are and not as one would wish them to be for self-gratification. The Gemini/Sagittarius nodes of Venus will naturally be highly active. Expression again becomes a key point. Clear expression is of the utmost importance. Expression that honestly expresses one's needs will be most accepted, assimilated and responded to. Shallowness of interaction along the axis of need fulfillment will not be tolerated or accepted. The conjunction will mark the beginning of a new era in which people can be truly who they are through the expression of what they need and want. Each person's perception of need can be understood (although not consistent with one's own need), thereby objectifying the human need dynamics. The path to satisfaction, fulfillment and intra-personal evolution can be sought.

Early in 1986, the Russians remodeled the archetype of Venus femininity forever. The Soviets embedded a new consciousness of femininity into Venus which women need do nothing to enjoy other than just be. After the deaths of Christa McAuliffe, and Judy Resnick in the explosion of the *Challenger*, and the commercial aviation death of child ambassador Samantha Smith, the Soviets namesaked three craters on Venus after them. Now inherent in the archetype of femininity are the qualities which these women symbolized.

Samantha Smith was an average young American student concerned about world peace and how it affected her life on planet Earth. She wrote to then Soviet Premier Leonid Brezhnev concerning Soviet and U.S. nuclear weapons policies. This young woman received an invitation to the Kremlin to discuss her thoughts on nuclear arms and disarmament. She symbolized the feminine, non-aggressive method of peace assertion. Diplomacy, territory and protection can exist without threat to others. Women maintain this perception and carry the responsibility to deliver this message in a world inured to violent methods.

Teacher Christa McAuliffe taught her students to push to achieve their goals. This educator truly personified the image of *Challenger*. She rose to the challenge of space, which is mythologically the unknown vastness of the superconscious. McAuliffe represented the urge to seek, to risk and to know. She etched these qualities of the intrepid spirit into the symbology of Venus and thus, into intrinsic femininity forever.

Astronaut Judy Resnick completed the trilogy of the Soviet feminine symbolism. Well educated and clearly intelligent, Judy Resnick also maintained a feminine beauty and grace. Her contribution to this female heritage is that it is a woman's right to be both bright and beautiful.

According to the images created by the Soviet Union, a new, softened imagery of the female model prevailed, whether relating to a male's access to femininity or a woman acquiring her intrinsic power divined by the principles of Venus.

Earth

At a relatively youthful four and a half billion years of age, the planet Earth occupies the third planetary position stepping outward from the Sun. Many perceptual oddities surround the sapphire colored planet which are not readily observable to the inhabitants of the sphere. Astronauts have reported that the Earth is one of the more attractive visual objects in space. Possible subjectivity on the part of the astronauts will be overlooked in the context of their statements. As seen in space the Earth and its satellite, the Moon, seem to maintain relatively comparable sizes. An alien observer might conclude that the Earth and the Moon comprise a double planetary system. This is precisely the situation that we see from Earth when we look at the distant planet Pluto and its newly encountered moon, Charon.

Imagine what it would be like for alien intelligences to send reconnaissance probes to examine our native domain. What would be concluded if the outsiders sent three exploratory probes to Earth and one landed in the Pacific Ocean, one in the Atlantic Ocean and one in the Indian Ocean? Inhabitants of this planet tend to forget that over two-thirds of the planetary surface is covered by water. Our subjective impressions of the planet created the name "Earth." One may speculate about the ultra-high levels of intelligence in a mammal of the sea, the dolphin. Perhaps the dolphins have named the planet in their own tongue and call it *Agua*. The name does indeed fit the coloration seen from space. The dolphins could even have the perception that they rule the planet on the basis of natural habitat constituting environmental superiority, not to mention likely mental superiority. Dolphins are comrade Earthlings!

Perception of both the Earth and Moon come from the feminine archetype. This manifests the dark principle (contrasted to light). It bears the receptive versus the creative; it is passive compared to aggressive. The Earth and Moon both represent the *Yin* of the *Yin* and *Yang*. The negative polarity resides in both polarizing the positive counterpart. The principle of Mother Earth gains additional perspective when considering that perihelion of the Earth occurs as it transits through the sign of Cancer, traditionally considered to be the sign of the maternal nurturing nature.

The Earth maintains added importance in heliocentric astrology because it is the home planet. A Jupiterian would accentuate Jupiter more in the heliocentric horoscope, and for good reason. The Earth is the ground upon which we stand. It provides a foundation, although the foundation of the Earth is ever-changing and shifting, regardless of one's perception of its inner tectonics (turmoil and adjustment). The Earth is an active, volatile planet, complete with shifting weather patterns, volcanic eruptions, seismic activity and extreme tidal forces. It is not exactly the sort of place that reads well in a travel brochure.

The Earth is surrounded by a magnetic covering known as a magnetosphere. The magnetosphere encompasses the Earth in a shape much like the head of a comet. The pattern of magnetic flux is shaped by the solar wind and responds to the polarity of the planet. Subsequently, all of the inhabitants of the planet are enclosed by this sheath of electro-magnetic energy. Since the magnetosphere constantly adjusts, shapes and reshapes to the ambient, inductive energies in space, the topical environment of the planet constantly undergoes revision.

The primary stimulations of the Earth's magnetic blanket come from the solar wind's initial shock wave interacting with the magnetism and the electrically charged particles shed by the Sun. Again, the nature of the vitality/survivability axis arises.

The Earth and all of its inhabitants (including the full spectrum of minerals, animals, plants and humans) respond to the energy received by the source of the solar system, the Sun. Reaction to solar forces determines much of the Earth's environment. Similar inhabitants in the same environment, subject to essentially the same solar interjections, react in highly divergent ways. The disparity in reaction patterns comes from the differences in the time/space relationships that the objects, things or entities have with respect to the planet. This receives astrological definition as the horoscope, regardless of the frame of reference. Uniqueness and individuality of response is definitely permitted upon the Earth. This does require that the entity responding formulate some sense of *solarity* (solar identity) with which to interact on the planet.

A frequently neglected factor in this perspective is that the individual overlooks the result of the response. Like it or not, each reaction solidifies a causal relationship on the plane of existence. Symbolically, the Earth represents the effect that an inhabitant upon the planet gives back to Mother Earth in response to growth obtained from living on the Earth. A *karmic* responsibility is incurred by each inhabitant of Earth.

One must draw from the resources of the Earth to support growth upon all levels. Natural resources contribute to physical growth and supply shelter and basic physical comforts. Air, another natural resource somewhat unique to Earth, flows as another natural commodity. People resources and, to an extent, animal resources, supply mental and psychological growth. Interaction with other beings establishes both emotional and intellectual reactions. Inhabitants and natural resources combine to solidify another form of need, which appears in a much more subtle manner. Spiritual needs are extracted from essence responses. Loving who one is, or being in touch with nature, are examples of the spiritual needs being fulfilled.

Each and every moment in space and time form growth experiences spanning over several need levels. Growth is the product of resourceful integration. Growth occurs whether one believes it or not. Rejecting the process of experiences is extremely detrimental to growth. Experiences must not be judged, deemed good or bad or mentally manipulated. Experience is part of the process of becoming. Experience itself is just fine. To experience is to be.

Each experience in space/time solicits a response. It is necessary to establish that even a non-response is a condition of response. Consider the reasoning behind the legal phraseology used within releases of liability which state "action or non-action." Something in a condition of non-existence is in polar opposition to existence. Action polarizes reaction. Not knowing polarizes knowing.

Response establishes the basis of return to the Earth of that which has been taken from the Earth. The process of reaping leads to sowing, leading to producing the harvest and bounties and so on *ad infinitum*. The regeneration of the resources and commodities of the Earth must continue to be perpetuated indefinitely for vitality to produce survival. This regeneration must take place for people, places and things. Application of one's learning polarizes the lesson. Use of one's growth makes the process of growing resourceful. Without use, abuse results.

The *karmic* responsibility of each inhabitant of the Earth is to give back to the Earth the product of each developing experience. Each experience, again whether recognized as such or not, induces the growth of the soul directly or indirectly, through action or non-action.

Spiritually, no waste or lack of resourcefulness manifest upon this physical planet. Physical and mental resources could be handled better. Something surely can be done about the emotional waste and atrophy which runs wild over the land.

The solution to resourcefulness is for each person to contribute and leave behind his or her mark. Everyone inscribes a personal legacy on the land. Some do this in a more obvious manner than others. Some even insist upon being obvious by omission. The most exploited, wasted and abused resource upon the planet is the life form known as human beings.

Many humans flounder through the experiences of their lives struggling for a basic sense of identity, purpose and meaning. The irony of their plea is that it is all in front of them. One of the indigenous traits of earthbound growth is the propensity to complicate the simple, overlook the obvious and expect the most negative manifestation to result. This natural inclination tends to allow humans to generate conflicting mental patterns.

Many of the human species choose to remain unaware that "thoughts are things and they have wings." This highly quoted metaphysical verbiage suggests that one's applied mentality and emotions are physical manifestations regardless of physical imperceptibility. One of the most referenced spiritual/philosophical texts upon the planet Earth, *The Bible*, also referred to this concept. *The Bible* refers to human responsibility extending to all of the following physical manifestations: thoughts, words and deeds. Most of the world's religious dogmas preach responsibility at these three levels.

When one absorbs responsibility for one's thoughts, words and deeds, growth increases. A person then has more to give, thus deriving more growth, followed by giving more back to the Earth, thus receiving even more. This effective chainreaction produces positive feedback loops which manifest in the form of perpetual motion.

Most people do not seem to use the full extent of their relationship to the Earth while living on Earth as the Earth is revealed in the heliocentric horoscope. These people then go about the condition of living at the survival level. Using this method of living no vitality can occur. These good folks do not usually recognize two-thirds of the power of manifestation contained within the soul. Interestingly, two-thirds of the planet is covered with water and most humans do not recognize that either. Human psychological symbolism suggests that water represents the creative impulse of the psyche. The natural brilliance of the human resides in creativity. So much of the time, most humans do not permit full creativity to blossom. One current theory in human development refers to this as "not owning one's experience." Much more resourcefulness could be cultivated. Most people on the planet could recognize purpose and contribute.

An outside observer of the planet could easily see the interaction of one person on the planet and to others. A person either contributes positively and creatively to the planet and others or goes into modes of non-action, understimulation and fails to use the spiritually stimulated, karmically motivated natural human resources that are self-contained. A lack of use constitutes abuse.

The Earth symbolizes the ground upon which one stands. This symbolism creates a foundation and sense of stability much like the fourth house would in geocentric astrology. In the human mind the stability of the Earth appears to be uncontrolled and insecure. The tectonics of the planet are such that huge subterranean plates slide against one another along lines known as faults. (Faulty things and negativity are recurrent themes upon the Earth.) Sudden shifts in the Earth cause Earthquakes (resulting from accumulations of pressure).

These potential shifts can occur virtually anywhere but some areas continue to remain more precarious than others. This provides the Earth dweller with a certain sense of instabililty. The feeling of instability is designed to free the inhabitant from relying upon external forces, causes and conditions unnecessarily or pretentiously. The theme of Earth based instability is that there are no guarantees that anything physical exists. This tends to be quite discomforting for those living on the planet. The tendency of the physical and psychological ego seems to be to set up guarantees and binding agreements, all of which on a larger scale may be seen as entrapment.

Humans try to guarantee relationships through marriage, children, houses and possessions. Humans try to guarantee jobs through contracts. Humans try to ensure that life will be everlasting on the planet through medicine, life extension programs and other physical remedies. This last example may seem strange to some, especially considering the innate difficulty of living on the planet Earth. Many people would question the benefits of living longer in misery. Presumably, these *homo sapiens* realize at some level of consciousness that the Earth provides one of the most intense environments for cultivating one's spiritual evolution and karmic fulfillment.

The quest for guarantees extends to treaties and a condition of response called fairness. Fairness means that one meets the expectation or qualification of another human. When one does not comply in totality with the expectation of another, unfairness exists. People then try to justify action through reaction. This explains the concept of an "eye for an eye, a tooth for a tooth," a phrase which crudely approximates the principle of *karma*—a Universal Law of Cause and Effect.

The picture from the Earth is only a point of view in space and a very minute point of view at best. What Earthlings fail to realize is that fairness and unfairness result from Universal Conditions of Natural Order in which balance precedes imbalance, stress yields to ease and thus ebb and flow magically manifest.

The consequential consciousness contributes to humans striving to control the physical plane. Natural sequence and order are not completely sensed. Mankind strives for conquest, power and domination. All of these dynamics are manifested through the symbolism of the planet of Earth.

Since the world of matter is surrounded by a magnetosphere, all things on the planet must agree to submit to the magnetic flux prior to entry into the field. Once the agreement is contracted with the Higher Universal Forces, whatever *IT* is, the form on the planet is subject to the influence of the flux and all things which affect the magnetism of the planet, including solar stimulation.

Most individuals sense a magnetic anomaly while on the planet, which is usually resisted and contested. This resistance generates Cosmic Persistence and sets up the human need for perseverance. Ultimately, control must be polarized by submission. The lust for power must receive balance by Universal Reverence so domination can yield to its polarity of absolute surrender. Control of the soul results.

It appears, then, that each human form (or any physical Earth form) brings along a lesson when entering the planet. The incarnation or manifestation upon the planet immediately sets the lesson into motion. One attends a spiritual schooling with strict rules and intense, silent teachers. Independent study is encouraged. Awards are subtle and cryptic. Scholarships often look like curses of eternal damnation. It is a school of paradox which teaches contradiction and double-bind as major lesson themes to reveal the Universal Polarity and the dichotomy of life.

The sooner that a human begins growing or studying within the school and doing homework, such as it is, the sooner awards and growth experiences occur. Through this education the lessons become legacies. The student becomes the teacher and the teacher becomes the student. Knowledge breeds wisdom, which leads to a realization of a lack of knowledge and greater growing/learning potential.

Upon completion of the basic lesson plan agreed upon between the individual and God, the human leaves the planet, making his or her final contribution back to the Earth . . . Ashes to ashes, dust to dust.

Considering the intensity of the emphasis upon the third planet from the Sun, it would seem appropriate to evaluate the zodiacal placements of the Earth. These polarizations will be considered upon the basis of the lesson and the legacy.

Typically, when analyzing configurations of the zodiac, one begins with the sign of Aries. This process will be conducted in this interpretation of the Earth. However, due to the opposition of the Earth and Sun the quest will actually start with the Aries Earth Sign (which is the Libran Sun Sign). The Earth Sign is always opposite the geocentric Sun sign because the heliocentic zodiacal vantage point is on the opposite side.

The Earth Explored:
The Lessons and the Legacies

Aries Earth (Libra Sun):
Lesson—The lesson involved in the Arien Earthling exists in the process of self-actualization. The individual must come to a full sense of self to allow functional relationships with others. These beings are highly interactive and not necessarily with other beings. Interaction at this Earth level may manifest through a direct confrontation or exchange with a person and it may also result with a thing or a principle. The interaction is secondary to the level of validation which they seek. A sense of self-worth independent of others must result for assertiveness to be complete. At some point, the individual will realize that with or without people, places and things the self remains intact. Until this process is understood, the soul continues to establish faulty interactions to create alienation, isolation and per-ceived rejection. This is all done in the interest of self-contained validation.

Legacy—Upon completion of self-realization and a self-contained sense of being free from the need of input from others, relatability becomes a primary dynamic in the individual's life. Interaction begins to provide a mechanism of on-going support for the individual as the person teaches others to recognize that which is self-disguised within their beings. This discipline can be taught by the Aries Earth with incredible compassion for the crisis of self-identity. The individual retains the ability to interact in a non-involved manner, allowing truth and personal integrity to prevail above all else.

Taurus Earth (Scorpio Sun):
Lesson—Many presume that the Earth rules Taurus. Perhaps one would then assume that the Earth in home territory would maintain a certain comfort or reliability in this Sign/Planet relationship. Perhaps that is true and only at the legacy level. These souls drop themselves into a body and begin an immediate struggle to learn absolute (Divine) worth without extorting, exploiting or destroying the value of the high worth item. The physical preoccupies the primal Taurus Earth mind, blinding all objectivity of what truly is important. Priority sys-tems must be established, the truth told and motivations revealed. This all tends to combine the positive aspects of the lessons to lead to

the luxury of the legacy. However, it is critical that the learning process for this Earthly student include doing his or her own homework with no ruses.

Legacy—Once optimized, these Earthlings quickly recognize the worth and value of a person, place or thing. They are challenged by intrinsic worth and seek to polish raw materials to a brilliant lustre. These individuals can become great motivators. This is often achieved through agitation and playing a negative role to produce a positive effect. Negativity is only used as a transformative.

Gemini Earth (Sagittarius Sun):
Lesson—This sign axis must learn to deal with an intellectually intense duality that teaches that the more consideration and objectivity, the greater the focus. These people perceive this postulate to be in direct contradiction to the basic programming of the mind. The blinders must be removed and a willingness to view polar opposition must result. A mental overload exists until the individual recognizes that missed objectives result from the inability to adjust or correct a course once in motion. Long range effects appear in little steps. As a Chinese proverb states, "a journey of a thousand miles begins with the first step." Such is the case for the Gemini Earth. Steps along the way allow for reconsideration, revision and resolutions to be refined without interruption to the natural direction.

Legacy—Once in a mode of receptivity and diversification, the Gemini Earth individual becomes one of the most directed and consistent contemplators on the planet. The lesson taught by these people is that there is no absolute way to get there. Many paths exist between here and there. Correction is taught as a positive attribute and not as an indicator of something thought or done incorrectly.

Cancer Earth (Capricorn Sun):
Lesson—Mother Earth herself reaches the closest point of approach (perihelion) to the Sun in Cancer. The Cancer Earth contains the need to respond to the most direct sunlight and illumination of all the Earth placements. Direct and undisputed contact with the nurturing action is maintained and requires useful, non-interfering incorporation. Domination tendencies must convert into a support mechanism. Those with this Earth must learn about responsibilities

and that each person owns a different sense of responsibility. This realization precludes being disappointed in one's offspring (anyone to whom the Cancer Earth becomes attached) and releases guilt, expectation and irritation. The pursuit of Earth dictates the need to frolic in the Sun. The ability to enjoy and align with nature establishes contact with the base of Earth. This eliminates an inability to appreciate beauty as it exists. This individual must reject cynicism in the soul to enable the heart to open.

Legacy—Cancer Earth people are among the most sensitive and caring upon the planet. They demonstrate this clearly when actualized in being through support and love given freely and without consideration of reaction or rejection. Love is given without expectation and the individual teaches how to love safely and responsibly without interrupting the flow of another person's development.

Leo Earth (Aquarius Sun):

Lesson—The development of the personality in an ego sense is the first portion of this soul's lesson. The ego must then evolve into a unique sense of self-contained individuality which functions without the need to compare the self to others. Confidence is the quality which stimulates the beginning of the work leading directly into the legacy. The lesson, though, is a tough one and contains intense periods of variation in self-esteem. Once the belief in and knowledge of one's own internal strength sets in, these people begin an active campaign leading others into awareness of the selves.

Legacy—The Leonine Earthlings strive to lead others in their realm to realize the need for a self-contained sense of individuality. They teach others how to own one's being and allow creative self-expression to flourish. The Leo Earth people discourage others from cloning or engaging in emulation techniques that establish superficial attachments to the projected qualities of another individual. These people stress uniqueness and strive to promote the confidence of everyone they encounter. This inspirational ability of the Leo Earth may manifest in both direct and indirect means of interaction with others. Personal contact is not necessary for the process to occur.

Virgo Earth (Pisces Sun):

Lesson—Virgo Earthlings appear on the planet to develop an awareness of the principles of integration on a minute level. Overall knowledge of the system seems to exist in these beings. A need for understanding the detailed simplicity of life's process must follow. Discipline becomes a key factor in the schooling of the Virgoan Earth as resistance to commitment and structure is taken for granted. This discipline, once implemented, allows these individuals to set into motion the plans, creative concepts and intuitive insights which flash through the mind. Discipline strives to eliminate the inability often experienced in prioritizing life's endeavors. The organized formats of discipline yield the ability to select an appropriate creative pursuit to manifest.

Legacy—The legacy of the Virgo Earth resides within the ability to adjust to a flowing system of discipline. These individuals are then capable of presenting to others the synthesis of the subtle and the gross, the sacred and the profane and the parts of the wholes.

Libra Earth (Aries Sun):

Lesson—At one level it appears that these people exist solely for the purpose of establishing identity of the self at the soul's core. The lesson adds a deeper aspect to the identity quest. It becomes imperative for these individuals to learn the active dynamic of interfacing with others on the planet. Self-assertion must be conducted in such a way as not to interfere with the will and identities of others.

Legacy—Once polarized, these individuals leave behind the lesson of interaction without compromise. The cultivation of the sense of self is a demonstrated blending with an ability to be and to let others be. Interference and imposition diminishes creating a clear approach in human relationship.

Scorpio Earth (Taurus Sun):

Lesson—The drive to transform need presents the biggest challenge of this Earth/Sun polarity. Attachment and possession must be overcome. Learning how to have and hold, and how the have/hold principle differs from owning/possessing, creates the crisis of reorientation. Scorpio Earth souls must learn to experience their feelings, especially feelings of material resentment, jealousy and emotional bondage. An innate understanding of the natural value of human resources must be learned. This resource of human potential must be understood from the standpoint of using people, not abusing people. Should this lesson about human resource not be learned, the Taurean tendencies only subvert deeper. The subverted tendencies appear through the use of others in a negative manner, creating a master/slave relationship.

Legacy—Once cultivated, these seekers become the masters of manipulating others into positive, creative spaces of existence. An understanding of when to intervene and when to not intervene becomes inherent. These individuals may become compulsive, not being able to see waste of a mind or creative potential. They constantly push, shove and work to apply every available resource. A unique ability to invest in the resources of others also evolves. True levels of abundance and prosperity consciousness can and must be taught.

Sagittarius Earth (Gemini Sun):

Lesson—These Earthlings must learn that focus does not rule out necessary pursuits. They sense that there is a lack of freedom of choice when, in fact, a simple level of mental discrimination strives to present choices. Short range planning must be relinquished to the long range projection. Distraction must yield to disciplined conscious direction. Simplification must be produced to gain distance, direction and result. Yet, the need to remain responsive to the subtleness of Divine Signaling is necessary so that single mindedness and dogma does not result.

Legacy—The Sagittarius Earth spirit strives to leave behind a sense of direction stemming from their abilities to focus. A directed philosophy results from knowing which needs to pursue and which not. Vicarious learning must be encouraged to prevent redundancy of the human consciousness effort. The value of thoughts and knowing is taught to others.

Capricorn Earth (Cancer Sun):

Lesson—The Capricorn Earth strives to generate an autonomous sense of self which can only be derived from a strong sense of support and foundation. This support initially extends from external sources and the individual resists receiving support (based upon a point of view that he or she renders support only). This unilateral perception must be terminated for the person to evolve to the fullest. Understanding the bidirectional nature of support assists these people in growth. The awareness of assumable responsibility, to take and not to take, must be assimilated.

Legacy—With the Cancer side understood and synthesized, the Capricorn Earth provides others with a quiet, parental type of support which encourages assuming total responsibility for the self; no more and no less. Sharing of support encourages cooperative interactions on all levels of the creative/receptive axis.

Aquarius Earth (Leo Sun):

Lesson—Within the natural Leo association to the Sun this axis assumes a stronger natural emphasis. The goal of the actualized ego bears the fulfillment of humanity, a lesson easier stated than learned. Overcoming the guru syndrome requires great attention and perseverance to cause. One must be conscious not to accept unwarranted praise and at the same time remain accepting of praise which is valid. Avoidance of idle flattery and yes-type followers must be included in the growth. Total identity as a unique and persistent individual cultivates some necessary isolationism for the growth process. Courage and commitment of the self requires more effort here than in any other case. One must obtain a strong sense of self that is referenced only to the self. This self referencing frees the ego from superiority/inferiority dynamics.

Legacy—Once actualized, these individuals strive to teach everyone to be who they happen to be and to become that which they strive to be. Courage and commitment are taught hand in hand with respect for the being that one happens to be. The creative process is accentuated, allowing them to exercise a purposeful lead in humanity. A choice must also be taught. That choice is the ability to help humanity from a non-involved point of view or from direct and inclusive involvement. A good example is a hermit who would pray over the dominion of humanity versus the leader who works with a group in the interest of evolution. The difficult choice is individual and must not be transferred to any other entity or oracle.

Pisces Earth (Virgo Sun):

Lesson—To flow in the dimension of experience creates the major crisis of evolvement for these Earthlings. When the Pisces Earth encounters a dynamic of growth, the tendency is to compartmental-ize the awareness in an intellectual or academic manner. This is fine as far as the process is understood. The only drawback to this system comes from the integration of the experience. To understand experi-entially creates a conflict for this sign. Once an experience is assimilated, the tendency becomes to translate the experience in a logical or mnemonic manner. On many levels of experience this is impossible, as no words can formulate a concise enough picture to represent the occurrence. Thus, the individual falls in the position of knowing and not being able to explain. The creative process builds up momentum from such a response, allowing the individual to be manipulated by perplexity into realizing an unrecognized aspect of internal ingenuity. Cognitive dissonance becomes the well known "A-ha!" of under-standing.

Legacy—The Pisces Earth person knows how to translate inexplic-able experiences into a system of reference, provided that when another flows into the same stream of consciousness the event will be understood for what it is. A Taoist teaching method arises, allowing great levels of individual creativity to be tapped without compromis-ing the process of logic, yet not allowing the mental to interfere with the flow of creativity. An extremely delicate balance of co-existence emerges guiding the person experientially and logically through all events in life. This balance utilizes every aspect of involvement in life to ascertain more of the process of growth and evolution.

* * *

Now what about the Moon? One of the more unique perceptions formed within the context of the Earth in heliocentric astrology originates in the new attitude of observation of the binary Earth/ Moon system. Science no longer maintains the view that the Moon is a satellite of the Earth, a captive vehicle subservient to the greater orbit of the larger body. Now the perception creates a pair of planets with a gravitational barycenter producing a nucleus of interaction of bilateral harmony. An element of integration now exists which had been precluded by the geocentric arrogance of lunar containment.

The first step to graphically symbolize the union of the spirits of the Earth and the Moon comes from a new glyph. The proposed glyph is ⊕. This representation allows for the Cancerian identity of the Moon to embrace the Earth with a hugging appearance. This symbolizes the warmth of nurturing and the availability of lunar nurturing while upon the planet Earth. Emotional actualization becomes one of the attributes of the Earth-born incarnation. The symbolic content of the glyph further strives to state that emotional fulfillment and contentment are, in fact, available upon the planet Earth.

Being purposeful contains the contingency in the basis here. When one perceives the self as totally and lovingly whole or in the process of fulfilling a greater purpose in life, self-esteem tends to rise. With that one becomes far more content, thereby asking for and receiving more emotional fulfillment.

Some deprogramming must be conducted to facilitate the acceptance of fulfillment into one's life. Eliminate contradiction with purpose. It is not true that money corrupts or that a relationship of a personal nature is an inhibiting force in the pursuit of purpose. If one continues to inbreed either of these concepts or other similar concepts of contentment disparity, then a denial of contentment is forced which reverts back to geocentric astrology when the Earth and the Moon were separate components striving to be part of the same.

Should one accept the ideal that heliocentric astrology does, in fact, give the blend of the Moon/Earth energies, then acceptance at large of contentment begins. The concept is simple to understand and difficult to experience due to the time in which denial and separation from overt contentment have been purported to be the way of life.

A separation between the Moon and the Earth also implies that the contentment is not attainable. It provides one with the "someday" *modus operandi*. In other words, "someday we'll have money," or "someday I'll be the boss," or "someday I'll be happily married," and "someday this and someday that." These "someday" wish manifestations lack purpose in their intent. They leave the individual wide open for infinite disappointment. The integration of the Moon and Earth "wishes" suggest that half the fun resides in getting there. A good deal of the Christmas anticipation comes from the excitement of looking at beautifully wrapped packages. Some of the best parts of sexual enjoyment come from leading up to and not actual orgasmic release. Accomplishment is often perceived best during the climb up the corporate ladder and not upon reaching the top. The Lunar/Earth theme is to enjoy the process of getting there. This re-enforces the "becoming" theme of the Sun/Earth opposition and adds to the initial incentive of fulfilling purpose. One becomes more open to fulfillment upon developing a sense of being during the process of fulfilling purposes. A positive feedback loop begins to cycle.

The process of Earth/Moon fulfillment notes that once a segment of deprogramming results it becomes necessary to fill the void to prevent replenishment of the void with inconsistent energies. This re-enforces and nurtures the process by validating the self with a higher level of self-acceptance.

Some lunar formation theories state that the Moon once was literally pulled out from the Earth. Regardless of the accuracy of this theory, the analogy maintains a concept of reclamation. The principle of karmic ecology, or recycling products of the Earth, prevails. The integration of the two bodies in space suggests a return to that which is completely whole and united. The Moon and the Earth are *a part of* one, not *apart from* one another.

Nurturing Embraces to the Kid Within: The Earth/Moon Integrated Need Level

Aries Earth/Moon—The nurturing sought by these people asks, somewhat apologetically, for acceptance of the self as is. Acceptance of the self when it is the new, improved version is not sufficient. These people require unconditional love and support for the identity they have right *now*. Once accepted, these individuals become the best givers in the heliocentric zodiac.

Taurus Earth/Moon—This combination needs support for self-worth. The individuals must be supported for what they are, not what they have, or what they can create with their own intrinisic resources. The value of personal attributes are paramount as is the need for support of the individual's ability to manifest positive activity and make life happen with ease.

Gemini Earth/Moon—These beings seek support for the attribute of listening. Their purpose of the lifetime requires objective consideration of external input (without that input seemingly invalidating the individual). Support for changing the mind, shifting direction, and changing horses mid-stream is needed.

Cancer Earth/Moon—This is perhaps the most intense of the Earth/

Moon systems. These individuals need support to have the space to cry, laugh, feel and not worry. Rest comes through emotional support and the relinquishment of the need to maintain control. Although resistance is natural when confronted with support, acceptance of support bears great rewards in all aspects of life, most especially the professional realm.

Leo Earth/Moon—To be an altruist and to dedicate one's life to humanity, much internal strength is prerequisite. Thus, these people require ego support, confidence building and listening to, especially for their most radical and unusual ideas. They need to shine and be emotionally polished by their support group to the brilliant personality lustre which results when purpose is pursued.

Virgo Earth/Moon—Support for order without criticism is required by these individuals. It is a tricky balance to integrate the creative and the logical. Encouragement to see the details, facts and processes required to fulfill the fantasy must be supported for these Earthlings. This provides the understanding required to follow inspiration from concept through to completion.

Libra Earth/Moon—These people require support for relating with others on an equal, cooperative level. To support this effort, relationships with peers become the starting block. Relating above or below the individual's self-perceived status only serves to complicate fairness. Equality comes from willing giving. To support these people, compliment all externalized generous efforts they perform and establish a system of cooperative giving by asking and receiving.

Scorpio Earth/Moon—Money is not power, nor does money ensure good sexual relationships. These people require support for intense, emotional involvement without external distractions like food, money and things. Performance must be discouraged. Fullness of being needs encouragement. Telling such individuals that they are worthy even if they have nothing takes a step towards the initially incomprehensible and seeds the needed message.

Sagittarius Earth/Moon—Support for the validity of one's ideas is required. These individuals must teach, in their own way, but cannot deliver this *dharma* without a realization that their ideas are valid, original and important. Support for thinking (especially out loud or on paper) provides the baseline for allowing acceptance of the importance of the individual's intelligence.

Capricorn Earth/Moon—Freedom from the responsibility of others sets the scene for support with these Earthlings. Allowing for the ultimate acceptance of responsibility solicits support. That responsibility results when one accepts conditions in life completely free from what others caused, needed or obliged the individual to do. Seeking and consciously asking for support is best.

Aquarius Earth/Moon—Originality of the human model requires validation to make this placement reach optimum performance. To inspire this person serves everyone. Ego is a temporary condition in which self-ness emerges. It is not to be feared nor denied; ego is intended to be supported fully and completely. "Be like the Sun at midday," as the I Ching points out. Shine on, fully and completely.

Pisces Earth/Moon—Support for openness to the unseen, unknown and the non-tangible best encourages these individuals into fullness. An etherial sense mutes the obsession with logic into a creative balance which allows for talent to emerge. This emergence takes ideas and gives them abstract form which ultimately yields a valid, logical result.

* * *

The perihelion of Earth occurs at 12 Cancer 36 (and aphelion at 12 Capricorn 36). Perihelion takes place each year between January 2nd and January 4th, in the midst of winter, for the Northern Hemisphere of the Earth. Imagine that the closest point of solar contact coincides with the time of year when the inhabitants of the top half of the planet, relatively speaking, are in the midst of snow, rain and cold. (Given that the Southern Hemisphere of the planet is larger, perhaps the inhabitants of the lower portion of the planet have a much warmer view of things.)

Receipt of ample solar energy is not seen as an energy crisis but as an entropy crisis and more light is shed on the Earth's perihelion. Quality as opposed to quantity again emerges as an Earth based theme. Use and application of efficiency prevail over bigness and non-use. It remains a basic issue of potential versus kinetic energies.

The point of perihelion of the Earth relates to the support necessary to provide one with motivation to ensure that the human kinetics receive total application. Potential is nice but totally unapplied from the perihelion's point of view. The connection to kinetic retains fulfillment as a keyword and annotates the need to use that

which is available in the interest of purpose and yielding contentment. The Cancerian vibration of the contact point installs significant amounts of nurturing. How can it be said that the release of one
in a cold, somewhat darkened winter world is not in the best interest
of one's purpose? It remains a point of rhetoric.

Perhaps the Cancerian perihelion of the Earth maintains the
quality of Mother Earth and the natural laws of natural forces.
Perhaps it is that the forces of nature merely strive to recreate the
balance of nature, spoken of so often in ecological circles. Earth's
perihelion appears in an ecological manner by establishing those
with kinetic power the channels through which to apply the power.

The aphelion of Earth in the normally perceived cool sign of Capricorn suggests a principle of a converse nature. It takes place each
year between July 2 and July 4. The Earth's aphelion indicates a point
of retreat in which one must contemplate potential and restore
energy for redirection in a quality manner of kinetic release later and
not now. A time of rejuvenation of mundane effort bears out in the
aphelion. A time for regrouping all physically based energy dynamics
exists. This storing up of energy and taking an inventory of energy
available ensures that when kinetic calls later appear one has the
potential to rise to the occasion in the form of action. It is recommended that the aphelion of Earth be treated as a point of physical
solitude and spiritual healing of the physical body. Refuge must be
taken before reintegration back into the collective. The time of pause
must be accepted and taken for full kinetic power to return later.
Otherwise, one will only be noted to have potential and be lacking
in application.

Mars

Mars completes the section of the inner planets in this planetary
parade. It maintains a rotation upon its axis of just over twenty-four
hours, creating a similarity of habituation to Earthly mechanics.

Habituation becomes a keyword applied to the mechanisms of
Mars in the heliocentric mode. This necessitates tremendous amounts
of consistent and repetitive efforts in the pursuit of purpose to ensure
manifestation. Mars notes the energy and effort required to initiate
and fulfill the purpose of incarnation. Mars bears a stronger implication of motivation in the heliocentric horoscope than its geocentric

counterpart. Mars at best notes the step beyond the perceived contentment, or at worst notes the lack of contentment and becomes motivated to move on in the direction of attaining one's purpose. It remains important to review, from time to time, the reasoning and motive behind the efforts extended.

Thrust is symbolized by Mars in the heliocentric model. In creating an analogy of a rocket in the greater and vast dimensions of heliocentric space, the regulation of appropriate levels of thrust to ensure economic and effective directions to destination looms as more significant. One must regulate, which is not to suggest impede, prohibit or inhibit, the efforts of Mars to obtain maximum result with the minimum of effort. One must learn the time to push and the time to relax. One must understand the ebb and flow of one's own physical cycle to allow for greater creative (masculine, light, assertive) thrust to be effectively extended.

Regulation of Martian energy prohibits the needless involvement in conflict often attained unintentionally (again motivation is an issue) through zealous extensions of the Mars dynamic at inopportune times. Conversely, it becomes necessary to incorporate the use of Mars when such a need is called to produce the support of the natural rhythm of attainment. Mars at this level receives positive reenforcement from the result of a timely nature accelerating the principle of cause and effect. This feeds back into the contentment level perceived in the quality of the Moon/Earth binary system, creating a greater sense of Venereal (Venusian) worth. More communication in a Mercurial manner is stimulated, allowing for greater emphasis to take place in solar centrality.

Mars maintains its North Node at 19 Taurus 24 with a South Node at 19 Scorpio 24. The overall theme of the Martian principle is to strive to attain its greatest worth. Mars actually intends to offer great insights into the dynamics of human potential. This awareness which Mars offers in this quest reduces the amount of conflict over those things which are of the Taurus/Scorpio polarity. This polarity contains: property, economics, economic controls, possession of any form, nuclear arms, mined or drilled resources and finally, the integrity of character. Modern day politics is filled with a renewed Mars type conflict on a daily basis. When striving to solve problems in the political arena that have to do with any of these issues, note that an attack of character takes place. The negative Mars push here strives to stimulate the Scorpionic South Node into a defensive posture.

The heliocentric Mars realizes that justification and rationalization stem from defensiveness which constitutes a loss of control of faculties (resources).

The optimum effort of the Martian nodal axis requries that the focus be placed upon the implementation of resource by pointing out the resource and, if necessary, digging to extract a resource of hidden potential. Further, it demands that all grievances or transgressions of the past be released and cleansed prior to moving forward. The Mars/Scorpio association by virtue of the South Node refers to a need for a more basic understanding of the flowing forces of life such as *kundalini*, DNA, healing and human sexuality.

Mars approaches the Sun in closest configuration at 05 Pisces 51, with its greatest extent into space opposing through 05 Virgo 51 (1990 positions). Given that Mars at perihelion would doubly re-enforce a sense of urgency, one might expect to find individuals with Mars at perihelion to have frenetic levels of motivation. This may or may not be true depending upon how the individual chooses to per-ceive the levels of the Pisces perihelion. Should one approach this sensitized point with ultra-delicateness of feeling, quite conceivably the individual could lose Piscean fears of unacceptability. Rejection of effort far surpasses the lack of extended effort. A retreat to the aphelion in Virgo allows the vantage to verify that maximum order prevails. Order intact, the next step must then be one of creative assertion.

The perihelion of Mars epitomizes creative thrust while the aphelion defines the background, research, writing, preparation and whatever is required to be in the creative mode. The aphelion sym-bolizes more of the receptive/following premise. The perihelion moves in a more overt direction, guided by a strong sense of intuition and will to follow.

Subtle distinctions must be carried through the Mars perihelion to prevent the Pisces placement from becoming the Christian Crusader who will sacrifice all of his or her energy for the emotional fervor of a potentially spiritual cause. Pretense in this case relies upon the nodal axis to provide a correct motive in the fervent pursuit of Martian energy.

Each of the bodies in this chapter create (with some mathematical creativity) a cycle of about eleven years. These planetary influences are grouped together for that common reason noting the effect that these combined energies generate in a persuading way to the center of the system, the Sun. It was previously noted that the sunspot cycle hinges upon the solar polarity reversal of eleven years. These inner planets participate with the Sun in creating the active, short term dynamics which affect the entire solar system.

To review these eleven year tropical occurrences:

46 sidereal revolutions of Mercury	11.079 yrs.
18 sidereal revolutions of Venus	11.074 yrs.
137 synodic revolutions of the Moon	11.077 yrs.
11 sidereal revolutions of Earth	11.000 yrs.
6 sidereal revolutions of Mars	11.286 yrs.

To which we may add:

10 synodic periods, Earth/Jupiter	10.919 yrs.
40 synodic periods, Mercury/Mars	11.061 yrs.

Each of the inner planets of the solar system finds at least one way each to combine and fit into the intrinsic resonance of eleven years. The music of these inner spheres dramatically cuts and creates the atmospheric conditions of the Earth via the Sun. Geometric logic would assume that the other inner planets receive as much significance as does the Earth/Sun opposition. Bear in mind that any planet under consideration in a heliocentric model maintains planet/Sun opposition innately. Each instant of time for which an astrologer constructs a heliocentric horoscope on this planet constitutes the heliocentric horoscope which for that moment of time fits each and every planet subject to the Sun.

Kepler, one of the sustantiators of the heliocentric concept, spent a large amount of time working to correlate the "music of the spheres." Perhaps it was this eleven year periodicity that he sought for the inner planets.

It is recommended that any astrological researcher begin to explore the rhythms and music of planets prior to exploring more typical configurations. This eleven year period, once applied to significant research, theoretically supports a tremendous amount of mundane causal forces.

Bear in mind that those forces which remain unknown create the more subtle influences with which an individual must contend. Once disclosed, the resolution of the influence comes far more easily. Such unconscious mechanisms of the realm of the undiscovered merely create more for contention and allow mankind to unknowingly follow the realm of these planetary persuasions.

Chapter Four

Planets of Persistence

It is now time to move into the realm of deep space and encounter the traditionally classified major planets (classified so due to size alone) Jupiter, Saturn, Uranus and Neptune as well as Pluto and its moon, Charon (the latter two often considered a binary planet). These wanderers in our solar system maintain slower orbital velocities, thereby yielding a slower period of revolution about the Sun and occupying more time per sign. As the effects of the motion of the outer planets in the solar system are experienced, the planets seem to operate with a greater level of persistence both natally and by transit.

Jupiter

Jupiter is the first of the bodies encountered in the advance into space. Jupiter, circled by a fine ring of silver, consists mostly of swirling quasi-liquified gases and a massive hurricane over 400 years old known as the great red spot. A microcosm within the solar system with its sixteen moons, Jupiter emulates the whole of the solar system on a reduced scale. It generates nearly as much heat as it receives from the Sun in a program of thermal exchange. Some speculate that Jupiter strives internally to be a star, but does not quite retain the necessary components for such an intensified combustion. The orbit of Jupiter's moon Io affects the radiation emission of the large planet, which suggests an affect on solar activity.

The process of Jupiter is embracing the concept of bigness.

Exaggeration and fabricated distortions may reside in the Jupiterian principles to create perspective in a philosophy. The Jupiterian burning urge for greatness does not contain enough substance to manifest fully. More is needed.

During the process of solar emulation unconsciously created by the gregarious and massive (influential) Jupiter, its many moons captured an external point of focus. This contains the key of Jupiter's heliocentric resolution. Note that Jupiter automatically recreated the central theme of the solar system and on a lesser scale—a galactic model. Jupiter strives to replicate Universal Order and seeks to create a model of reason as to why, how and what It is. The grandiose planet need look no further than within its own dimension. The effort to possess that which is external is misdirected. The Jupiterian obsession with higher mind, philosophy and the primal urges of religion (usually Fundamentalistic in nature and application) continually seeks from outside itself the essence of it all—God. Ultimately, the Jupiterian perception contracts to within its own dimension and notices the action which it, established itself. Emulation is realized. The ultimate of primal consciousness puts itself up for inspection: If you seek God, act as God would act. God is not external, nor can God be perceived through any amount of didactic learning, disciplining or regurgitated prayers. God manifests in the heart and soul when one acts automatically and autonomously in accordance with God. The epitome of being able to practice as one preaches results in Jupiter's actualization as a planet.

The Jupiterian process is very simple, so simple that it often needs complication to be comprehended. Sometimes it is necessary to step outside of oneself to understand the emulation of this dramatic perception of the complex solar system that the individual has created.

Jupiter far too often fails to sustain the geocentric interpretations offered by many astrologers (especially in prognostication). The reason behind this apparent astrological shortcoming personifies the Jupiterian nature. The tendency to examine the horoscope looking for the prizes of Jupiter in the old school benefic manner merely induces one to look outside the self for luck. The solution to the situation requires self-examination and reaffirmation of the qualities of the Godself establishing fortune, the higher polarity of luck. The difference is that luck remains totally external while fortune prefers to go within for manifestation in the outside realm.

The principle with which Jupiter speaks in the heliocentric horoscope notes that one must abide in total accordance with Divine Law as the individual understands it. An individual implementing aspects of Divine Law does not function in accord with the essence of Jupiter and may feel as if God holds some sort of personal grudge. This is not the case. The only difficulty is in the inability or unwillingness to follow the basic understanding of God held by the individual.

The nodal axis of Jupiter and the perihelion/aphelion polarity both relate to this Jupiterian premise through a cardinal influence. Jupiter's North Node occupies a point at 10 Cancer 14 and the south node subsequently falls at 10 Capricorn 14. These points are virtually in a square to Jupiter's perihelion of 14 Aries 29 and the aphelion at 14 Libra 29.

Beginning with the nodal orientation, one may surmise that Jupiter's North Node in Cancer, like the perihelion of Earth, strives to establish a support mechanism. The Cancerian implication pushes in the direction of a strong foundation, perhaps a home base. One interpretation of inner environment which applies to the Cancerian archetype defines the individual's aura space of energy. This aura stems from the inner alignment (or lack of alignment) of the chakras or inner energy cells which interact in alternating patterns of exchange. Again, the inner dynamic of Jupiter prevails to create a condition of external support. One must heal and soothe the aura from within. Any aura balancer or healer will reveal that the effect of his or her work depends upon the inner integration of the individual. The process of the balance work or healing is symptomatic in nature and fails to resolve the cause. For the external support to be received, the individual being healed must agree, in consciousness (Jupiter), to allow for internal understanding of the lack of alignment with the basic God principle as understood by that individual. This requires that the pull from Jupiter's South Node in Capricorn establish a strong sense of inner integrity, confidence and responsibility (responseability) in order to support and re-enforce the mechanism of the North Node. This effort clearly demarcates the difference between being strong and being tough. The former is internal and the latter is external.

The perihelion of Jupiter pushes the individual to become more of the Arien polarity—more of the self. Again, it is imperative to stress that Jupiterian awareness is a matter of individual interpretation and that as many interpretations will exist as there are interpreters. No one is right or wrong. No one is more correct than another; no one is more incorrect than another. Jupiter requires that the perihelion be as personalized as the Aries dynamic can connote.

The aphelion of Jupiter in Libra creates a need for periodic retreat in which one can experience intimate one-to-one interaction with those of similar disposition. A problem which so often occurs in any Libra phenomenon astrologically is that the balance of similarity is neglected. This precludes re-enforcement of a positive nature and establishes unnecessary confrontation. The Libran dynamic, in its search for support, under worst case conditions can change perception to accommodate and follow the interpretations and beliefs of others. The negative side of Jupiter thus manifests again with externalization when internalization is implied. The Libran pursuit of Jupiter's aphelion requires retreat with those of similar belief and spiritual development.

Saturn

Saturn appears as the next planet of discussion. It still astounds, with as much as it endeavors to do in cooperation with a horoscope as how much malicious press it receives. This effect still prevails, and as of yet has not managed to become past tense. The heliocentric view of Saturn contains a miniature paradigm shift within itself. No longer can the malefic effects of Saturn render ineffectiveness, despair and misfortune to mankind. These effects, on a more primal level, can no longer be perceived.

Albert Einstein is credited with asking if the Universe is friendly or not. Saturn provides us with the first coherent look at such a question. The basic premise of karma (cause and effect), Newtonian Physics, sowing and reaping and synchronicity need not fall into the category of punitive actions. Punitive perceptions of Saturn merely etch the dogma of old geocentric forms of astrology into the interpretive consciousness of astrologers and re-establish scolding tones in the horoscope.

How many times has the following flowed from the presumably astrologically or metaphysically wise? "It must be my karma." "I was very evil in a past life and this life is retribution." "My karma says that I cannot be whatever I really want to be." "Karma does not want me to be full or happy." These disillusioned proclamations fall into the category of unactualized Saturn. Such perceptual limitations must evaporate before the heliocentric Saturn fits smoothly into the horoscope. Let us begin to reconstruct a new image of Saturn.

Saturn formerly guarded the perceived edge of the solar system. Since 1781 and the popular recognition of Uranus, this image melted in visual perception and somehow snagged on the seams of the subconscious in the astrological community. Pluto now (for now) reigns at the outer edge of the solar system. The etching that Saturn carves the outer extent of the solar system is no longer true. This, the interpretation that it represents the limits of space, must be released. That duty now belongs to Pluto (that aspect of Pluto's role comes later).

The perception of limitation stemming from an outermost configuration intended only to communicate the essence of perimeter, or even more succinctly, parameter. A parameter represents the operating characteristics of any given system, not exceeding the effective viability or functionality of that system. Saturn's efforts merely intend to define the effective limits of operation. This definition allowed for maximum efficiency in effort and subsequent attainment by staying within the realm of natural capabilities.

An attitude problem now arises. Should an individual decide that his or her natural capabilities fall short of the demands of the time, the individual would often strive to attain more and thereby run the system over redline. A consciously invoked stress test results in which the individual elects arrogantly (possibly as the result of an externally motivated Jupiter) to exceed his or her own capabilities. It is only a matter of time before the system stresses beyond its natural resiliency and structural fatigue destroys the foundation of mundane life. Such fatigue may be physical, mental, emotional or spiritual—all of which Saturn characterizes in this context—all impacting on the mundane.

A return to Jupiter at this point of fatigue proclaims the failure of the belief system and declares a vengeance which Saturn seems to hold for the individual personally. The process of examination of rational parameters is all that is needed now, not rationalization.

Saturn quite comfortably allows for periodic intervals of rest and recuperation in the flow of life. Often plateaus in human experience are negated by the perception that life is an onward trudging effort. Re-enforcement of fatigue again results. It appears that Saturn's graces must be accepted before effective levels of manifestation begin to consistently arrive in one's daily experience. It is only through such experiences of timely consistency that one can maintain the levels of persistence required to fulfill an enduring purpose. Acceptance of support and times of refuge and solace need noting and integration. It is up to the individual to attain such an attitude of acceptance. Saturn's parental persuasions are silent, subtle and unconditionally supportive qualities of emulation for any parent. It may be that if one expects Saturn to clobber the consciousness within heliocentric horizons that great disappointments of perceived parameters form dark clouds on that horizon.

Saturn will not make you do anything. It just seems that way in the mundane thicket of Saturnine influence. Choice always prevails in the operation of the system under the Saturnian parameters. Further, one may even choose to shut down the system and not work with the parameters of the design of the time. One usually believes under such conditions (again an external Jupiter) that no choice exists.

Saturn, interestingly enough, shifts operating speeds when working within a heliocentric system. Saturn's speed runs smoother, with less stress than in its geocentric counterpart. It resembles the model of an automobile engine running at high revolutions near its redline rating. Then, the operator engages the clutch and shifts the gears. The shift into higher gear releases the engine's revolutions and eases the overall operation. Saturn gears up from the geocentric to the heliocentric.

Gearing up to the heliocentric requires a conscious attitudinal choice of selection. No one may indicate the time or the manner in which to shift. That remains as a personal and intimate perception according to individual Saturn parameters. The benefit of working with the higher heliocentric bendix comes in the form of less mundane distraction. Believe it or not, when operating within the parameters of the more highly energized heliocentric system, one experiences less mundane disorder. This comes from the elimination of mundane distractions; conditions held within the geocentric system. One eliminates activities and events which no longer matter. It appears to be an element of mind over matter. Purpose prevails over pettiness of effort.

Both the nodal axis and the solar contact axis of Saturn hold Cancer to Capricorn configurations. The North Node of Saturn resides at 23 Cancer 30 with the south node at 23 Capricorn 30. The perihelion occupies a residence of 02 Cancer 37 allowing a domicile of 02 Capricorn 37 (1990 positions) for aphelion. Wouldn't you know that Saturn would spend the most time in Capricorn, the sign it is said to rule?

The nurturing theme of the solar system again appears in the Saturnian context supporting the parental role of the ringed planet. Balance in a bi-directional manner of giving and receiving support enters into the Saturnian nature. Much effort is extended through the Cancerian North Node to give support. Such support, though, can only be rendered when one resides within a supportive foundation. One cannot give that which one does not have. The crisis of accepting support and having that support create dependence upon something or someone also exists. To have a supportive foundation merely suggests that one experiences a level of stability. To stand upon something denotes that the something stands under the person. To translate this more literally, support *understands* the individual.

A Cancerian perihelion demonstrates the need to render active levels of support and nurturing. Again, how can this be done without foundation? The foundation implied in Saturn's energy recommends an inner retreat from time to time to adjust the perception of how the individual is functioning within prescribed parameters. The retreat complete, an individual can now perform as a consultant to others seeking to go within and explore the dimensions of operation in their respective parametric systems.

Saturn's nodal orientation combined with the perihelion/aphelion axis creates a precise balance of inner and outer dimensions of supportive/nurturing mechanisms. Sometimes re-enforcement is needed, sometimes it is not. The choice is individual, as throughout Saturn's theme. Saturn's power drain, however, must be understood and support accepted when needed, from within or without, to prevent parametric impotence.

Uranus

The wanderer Uranus is next following in sequence from the center Sun of the solar system. This planet has an unusual 98° axis of inclination mixed with an almost vertically aligned ring about its body. Awareness is the most significant keyword of Uranus. This planet, with just over 200 years in popular understanding, falls subject to a variety of misconceptions which awareness resolves. To be aware is to be cognitive, responsive and sensory. Uranus is not so much concerned with the development of the lucrative and illusive sixth sense. The planet much prefers that one first utilize the five physical senses. Hear what is spoken. See what is viewed. Smell what is available. Touch what is touchable. Taste that which is ingested.

Perceiving the above senses establishes a new dimension of awareness, pay attention and be conscious of what is in the environment of the system. Such awareness takes away surprise and reduces the emphasis on discovery. Discovery is a word which refers to the fact that at one moment something was not present but now it is a function of awareness. For instance, the discovery of new planets does not mean that on Tuesday the planet did not exist and on Wednesday it did. It notes that on Wednesday the awareness of the planet took conscious form.

Awareness very often contains something undesirable. The more aware one becomes, the more a collective Aquarian sense predominates. More pleasure is perceived. More pain is perceived. Uranus does not discriminate polarities in perception. Many of those evolved in the ways of perception indicate that the more aware they became, the more impersonal pain they perceived. There are distinct disadvantages to being perceptive or sentient in a psychic sense. The reason for perceiving pain often manifests in a motivation to be strong within the self and to pursue a path of action which reduces the collective (and personal) levels of pain. Non-judgmental perceptual abilities result from this effect.

Uranus encourages the individual to be true to self, no matter what. Individuality is a key of being. The balance of individuality comes from not flaunting the uniqueness of self, but knowing and being the total self. The element of conformity dissipates. The internal mechanisms of the individual (Saturnine support) generate a core knowledge of being. Comfort exists in being at one with the soul; comfort does not exist in conformity. Courage, commitment to the self and compassion for others must exist for the Uranian element to reside visibly in the horoscope. Heliocentrically, Uranus is a key thrust in the chart. This thrust originates in the Uranian association to Aquarius, the sign opposing Leo, which associates with the Sun. Uranus focuses the use of an actualized being. This amplifies the need for a lack of conformity and indicates emphasis on the need for uniqueness of being.

In this way, Uranus erases the implication that the planet has held regarding rapid, destructive change. Changes of those proportions extend from an inability to perceive, blocking the natural flow of transitional energies. This blockage pattern builds tension which results in such intensity that only a physically debilitating force can release it. Change of Uranian fashion is destructive only if resisted. Saturn clocks the changes and Uranus provides the alterations to the parameters of the system, indicating the need to move up and add to the system in a revisionary improving manner. Some level of uncertainty may be perceived during Uranian transitions and the need to move in the direction of the change is required, regardless of the anxiety.

Uranus maintains a north node at an even 14 degrees of Gemini and a South Node at 14 degrees of Sagittarius. The essence of the pursuit of Uranus is diversification. This diversification reveals alternate ways of performing tasks. These alterations often initially appear wrong and the validity or invalidity will not be known until tested. Should the Sagittarian South Node prevail over the North Node, dogma sets in and the rigidity of an old philosophical form hinders efforts needed for change. The progressive quality of the south node stimulates the need for retaining all concepts, techniques and thought forms that maintain a level of validity. These become the foundation for utilizing new steps in divergent directions without scattering or negating completed efforts. This axis demonstrates that it remains as important to note what has not worked and why as noting what does work and why.

Perihelion for Uranus is at 18 Virgo 36 in the ecliptic with a zodiacal counterpart at 18 Pisces 36 for aphelion (1990 positions). Here a need for urgency in regard to attention to detail may not and can not preclude the systemic overview. Change comes best when the big picture, as indicated by the aphelion, and the details warranting attention, are held in balance to complete the perspective. Focusing on detail (perihelion) while allowing for a retreat to obtain perspective (aphelion) facilitates the mobilization of change in true Uranian form. The Uranus process of advance/retreat can not be assumed to relax over an interval of an eighty-four year orbit. Thus, a perpetual process of going in and out of focus to obtain clarity becomes the integrative point of the two extreme solar contacts. This requires that the full thrust of all senses (and any extra senses available) are used to ensure total integration and completeness of unique identity.

Neptune

Neptune normally holds the number eight spot in the planetary sphere of orbits. Currently and until 1999, the nebulous Neptune resides at a greater distance from the Sun than the ninth planetary entity, Pluto and Charon. Neptune, though, will be treated next in this discussion to accommodate the perceived normalcy of the solar system irrespective of this temporary anomaly.

One of the great beauties of Neptune seems initially to be a curse. When one embarks upon the path of spiritual pursuit and growth, one immediately experiences more confusion and distortion of images. The purpose for this period of perceptual uncertainty exists in its promise to later include awareness and enlightenment. Sometimes it is just not appropriate for one to see beyond the realm of the current situation.

Neptune further facilitates the process of growth by providing one with a high level of confusion each time serious thinking is assayed. The solution that Neptune provides is too easy. Stop thinking. Soon there will be the time for contemplation but not now. Most importantly, it is *not* a thought oriented process. Neptune encourages, through its ambiguous fogs, a flow with the *Tao*. This flowing is tidal in nature and realizes all of the subtle needs of the varying times— times to advance, times to retreat, times to pause, times to be visible, times to be invisible, times to think, times to feel and times to be void. An intuitive sense of flowing and timing results. This affords later motion at a precisely perfect time; all based upon contemplation, the higher form of thought.

Neptune defines spiritual values. To find spiritual value in each and every thing encountered characterize Neptunian perception. The veils of Neptune soften one's focus just enough to reduce the sharp edges of criticism and judgment. Neptune allows an altered point of view—to see a subject in a way never seen before, thus capturing a natural state of beauty. Neptune represents simplicity of form, not complexity, neither of form nor essence.

Neptune also captures the purity of being and allows one to completely confront the receptive part of one's nature. This symbolism aligns with to the natural need to follow the flow and to deal with what is given in a creative way (not through abject dejection and resignation). The principles of darkness, the feminine and the receptive follow in the wake of Neptune's subtle pushes. One must confront the most spiritual side of Neptune, recognize its susceptibility to seduction and protect it from seduction. If seduction is believed to be an external effect seduction will surely follow close at hand. Seduction defines a subconscious urge for manifestation which can not be given form due to a concept, notion or chosen mode of behavior. To prevent seduction, one must feel free to flow through the psyche on the road to what could be hell without fear of what may come to pass. Only then will Neptune implement fully. The natural intuition of Neptune is all the protection necessary should the individual choose not to be naive.

Neptune's North Node reigns in Leo, specifically 11 Leo 31, with a tailing node at 11 Aquarius 31. Neptune's south nodal foundation may actually manifest in compulsive assistance to humanity. An overwhelming drive to have good intentions and be altruistic may pressure the individual into service to others through an immolating or self-sacrificing mechanism. Immolation is not an answer, as subservience to all others negates the spiritual needs of the self (rendering it ineffective in service). The Leo polarization, when active, allows the individual to first claim the needs of self in a conscious and honest manner and to then be capable of meeting the needs of the rest of humanity. The balance of the Leonine aspect is achieved when one realizes that the response of greatness often rendered to the server can create the condition of the server being the served. Such ego glorification is counterproductive to the process of altruism. Nonetheless, many must go through the period of personality distortion stemming from the quest of ego fulfillment without the memory of the soul's motive for being.

Neptune's perihelion/aphelion axis makes fairly wild zodiacal shifts in comparison to the other planets' axes. For example, simply during the last two decades of this century it varied (in a back and forth motion) from 23 Pisces to 01 Gemini. It is therefore difficult to integrate Neptune's perihelion/aphelion axis into a brief, generic interpretation of the planet's significance. Certainly this fits the archetypes of elusiveness usually associated with this planet. (See Appendix D for a visual depiction of variance in this axis.)

Neptune's perihelion/aphelion axis slipped into and out of Gemini during a three year period roughly from 1978-1980. Since that time corresponds with the formative mental/idea stage of this book, it seems appropriate to delineate these peak orbital points in their Gemini/Sagittarius polarity.

Balance is the keyword here. The urgency of cause induced with the Gemini based perihelion requires maintenance of both points of view for integration to complete. Dualism in Neptune is a must. This dualism allows for the pursuit of that which is fragile without fear of the fragility and yet with an intimate respect for the delicate nature. The point of darkness of Neptune falls in Sagittarius and at an expansive distance in space. This point requires periodic refuge from thought in order to contemplate through situations and develop contact with the basis of the primal philosophy. With reactivation of belief and faith, the individual can again move back into the depths of interacting in the realm of thought without contradiction of awareness.

Armed with the information in Appendix D, you are called up to test your wings with your own interpretations of Neptune's perihelion/aphelion axis in Pisces/Virgo, Aries/Libra, and Taurus/Scorpio. Think of the archetypes associated with these polarities and go for it.

Pluto/Charon

The planetary pair of Pluto and Charon rests on the outer edge of the solar system. Pluto and its companion Charon (once thought to be a captive satellite) have an even more intimate relationship than do the Earth and Moon. The mythological associations of the pair fit hand in hand. Charon was the ferryman on the river Styx who steered the souls across the river at the entrance of Hades (Pluto). Still, even within the apparent grimness of this operation, choice existed prior to a soul's crossing. The individual held the choice to enter or not to enter.

Pluto and Charon do not constitute a pair of bodies dictating the realm in which the depths of consciousness must exist. That choice is individual. The Pluto/Charon team does, however, establish the need to choose and reinforce choice. Absolute power resides in this combination. The deepest thoughts, the darkest secrets and the isolation of self-awareness prevail in Pluto's realm. A level of infinite embarrassment always finds its way into the darkness of the Plutonian cavities in consciousness. If embarrassment or evil lurks, it lurks in the dimension of Pluto; worse yet, it lurks deep within the consciousness. Why is it that so much extreme embarrassment exists regarding something done poorly? Why must it remain such a repressed secret? Can it be understood that the repression merely adds to the depth defying pressure which caused the situation to resurface with greater ramifications and turmoil? Could it be that everyone has such deep secrets stifled away? Not only could it be—it is.

The retention of those embarrassing aspects of the self merely causes those aspects to become the limitations of totally self-imposed consciousness. The devil raves in the mind and is apparently real. Hell is a condition of negative consciousness much more limited than Saturn ever thought of being even while in a malefic mood. Pluto's cohabitation with Charon on the edge of the solar system defines limits to the possessed soul and only to the possessed soul. Any obsession and repressed compulsion constitutes possession. It would be too easy for Pluto to become astrology's new Saturn, to brand Pluto with qualities which consciousness simply refuses to recognize within. The humor of it all is that in even creating the thought of accusation or projection one confesses for the soul.

The key to Pluto's lack of limitation as a boundary began in June, 1983, approximately eight months prior to its entry into Scorpio, when a *Voyager* space probe pushed past and through the perimeter of the solar system. This probe extended the essence of mankind into the deep, dark, depths of space. For this reason alone, humanity will never again be limited to the consciousness contained solely within the dimensions of the solar system. This symbol, although small in size, is monumental in nature.

A second such event occurred in September of 1989 when the *Voyager* space probe passed by Neptune (during the interval of the Saturn/Neptune conjunction), and also plunged into deep space. *Voyager* provided dramatic and concept altering photographs and data for the planets Jupiter, Saturn, Uranus and Neptune, establishing rings for all four. As *Voyager* pressed on into the depths of space defined by the Neptune/Pluto orbital interception, many felt as if they were off the deep end. Uncharted waters (Neptune words) set the sea state of emotional transformations controlled by the introspective nature of Pluto. New, unusual, cathartic processes and releases affected individuals singularly and collectively. A voyage in consciousness had begun and many were seeking answers. One small problematic point surfaces here; before answers can be found, the questions must be formed.

A Plutonian key appears in the associations of *Voyager*. That key is interrogation. Interrogation exists in the interest of discovery. The mechanism of Pluto uses the tool of questioning to provoke the consciousness into awareness. Pluto knows that sometimes the answer stands secondary to the question. Pluto through actualizing consciousness strives to find the right questions, placing little emphasis on the answers. The answer is in response to the question regardless of the answer. For instance, if one is asked a question and defensiveness creates the tone of response, why is one defensive? If the question were not an issue to the subconscious and if there were not a corresponding level of embarrassment with it, no need for defensiveness would exist.

Pluto, with its association to the defensively postured Scorpio totem, knows the mechanism behind questioning. Timing prevails as of the essence as well; this too, both the Scorpio and Plutonian person knows so well. A scorpion will let its prey walk all over it, waiting for the right moment to strike. The point here is not the destructive sting of the scorpion, but the innate sense of knowing when to destroy that which resists change, perception and vision. Pluto has the power and prowess to strike down the levels of misconceptions and to stalk out the lies designed to repress embarrassments into nonexistence. Pluto at this level of manifestation fulfills great magnitudes of Cosmic Order.

It is not recommended that one seek out the Plutonian role in life as the inquisitor of the subconscious of others. This smacks of the Catholic Inquisition. The Pluto guardian of the unconscious will be sought out by those desiring or needing self interrogations. Sometimes it is the most innocuous statements which set off subterranean consciousness reverberations throughout another. One's intent must always be clear.

Pluto's final keywords are, "The truth is." Pluto requires absolute truth that yields to absolute power. Total reclamation of power is the benefit. Currently this process of power reclamation may be more difficult for the female of the human species due to the conditioning which has taken place in society with respect to women. Ironically, women now have a greater collective drive to encounter the full grasp of their power. A balance in this dynamic was completed when Pluto achieved perihelion in September, 1989.

The North Plutonian Node at 19 Cancer 56, polarized by the south node of 19 Capricorn 56, completes the roster of planetary nodal implications and finishes the natural nurturing tendencies of the solar system's orientation. Three planetary north nodes fall in Cancer along with two of the perihelia. Pluto summarizes the finished product of the support/non-support axis of interaction. The Truth

(Question) is: Was support accepted or rejected? Was support even needed? Was support given when called for from another? The South Node of Pluto creates that condition of psychological limbo known as purgatory wherein one revives past experiences. Self-imposed penance may be executed to relieve any stresses and rewards must be submitted for altruistic acts. The overall inventory of the self, including motivation, takes place on Pluto's posterior node, ultimately creating forgiveness.

Pluto reached perihelion on September 4, 1989, in Scorpio, the sign it rules; thus, extra significance is attached to this closest point of solar approach. Many feel that the Pluto in Scorpio perihelion stood as a turning point in collective consciousness and marks either the decision to transform the world or to terminate the world in apocalyptic fashion. Pluto has hit its perihelion before; however, this is the first perihelion since general conscious awareness of the planet took hold in 1930. This point indicates quite clearly that a decision will be collectively made as to whether the wheel turns again in the same way, setting a trend for some 250 years to come. It is pivotal. It is critical. It is not the end of the world.

Pluto at perihelion marks an ending and a simultaneous beginning. Choice occurs as to the rotation of the next revolution. What collective, world wide trends began then that need to end? The nuclear reduction efforts, the opening of the Berlin Wall and economic uncertainty all fit this archetype. The theme of squabbling amongst ourselves over possessions which are not possessions (totally Pluto, aphelion in Taurus) must end. Power, control and ownership must be transformed. They must be owned and not possessed. Possession merely brings within the grasp a loss of control. To possess requires that one be possessed by the possessed object. Pluto at perihelion seeks to bring ultimate freedom from the material plane, all the while experiencing total participation in the material plane *sans* spiritual impedance.

Two major technological events symbolize Pluto at perihelion. The first, superconductivity, arose into public view following the Harmonic Convergence and gained household word recognition status. A superconductive device, unlike a semiconductive device, has no resistance. Subsequently, it achieves levels of cool power never before attainable. A nice metaphor for superconductivity is of flowing, not resisting, and creating one's unlimited power. Secondly, nuclear fusion, also produced in cool environments (chilled out, man) defined a new aspect of power creation. The fusion analogy notes that within the context of complete, uninhibited merger, both merging entities gain strength. In regards to relationships, Pluto's analogue suggests that two people become stronger through union; their individual autonomy is supported, not compromised. Individuality must be reassessed within the framework of personal relationships. Nothing of self is lost in fusion; strength is gained—a new metaphor of relationship evolution for those feeling like Voyager, having gone off the deep end in affairs of the heart.

* * *

The four major planets have already been noted to create a mean resonance in the solar system of 178 years:

6	sidereal revolutions of Saturn	176.746 yrs.
15	sidereal revolutions of Jupiter	177.933 yrs.
9	synodic periods, Jupiter/Saturn	178.734 yrs.
14	synodic periods, Jupiter/Neptune	178.923 yrs.
13	synodic periods, Jupiter/Uranus	179.562 yrs.
5	synodic periods, Saturn/Neptune	179.385 yrs.
4	synodic periods, Saturn/Uranus	181.455 yrs.

It is interesting to note that Pluto, the inter-system vagabond, does not fit into any of the 178 year resonances. Perhaps earlier speculations that Pluto is time shared with another system is not so absurd. Regardless of Pluto's lack of involvement, the 178 period prevails establishing the larger rhythm of the solar system.

Cycles prevail, cycles push and cycles persist. The cycles of planetary origin create the dynamics of the interactions of the solar system. These dynamics extend down the planetary ladder to the inhabitants of the planets all striving in common to attain the same resonances and rhythms. A conscious turn is at hand with the awareness created by the examination of the heliocentric horoscope.

Chapter Five

A Note on the Solar System at Large

In November of 1983, the United States based National Aeronautics and Space Administration (NASA), announced the discovery
of three rings encompassing the solar system. These bands of dust
were found by IRAS, the *Infrared Astronomical Satellite*, a joint venture of the United States, Britain and the Netherlands.

The bands of dust appear to feed off of the asteroid belt between
Mars and Jupiter. The inner ring circles the system at 200 million
miles from the Sun and the outer ring some 100 million miles farther.
These three highly stable symmetrical rings seem to defy the laws of
physics as astronomically perceived. However, the defiance, if real,
would allow for the simultaneous destruction of the rings, which is
not taking place. Obviously, some reformation of concepts of particles in space and space plasma requires attention.

The idea of rings prevails again. It used to be that astrologers
were obsessed with the containment and confinement suggested by
the multi-levels of rings about the planet Saturn. The discoveries of
rings about Uranus and later around Jupiter and Neptune disbanded
that theory of limitation. To maintain the rings of Saturn as a symbol
of restriction, would logically require that the rings of Jupiter and
Uranus be perceived in restrictive contexts as well. The theory falls
by the wayside since the experience of both Jupiter and Uranus is
inconsistent with restriction. Recent observation from *Voyager* con-
firms the speculation that Neptune contains rings. One may choose
to experience rings collectively as containment and now note that the
rings banding the solar system together create just another trilogy of

restriction. Perhaps the rings in space will never end.

The newly discovered rings banding (bonding?) the solar system in breadth seem to stem from the asteroids. Perhaps the asteroid belt comes from an exploded planet ripped apart by some unknown force, resulting in devastating fragmentation. Such a planet may have circled the Sun near the asteroid belt. Yet, from this source, the subtle essence and stuff, the dust merges together in an integrative pattern to bond the solar system at the point of apparent injury. The dust almost appears as three large band-aids mending the wound of disintegration.

Speculation exists now, astronomically and astrologically, as to the meaning and symbolism of the rings. Time, good time, will provide more meaning.

Our entire solar system is but a speck of dust swirling about a more massive core—the Galactic Center—residing late in the degrees of Sagittarius. With a rotation about the Galactic Center of some 250 million years, the Sun and its solar system looses significance in the greater cosmic scheme. Other systems may be found to exist, such as the one recently speculated to be centered about the star Vega. Our solar system would ultimately have the same relationship to Vega that Jupiter has to Saturn.

It just goes on and on. Each new discovery which defies physics and natural laws as we know them merely implies a new paradigm shift. Heliocentric astrology could then prevail with a sense not only of universal, but systematic prevalence.

Chapter Six

Aspects to Consider

One of the most dynamic components of any horoscopic system is the analysis of the angular relationships between the horoscopic commodities. These angles, noted to be of significant effect, are the aspects. An aspect is an angular relationship between any two configurations in the horoscope. Technically, any angular relationship whatsoever constitutes an aspect, but throughout the ages astrologers have maintained that certain angles contain more inherent potency than others.

The purpose of this chapter is not to interpret the traditional astrological aspects. This effort has been performed many times over (some performances being far better than others). The intent of this chapter seeks to put forth new information regarding angular relationships which falls more specifically into the realm of heliocentric astrology.

Previous astrological dissertations sought to relate an orb of influence or an effective range of longitude through which an aspect is effective. These definitions of orbs found reference to the angle in question. The speculation submitted herein states that a second orb of influence finds reference to the intrinsic mean motion of the planet involved, with the faster moving planet prevailing. Two forms of translating orbs arise; one with respect to angle of longitude and the other with respect to time. It is recommended that the longitudinal orientation of orbs be used for natal interpretation and that the time influence be applied to the effects of transiting motion in terms of speeds of approach and separation.

It is recommended that an orb of not more than 5° be applied to an aspect. The aspect retains greater dynamic potential within an arc of 2½°. Work done by John Nelson implied that angles of out to 10° remain effective; however, such loose application of orbs weakens the dynamic.

The following reference table notes the effective orbs for the planets both by degree of the arc and corresponding time element. These orbs are effective for longitude only and do not refer to declination.

Planet	Degree	Time Element
Mercury	± 7°	1.7 days
Venus	± 3.5°	2.3 days
Earth	± 2.5°	2.1 days
Mars	± 1.5°	3.1 days
Jupiter	± 1.25°	6.8 days
Saturn	± 2.4°	14.4 days
Uranus	± 1.25°	21.3 days
Neptune	± 1.25°	26.8 days
Pluto	± 5°	40.0 days

The following orbs of parallel and contraparallel result for those choosing to pursue these aspects in heliocentric astrology. Orb measurements are in minutes (') of arc, 60 minutes comprising one degree.

Planet	Orb
Mercury	± 45'
Venus	± 21'
Earth	± 15'
Mars	± 7.5'
Jupiter	± 7.5'
Saturn	± 15'
Uranus	± 7.5'
Neptune	± 7.5'
Pluto	± 2°

Sensitive Points

Four unusual contact points appear in heliocentric astrology, presenting significant importance to any tropical (seasonally based) system of astrology. These points are: the Vernal Equinox (0° Aries), the Summer Solstice (0° Cancer), the Autumnal Equinox (0° Libra), and the Winter Solstice (0° Capricorn). The first glance at a heliocentric horoscope often creates the perception that the natural Cardinal Cross represents the angles of the horoscope. That perception stands as a misperception. The solar basis of the chart and the lack of attention focused upon the axial rotation of a reference point eliminates the existence of a rising sign. The angles of the horoscope evaporate and new considerations appear, witness the solstices and equinoxes.

Contacts to these points will occur primarily from planetary placement as the nodes and perihelia/aphelia do not presently reside in orb to these contacts. The aspectual stimulation results from direct planetary alignment (± 1°) to the zero degree Cardinal points (Aries, Cancer, Libra, Capricorn).

These points all share the changing of a season and thus, imply a significant environmental alteration. The ratio of light and dark of the twenty-four hour period known as a day shifts with respect to these contacts. For instance, on the first day of winter maximum darkness is perceived and on the first day of summer maximum light falls on the region. Interestingly enough, the first day of winter marks the increase of the forces of light and the first summer day brings with it the rise of the dark power. The equinotical points, Vernal and Autumnal, carry within the balance of light and dark. The Vernal Equinox carries the balance from dark into light and the Autumnal Equinox equates equilibrium of lightness yielding to darkness.

The balance of light and dark may be translated into several other dimensions of relating. These are (all respectively to light/dark): *Yin/Yang*, Creative/Receptive, Masculine/Feminine and Assertion/Passivity. Other similar relationships include: Strong/Devoted (yielding), Heaven/Earth, Father/Mother as well as Positive/Negative.

Summer Solstice

The analysis of these points begins with the Summer Solstice at the precise moment that the light force culminates at its zenith. The Summer Solstice carries with it qualities of perseverance, timeliness, assertion, strength, originality, leadership, sagacity, cultivation of spiritual power, repetition, the sublime and success. The implementation of this wide array of attributes requires activity in the pure interest of creating order and restoring peace. Unimpeded steps suggested by the very nature of this solstice lead to success. Six steps are implied in this great point of manifestation, two sequences of three steps each. Duration is required as each step must be taken upon the actualized basis of the preceding step. Most importantly, the first step must be taken.

This light switch works through principles of change and transformation. The individual with contacts to this point strives to obtain clarity in perceiving the beginning and the end. The tapping of the natural power of the Universal Sources and the pursuit of the ultimate manifestation of the Godhead need to be sought with great diligence.

Winter Solstice

The Winter Solstice connotes the culmination of the dark forces. Note that the Winter Solstice does not compete with its summer counterpart, but completes it. The combination of the solstice points represents the archetypical male/female relationship and combines the nurturing forces of both father and mother.

Devotion to the primal power of the Universe requires entering a time of following. This includes the total relinquishment of urges to lead. Leadership roles in connection with this point compete with the creative forces and connote conflict of forces or evil. This point of 0° Capricorn normally translates to the leadership needed to attain, accomplish and conquer. It notes here, however, that one must stop and listen before leading.

Conformity within a situation, not with resignation and condescension, but with devotion and gentleness, allows for the ultimate advance. Guidance sought and guidance followed completes this natural effect. Cultivated breadth and purity of character combine with sustaining power so that one achieves the ability to tolerate all people and things.

Nurturing receives substance from this solstice through rest, friends and family. Utilization of a womb-like rest creates ultimate success.

Vernal Equinox

The Vernal Equinox refers to spring. The blooming and flowering of life is visible again. The balance of light and dark shifts toward the increase of light, allowing the essence of peace to prevail. It appears as if Heaven descends upon the Earth. In effect the Sun returns to warm and contact is again made with that which is the life giving influence.

Social harmony becomes the theme of individualized manifestation. The animal nature reveals itself in human form and must be dealt with in such a way as to continue social harmony, not upset it. Brusqueness must be refined. One must ultimately do what is in accord with his or her nature.

The balance of masculine and feminine is induced at this point. This may suggest the social interaction of male and female or may imply an effort to attain gender equality, androgyny or neutrality.

Good conduct yields contentment. The development of an intimate inner circle is implied. Long range goals thrive through short range actions.

Autumnal Equinox

Finally, the Autumnal Equinox completes the markings of the seasons and the calendar. The time of harvest, standstill and decline comes into being as the light/dark balance presides with the increase of darkness to follow.

Resources, especially resources of inner worth, stand as the paramount commodities of the time. Due to the inner awareness of decline, one may submit to and be adversely affected by monetary offers, flattery or dazzling offers in the public arena (note that the fall is often the time of political elections). Withdrawal and inner contemplation need manifestation to ensure that one stays in accord with a Godhead. Faith in one's principles creates the enduring action.

A sense of becoming disunited prevails, but one should realize that this point merely annotates the waning portion of a perpetual cycle which will later begin to wax. The Sun is sinking away and the life force appears to dissipate. Yet, the harvest of the time creates the sense of nurturing and abundance needed to persist until the next seasonal change occurs.

Planetary Nodes

The planetary nodes stimulate an area of influence in the heliocentric horoscope. Early work by John Nelson found that a planet was stronger[1] when within five to ten degrees of either node or bisection of the nodal axis. He was not clear as to whether a planet

---

[1] Dean, Geoffrey, *Recent Advances in Natal Astrology, A Critical Review 1900-1976*, p. 264.

interacted strongly only with its own nodes. It is submitted that any planet to any other planetary node may be considered to be an effective aspect—five degree orb maximum.

Planetary nodes in heliocentric astrology advance at a rate of about one degree per 100 years. This does not represent an effect of precession since precession is a geocentric perceptual phenomenon. The slow motion of the nodes creates a generational influence in which virtually any person born in any given century has the same nodes. What could be the fuss?

The planet in contact to the node represents the personalized connection to a collective issue. The planet reveals the impetus that the individual possesses to exert an effect in a larger issue of humanity and in context of the planet's symbolism. North Node connections induce the individual to push for advance, change, reform and progress—worst case: rebellion, malcontent and antiestablishment attitudes prevail, often polarizing the opposed force into greater manifestation; protest and resistance fail to function at any level. South planetary nodes contain heritage, tradition and foundation. Contacts to the south node support such historical bases with great chauvinism. Other times, the tailing node contact represents dogma, resistance to progress, fear of advancement and the inability to adjust to technological progress. A point of equilibrium and balance must be maintained.

It remains relatively simple to delineate planetary contacts to nodes. Do realize that examples presented are out of horoscopic context and could be modified significantly by other aspects in the chart.

Consider the instance of an individual's Mercury in Gemini conjoining the Venusian North Node. A double Gemini influence prevails from Mercury and its association to Gemini and the sign of the North Node of Venus. This inspires the individual to speak actively regarding social issues, monetary conditions, or the sphere of social relationships. Best case, this person effectively occupies a platform for social and economic reform. Worst case, the individual reduces the self into the realm of idle gossip—misdirected, unapplied, frustrated by the collective conditions at hand. His/her overall morality would feel violated without source to rectification.

Should an individual's natal Mars in Capricorn fall upon the Saturnian South Node, the individual would be an archeologist. This archeology need not manifest in the physical let's-go-dig-a-hole-in-Egypt mode. The digging into the past could be mental, philosophical or emotional. This individual strives to extract the value and benefit of what was done, noting the downfalls in the interest of avoiding future tautology. At best, the person advances great insights into dimensions of development and realizes a variety of ways to transcend past errors. When operating at a less than optimum level, the owner of the map becomes obsessed by tradition, allowing an antiquated heritage to go unchallenged by the motions of progress. Such action merely seals the fate of the collective force to replicate old procedures enabling accurate recycling of the same efforts at evolution—ultimate redundancy.

Nelson's work pointed out sensitivity of a planet bisecting the nodal axis—the midpoint of the North Node/South Node or South Node/North Node. A moderately different flavor may be applied to each of these nodal midpoints. The direction of the natural zodiac constitutes the from/to direction, these points follow a from/to format, that is, from South Node to North Node (℧/☊) or from North Node to South Node (☊/℧).

The motion in the direction of the North Node from the South Node shows a movement out of the past and into the future. Integration, balance and synthesis of the two worlds of existence becomes paramount. Taking the best of the old and applying it as foundation provides a key as to this necessary integration. Elimination of old formats which exceed effective application propels the issue forward even further. A moderate approach to progress blending with the firmness of tested effort combines for a successful approach to a planet's theme.

Moving from the North Node to the South Node requires more emphasis to be placed on exploration of the past. Previous forms hold many keys to ensure that progressive effects do not fall short of the goal through lack of preparation or expectation of the unforeseen. This nodal moderation calls for a conservative attitude in growth and progress. Examination of the former reveals potential problematic situations. Such avoidances, perceived in advance due to retrospective analysis, save great time and energy in the interest of forward motion and growth.

Perihelia and Aphelia

These solar contact orientations establish another set of fixed configurations to examine in order to understand the pursuit and purpose of the individual with respect to the collective. As with the nodal nuances, these points generate interest in destiny and meaning in life, thereby inspiring the person to continue forward in life with zest and zeal.

At the perihelion point the Sun occupies one of the foci of the planet's orbital ellipse. The persuasion of the planet strives to find focus at the perihelion and does so with great urgency. The urgency is established by the rapid motion of the planet at perihelion and the relative proximity to the Sun.

Consider the implication of John Nelson's work again. He substantiated that a planetary connection to either perihelion or aphelion significantly strengthened the influence of the planet.[2] No direct reference was made to perihelion/aphelion bisection; however, the influence is implied. Suppose that an individual had natal Jupiter in the heliocentric chart in a partile conjunction with the perihelion of Mercury in Gemini. Note that Jupiter would also conjoin the North Node of Venus, and to a lesser degree the North Node of Uranus. To contemplate solely the Jupiter to Mercury integration in this planet/ perihelion configuration, the individual would carry strong teaching abilities into this incarnation. An urgency to guide or instruct would prevail until the individual found manifestation. Idle bossiness or voicing arrogant opinions are good examples of this aspect in an unintegrated form. Still, the prevalent urge carries the need to contact, at close distance, those with whom one can share information of an experiential nature.

Ponder upon a Mars in Scorpio on the perihelion of Pluto. This aspect guarantees a strong interactive influence geared to provoke, push, and persuade a deep level of transformation. Regardless of how this aspect looks at a distance (even when Pluto is closest it is still some thirty times the distance of the Earth from the Sun) the goal is to produce massive change and possibly painful evolution, even at the risk of complete isolationism (not a purpose to be approached lightly).

Venus falling upon Jupiter's aphelion in Libra should stimulate some interesting relationship interactions for the individual. Despite discreetness, this individual's relationship life would attract the attention of the collective, especially that part of the collective which thinks it has the right answer. The individual bears the lesson to teach the collective how to relate to others within one's own standards. Retreat, as the distant aphelion implies, provides the point of essential refuge and perspective. Retreat from a relationship allows

---

[2] Dean, Geoffrey, *Op Cit.*

for participation in the same relationship, forming a statement of synthesis.

The midpoint of perihelion/aphelion (q/Q), moving from perihelion to aphelion direction created by the natural zodiac, demonstrates a braking motion. The planet theoretically reaches a mean speed of revolution about the Sun, striving to obtain a point of normalcy. Some remorse may be felt during slow-down. Otherwise the retreat may be anticipated in a vacation-like atmosphere. Enthusiasm for the plateau results.

Pluto's q/Q midpoint falls in Aquarius. Should an individual have the Earth in Aquarius aligned with this point, the individual feels an environmental urge to deal with ecology of the planet. This ecological interest can thrive without impeaching the Secretary of the Interior! It may appear in a psychological, mental, philosophical or spiritual sense. These individuals try to manifest the essential resources upon the planet in the interest of the planet's transformation. The "putting on the brakes" theme of the midpoint stresses the need to pause and review, ensuring effective and conscious effort of resources before moving forward and using (exploiting) other resources. An earthier analogy is reviewing the refrigerator for potential leftovers prior to cooking a new meal. This investigation requires the jettison of the decayed foodstuffs to prevent decay of good foodstuffs.

Mars resting upon the midpoint Q/q of Saturn in Aries represents the point of planetary acceleration as it passes through mean orbital characteristics. This creates the need for renewed thrust and pooling of resources and guarantees that the effort extended has sufficient impetus to produce the intended structural manifestations implied by Saturn. One demands more individualized energy, great persistence and an overwhelmingly positive attitude toward success.

With all of these contacts analyzed, a return to more traditional aspect operations is in order. Nelson noted the following descending order of importance in aspects:

    a) squares and oppositions
    b) conjunctions
    c) trines to tense aspects
    d) trines to ease aspects
    e) sextiles, semi-sextiles, inconjuncts to tense aspects
    f) sextiles, semi-sextiles, inconjuncts to ease aspects
    g) seven and a half degree multiple aspects[3]

---

[3] Dean, Geoffrey, *Op Cit.*

The seven and a half degree aspect family, familiar to those of the Uranian school of thought, stirs some initial puzzlement amongst other astrologers. In many systems of astrology these angular relationships repeatedly demonstrate their potency and viability. The simplest way to encounter these contacts is to make a listing of angular separation among all planets and points in the horoscope. Orbs to the seven and a half degree family should keep to one degree.

A reference table of the seven and a half degree family follows:

7.5°	97.5°	187.5°	277.5°
15.0°	105.0°	195.0°	285.0°
22.5°	112.5°	202.5°	292.5°
30.0°	120.0°	210.0°	300.0°
37.5°	127.5°	217.5°	307.5°
45.0°	135.0°	225.0°	315.0°
52.5°	142.5°	232.5°	322.5°
60.0°	150.0°	240.0°	330.0°
67.5°	157.5°	247.5°	337.5°
75.0°	165.0°	255.0°	345.0°
82.5°	172.5°	262.5°	352.5°
90.0°	180.0°	270.0°	360.0°

These aspects imply efforts towards manifestation. It is worth noting that the seven and a half degree aspect family contains all of the major aspects within the aspect genealogy.

A final note on aspectual orbs comes again from the works of John Nelson. Nelson's work implied that an applying orb of five degrees and a four degree departing (separating) seemed highly effective.[4] For mundane analysis wherein timing is foremost, tighter aspects of 15' applying and 30' separating function accurately.

The initial encounter with the heliocentric horoscope induces one to look for similarities and differences especially with regard to the planetary positions. One will notice that the planets beyond Uranus reside within two degrees of the geocentric position, Saturn within about four degrees, Jupiter within some twelve degrees, Mars within roughly seventy degrees, and the Earth in exact opposition to

---

[4] Dean, Geoffrey, *Op Cit.*

the geocentric Sun. The inner planets Mercury and Venus experience no placement restrictions whatsoever.

Most individuals experience a new zodiacal position of both Mercury and Venus. A great beauty exists in this analysis. As soon as one submits to the nature of the heliocentric horoscope, finding one's ultimate purpose in this incarnation exists, a new format for communicating (Mercury) one's needs, both personal and material (Venus).

Not only do new signs generally prevail for Mercury and Venus; new aspects between the two rapidly moving planets form. One may now experience an opposition of Mercury and Venus when in the geocentric format no such angular relationship was possible (only conjunctions semi-sextiles, semi-squares, sextiles, and quintiles are possible). This example would now indicate great levels of objectivity which could result in an expression of need that increases potential fulfillment. More clarity and conciseness would intrinsically develop.

A comparison between the aspect breakdowns of the geocentric and heliocentric charts, is now appropriate. To do this, make a list of all aspects in the chart by type, i.e. trines, sextiles, squares, etc. Next, compile the aspects into categories of tense aspects and ease aspects. Ease aspects include: semi-sextiles, sextiles, trines, quintiles, bi-quintiles and perhaps conjunctions. Stress aspects consist of: semi-squares, squares, sesquiquadrates, quincunxes and oppositions. Weigh the ratio of stress aspects to ease aspects. Whichever family of aspects contains more occurrences, the chart receives definition from that family. The chart now appears to be either ease dominated or stress dominated (with the exception of those charts which show a nearly even distribution of stress and ease aspects).

A comparative look between the aspectual nature of the geocentric horoscope to the heliocentric horoscope begins. One of four combinations result. (Use E = ease domination; use S = stress domination.) These are (geocentric to heliocentric): E/E, E/S, S/S and S/E. The contrast of these aspect dominations loosely notes one's reaction to the transition and use of the heliocentric nativity.

Individuals with either the E/E or S/S patterns notice little distinction between the systems. The E/E individuals find each astrological point of view just as simple as the other, only in a slightly different way. This is also true for the S/S individuals. It is difficult for the S/S person to see what the difference is since both dimensions of life appear to contain the same amount of turmoil. It just seems that in the heliocentric point of view that the placement of the major tension exists elsewhere.

The E/S dynamic stands to realize more with approach to the heliocentric map. These people embrace an increase in the difficulty of life. Although this represents an initial test, these individuals may turn back in an early stage of heliocentric development only to return later. They realize the increased level of commitment, persistence, responsibility and integrity required in a conscious approach to life. They simultaneously recognize the need and demand to continue upon the heliocentric road whether or not they want or choose to.

The S/E individuals experience quite a different perspective. These purpose pursuers look at the heliocentric horoscope with a spiritually based where-have-you-been-all-my-life look. Finally, at long last, these persons find their respective niches in life. Life becomes simplified and less difficult when following the path of growth and attainment. How nice it feels to be in tune and guided by the natural flow of a larger solar system cycle. These individuals ultimately stand to be some of the strongest proponents of the young model of heliocentric astrology.

With these considerations in mind and a heliocentric centered heart, the distribution of the planets in the heliocentric horoscope steps forward for accountability. That is just the point. It is another view with a different aspect.

Chapter Seven

General Quadratics

Fortunately or not, the term general quadratics bears no reference to the notorious equation which perplexed many in the introductory algebra. General quadratics merely describes a system of dividing the heliocentric horoscope to obtain an alternate set of revealing variables about the map.

Given that the rotation of the Earth upon its axis no longer affects the realm of astrology as a variable, then the configurations known as the rising sign and the midheaven no longer exist. The houses of the horoscope, following the ascendant and midheaven evaporation, also cease to be indicated. The question arises as to how to lay out the planets of the Sun centered system. Granted, the dispute over house systems and technicalities between zenith, culmination and midheaven disappear. Still, one must establish some form of reference wheel to begin the interpretation.

Though Rudhyar preferred an eight sector division system, a quadrature approach seems natural and receives demarcation by the natural flow of the seasons. The Vernal Equinox, Summer Solstice, Autumnal Equinox and Winter Solstice configure the perimeters of the quadrants. These points correspond to the zero degree points of Aries, Cancer, Libra and Capricorn. It is suggested that upon the wheel of the zodiac that these be the only outer ring markings for clarity and simplification. No intermediate sign markings need exist as no intermediate houses hold any relevance.

Each quadrant possesses a quality of association to flavor the region it contains. Quadrant one which contains Aries, Taurus and

Gemini, bears the quality of *expression of will*. The second quadrant containing Cancer, Leo and Virgo, maintains a tone of *expression of space*. The third region occupying the signs of Libra, Scorpio and Sagittarius, receives flavoring from the quality of *application of will*. The fourth and final quadratic division bears the signs Capricorn, Aquarius and Pisces indicating an emphasis of *application of space*.

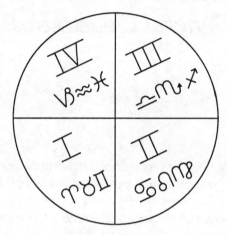

The heliocentric horoscope can now be interpreted with the planets intheir respective divisions through the use of the quadrant system. Merely place the planets into the quadrants by zodiacal sign. Notice the domination of quadrants parallels the effects done in geocentric astrology with quadrant analysis. Be aware not to include lunar nodes, vertex and *pars fortuna* as these effects all refer to specific configurations in geocentric astrology. Should the newly discovered planetoid, Chiron, be used, it maintains a full planet weight. All asteroids, including the newly categorized spread of minor planets, each operate with a half planet weight. The quadrant with the most planets and minor planets becomes the most emphasized sector. Natal charts often contain two, sometimes three, quadrants of equal emphasis.

Generational dominance also occur. In the early 1940s when Jupiter, Saturn and Uranus all passed through Taurus, the first quadrant received emphasis. The inner planets in one of the first three zodiacal signs periodically added to the domination of the first quadrant. Those born in the pre-World War II era grew up with a strong impending sense of insecurity based upon the imminent threat of war. This precognitive response formed the materialism consciousness of the possibility of rationing, need for conservation of resources and total support of the country's effort. These people sought self-identity and looked for manifestations of the will to validate their existence. The crisis became one of identity and the ability to assert, express and create despite the tribulations politically generated in the time.

Another such generational influence began in July of 1988 as Saturn joined Neptune in Capricorn followed in September by the Uranus' entry into Capricorn. This supports the heliocentric quadrant theme of application of space presiding until Saturn enters Aries in June of 1996. Jupiter enters Capricorn in February Of 1966, adding a fourth major planet to the quadrant perspective until Saturn's passage into Aries. The inner planets add their period stimulations as frequently as Mercury offering its fourth quadrant passage for about three weeks every three months.

The first quadrant contains Aries, Taurus and Gemini and bears the tone of intent of expression of will. Self-assertion looms as the fundamental quality for these individuals to cultivate. Without some form of assertion, how is it that anything would get done? The nature of assertion requires modification from the archetypical notion of forceful thrust. Assertion needs support of cultivation, refinement, contrast and basic mental developments. Initiation starts the effort in motion. It must be understood that immediate effects of initiation may not appear. Consider the springtime when seeds are planted in the ground. Some time must pass before even the first signs of effective germination make evidence. Only after the sprouts arise to certain heights can weeding, or shall we say refinement and cultivation, occur. The comparison of seedlings to weeds must be conducted and aspects of defined learning warrants application.

Great disappointments lie in store should one anticipate immediate response to extended efforts within the first quadrant. Individuals often scatter seeds about the Universe, running hither and yon, never staying in one place long enough to see if the seed sprouts or not. These individuals seal their own fate of not creating a sense of existence. They see no result from the expression of will and the primal use of creative force in life.

Results do come to individuals utilizing any level of patience and persistence within the first quadrant. The realization that the perceived results stem directly from extended efforts and the creative free flowing expression of the will occurs. It then happens that many see the result as the self, establishing a reliance in life upon external results.

These externalized perceptions take away the perception of expressed will achieved, and this undoes the entire result. Attachment of the self (will) to that which is outside the self produces slow, static functioning.

The feedback cycle then pushes the motivation mechanism within the individual to assert more dramatically and with greater demand for results. The whole essence of this quadrature stresses that such efforts inhibit the expression of will. The impedance of will results from the control of the will by the result. No longer can the individual cast seeds knowing that some will germinate and some will not. This level of assertive insistence demands that all seeds grow. In the sphere of social interaction, this debilitated view of one's will leads the person into relationship interference through imposing the self onto the wills of others.

Pure, unimpeded, clear extension of will idealizes this sector. The primal quality of expression without expectation and anticipation clears the way for infinite margins of self-awareness, completing the nature of the quadrant. Subjectivity in consciousness disintegrates permitting clarity in relations with others. The will expresses and receives acknowledgement (not to be perceived as agreement or compliance) and the level of acknowledgement feeds positively back to the will, enabling a clearer expression in the future.

Think of the unimpeded way a young child cries. The essence of the feeling spews out of the stomach, defining the gutteral level of response and reaction. Uncontrollable sobs fail to regulate the breathing. No inhibition takes place in the release of emotion that demonstrates only a portion of the will—that portion of ego expression relevant only at that time. This ego expression works well until a parent decides that there has been enough crying. "Don't let me hear you crying," bellows the parent into the child's room. "You stop that stupid sobbing right now."

Many children hear this. The nature of the force is inhibitive. Incidentally, this example does not suggest at any level that the parent is bad. It also does not suggest rightness or wrongness of the child. Consider another example of the same situation with an equal level of will-impedance. The child cries because a schoolmate used names which defamed or took away some margin of the child's experience of will. The child bursts through the door crying and exclaiming a story of woe. The helpful (or so it seems) parent holds the child and says, "There, there, it's alright." Like hell, it's alright. If it were alright, would the child be crying in the first place?

The individual dominated with planets in his or her first quadrant must contend with such issues of expression of identity continually upon the path of purpose. The integration comes, but not immediately or with great certainty. The person must note the transitional nature of acknowledgement, positive or negative, and file the acknowledging information under the category of will validation. Only then, with all levels of response, validation and invalidation utilized, does the individual emerge at the primal levels of total self-assertion.

The Second Quadrant

Expression of space demonstrates the qualities of the second horoscopic quadrant. This sector of solar system space splices in the signs of Cancer, Leo and Virgo. A somewhat mental quadrant, these individuals either use logic to assist in the path of growth or to impede the path of growth.

The logical axiom applied in the second quad is the classical "If . . . then . . . " principle. If this, then this, states the person, with abundant levels of arrogance. Initially, this axiom creates havoc for the person to sort through in order to find a destination. The essence lies in the awareness of all that which is available and how to utilize it on the path of purpose.

Classic manifestations of this sector sound like this: "If I did not have to work so much, I could get so much done." "If I had an office at home, then I could set up my own business." "If my mother had loved me more, I wouldn't be so demanding of my spouse today." All of these statements hold one great error in common. All of these affirmations, such as they are, ensure the individual's correctness of position regarding the conditions prevalent in life. This externalizes the need for responsibility for one's life and removes connection with the creative part of one's nature.

Part of the theme of the second division requires total extension of one's creative force into all that stands about the individual. To begin, the individual must first remove the need to justify the lack of attainment or completion of purpose in life. Note that the statements of "if, then" arise out of a sense of wrong doing for not having done more in life. None of these statements create a sense of capability to fulfill life's purpose. The statements attenuate, debilitate and castrate. Potency vanishes.

The individual willing to be wrong about these conditions and their proclaimed inevitability of outcome stands to change the outcome and to regain the pure ability to apply the self in the surrounding spaces of life.

Space, at its most primal, is one's aura. Upon creative interjection of energy into the aura, one begins to magnetize far more creative attributes. The process of attraction multiplies and suddenly availability looms at every nook and cranny in experience.

The opportunistic mode of life motivates one to participate in the openings of offerings. One must learn to utilize partial opportunities, transforming those efforts into the full-fledged manifestation. Acceptance of that which is incomplete and available must occur to produce the subsequent manifestation. This overcomes the "if, then" logic box and frees the person to create via the expression of available space.

The Third Quadrant

The third quadrant of the chart carries the theme of application of will. The signs of Libra, Scorpio and Sagittarius make up the zodiacal components of is dimension. These people are perhaps the most difficult to work with in the interest of their own growth.

The individual with a domination in the third quadrant already possesses a strong sense of self and knows much of the capacities of the self. This awareness resides at a deep level in the mind and may not seem consciously accessible. Yet it is accessible.

These people strive to manipulate others into the process of self-validation by having another tell them precisely what they wish to hear. Others usually comply with stunning accuracy of imagery, supporting the visual picture established in the mind of the third quadrant person. The person then rejects the input of other people as being invalid and unimportant due to judgments of others' perceptual deficiency. The third quadrant dimensional being now forces the self back into the hidden portions of the consciousness to recapture the known sense of soul.

People near a third quadrant personality can do nothing to support the growth of the individual. It is absurd to try. Third quadrant individuals double-bind others. They request input and then reject it, thereby rejecting the individual giving the input as well. Despite the growth being sought, this manner of human interaction remains far below minimum standard in relationships. These individuals, when in the midst of their own intimate processing to attain a spiritual or psychological goal, can only be left to their own devices. Those devices are numerous and the individual instinctively knows how to make contact with them.

The actualized third quarter person, complete with a sense of inner knowing of personal resources, begins to notice such resources in other people. The individual begins a campaign to bring others to the same level of inner awareness. Typically, this takes the form of the third quarter individual being available to one who appears to be in need of inner support. The third quarter individual starts a process of questioning which enables the seeker to arrive at the conclusions of the self by the self. A word for this process is motivation. The third quarter individual owns great motivation potential and fully realizes that one can not in any way, shape or form motivate another individual. It is often stated by professional motivators that motivation is 10% the motivator and 90% the person trying to be motivated. Third quarter people manipulate others to become the self-motivators in a package so slick that the other individual never realizes the shift. Resistance to motivation falls off and progress is made. It is in this way that the third quarter being comes into full application of the will.

Third quarter individuals also need to gain awareness of the sense of creating one's own destiny. Manifestation powers and the use of manifestation can and must be developed by these people. Should manifestation not be incorporated into the life experience, these individuals generally become cynical and seek to manipulate others to meet their needs. This too could be considered to demonstrate a form of manifestation power in a very left-handed way. The pure intrinsic manifestation power comes from within to without, not from outside to within. Actualized third quarter personalities clearly recognize this premise; unactualized inhabitants of this segment bear no consciousness of this reality. The unactualized swear that others control their destinies.

Cause and effect forces of creation must be concisely understood. Power to apply the will lies within such forces of creation. The application of the will in a direct and collectively demonstrated manner provides the push to gain purpose.

The Fourth Quadrant

Fourth quarter emphasis takes in the signs of Capricorn, Aquarius and Pisces. This quadrature carries the tonal quality of application of space.

This portion of the heliocentric pie bears the strongest collective emphasis of all the regions. It appears that these people have no choice but to become immersed in the collective activities which surround them in their inner and outer environments—space. Perhaps the true humanitarians reside within the perimeters of this astrological atrium.

A fundamental realization must occur first before the manifestation of the ultimate altruism can begin. These individuals first need to realize the thrust of the purpose in life. A dedication to purpose prevails over personality. This dedication cannot take place in a manner which creates the tone of sacrifices in life. Such sacrifices remain totally counter-productive to the process of evolution. These people must rise to a sense of destiny, gain a sense of making a difference in life and strive to fulfill the maximum difference which can be created with the efforts of the self in the collective world at hand.

Realization of destiny inspires the individual to seek purpose and reach out to gain all possible responsibilities in the transformation of the collective consciousness. However, one must not try to save the world. World-savers often go on fanatical binges that alienate precisely those most in need. Perspective of the realm of effective influence should develop. One must consider the collective receptivity. If this receptivity does not exist, then the condition is not inclined to change.

Questions of merit for the fourth quarter inhabitant include: Does the effort meet a real need? Does the effort stand clear of all selfish motivations? Does the effort tend to replicate previous actions (thereby recreating the wheel)? Is the time correct for such an effort?

Great change can take place only from within the collective power structure and not form without that structure. This is the truth of polarity. The truth of polarity points out that with each anti-nuclear rally more fuel is added to nuclear reactor potential. The polarized truth notices that war protests only aggravate the hawkish attitudes towards war.

With these considerations completed in consciousness, one can now pursue the activity necessary to persuade collective change.

One final polarized point remains. How does one heal the masses? Two possible manifestations result, either of which could produce the intended results. Consider each.

One could go to Ethiopia with 100,000 bushels of grain. A complete bushel of grain could be given to each of one hundred thousand Ethiopians. This effort strives to end the agony of starvation and the misery of hunger.

How long does one bushel of grain last one individual? Does the grain sustain a person's malnourished condition back into total health? Will this dispersion of food be effective? Would other techniques of distribution be far more efficient?

Taking the same bushels of grain, 1,000 bushels could be given to each of 100 persons. This grain lasts longer per person and could nurture the individuals long enough for those 100 persons to generate more grain for the multitudes. How much grain can 100 persons produce, in cooperation with nature, while feeding off of the 1,000 bushels of grain they now own? Perhaps a more effective distribution would be to give 1,000 persons 100 bushels of grain and include the workers in a profit sharing program of receipt of the grain they now farm.

Which solution holds more potency? These are the types of questions that the individual of fourth quarter domination asks. A hazard in questioning is that so many questions can be formulated with so many rhetorical answers that the spirit could be demotivated by the complexity of the problems and solutions. There is so much to be done and so little time and so few resources to work with. This attitude blocks results by stalling the individual with frustration and ambiguity. Apathy and rationalization at their worst prevent even minimal exertion in the direction that the individual knows must be taken. However, action must be taken regardless of the perceived likelihoods.

The quadrants of the heliocentric horoscope contain a much broader base and fulfill a higher need, than the geocentric houses. The geocentric houses tend to put the individual in a coping position with the mundane influences in life. The converse is created in the heliocentric quadrant system. The individual establishes a position to do something with and about the surrounding conditions either through the application and exertion of the self or by creating something from the given ambient conditions.

These territories of influence are designed to be transformational in emphasis, inspiring the individual to produce any variety of solutions out of the existing environment. The process resembles the algebraic application of the general quadratic equation. One may produce a positive result, a negative result or a condition for which there is no resolution. In the heliocentric horoscope that choice remains up to the individual.

Chapter Eight

Interfacing
Priorities in Delineation

The background material for the heliocentric horoscope is now behind you. Now comes the simple task of putting the horoscope together and making sense of the new style of map.

The interpretation of the heliocentric chart **IS** a simple task and requires no complication by the astrologer. Logically, from a purely technical point of view, the process of the heliocentric interpretation stands to be more simplified than a geocentric interpretation. With this presupposition in mind, let us proceed.

Some of the pioneering proponents of heliocentric astrology have suggested the integration of the geocentric and heliocentric systems. This integration occurs by placing the heliocentric planets on the geocentric wheel and comparing the aspects between the two systems. Although that process works and gets revealing results, the present work does not support that interpretive technique. One of the promulgators of this theory of geocentric/heliocentric interpretation stated "that it's like mixing apples and oranges and making fruit salad." This mixing of systems does not allow the heliocentric horoscope to speak of its own accord. It is recommended then that you read the geocentric horoscope along side of the heliocentric horoscope, each as its own distinctive entity with a clearly defined and separate theme. The overlay system reduces the significance of the purpose and spiritual implication of the heliocentric map.

Some configurations in a horoscope stand out as more energizing and mobilizing than others. It is as if some components create activity within the individual or event and others merely set the stage for the players. The active components in the horoscope are dynamic influences and provoke responses. Dynamic heliocentric influences are: planets, planetary midpoints and aspects. assive levels of influence come from more conditioning or environmental issues and are static: planetary nodes, perihelia, aphelia, solstice and equinoctal points, and lastly, signs.

Aspect patterns in the heliocentric horoscope contain the greatest level of dynamic influence and should be considered first.

Aspect priorities listed in descending order of strength:
1. planet to planet
2. planet to midpoint
3. planet to perihelion or aphelion
4. planet to node
5. planet to perihelion/aphelion (or visa versa) midpoint
6. planet to nodal midpoint
7. planet to solstice or equinox
8. midpoint to planet
9. midpoint to midpoint
10. midpoint to perihelion or aphelion
11. midpoint to node
12. midpoint to perihelion/aphelion (or visa versa) midpoint
13. midpoint to nodal midpoint
14. midpoint to solstice or equinox

Breakdown of delineation priorities follows:
1. aspects
2. dynamics of planetary motion (i.e. speed), q, Q
3. quadrant emphasis
4. midpoint analysis
5. planets in signs
6. distribution of midpoints by signs

The interpreter stands to benefit greatly from a computer production of the heliocentric map. Such a computation and printout saves hours of calculations by including midpoints, angular separations or aspects, Chiron, an analysis of midpoints, distance values and the precise perihelia and nodes for the solar system time of birth. These factors then extrapolated onto the chart blank give a greater quadrant perspective. Such a computerized horoscope contains the capability to conduct the complete investigation of aspects recommended as well as an interpretation of the midpoints.

The interpreter, if following the listings of aspect and delineation priorities, merely goes down each list noting and documenting the results in each category. This can be done one step at a time. The beauty of heliocentric astrology comes from the fact that all geocentric astrological groundwork is relevant. Aspects maintain the same meaning; planets remain in the same basic contexts; midpoints add no new perplexing qualities.

The main question asked at lectures on heliocentric astrology is, "Okay, wonderful. So what good is it? Why would an astrologer ever even want to explore the meaning of the heliocentric chart when the everlasting geocentric horoscope works like a champ?" Good question.

The creation of an analogy serves this answer best. Consider some regions of the United States in which the average household income soars above the national mean. Such areas are invariably saturated with a high proportion of members of the helping professions— psychiatrists, psychologists, counselors and holistic mental and medical practitioners. Why? Why is it that when individuals obtain the long-sought-for fulfillment that something seems missing? Why is it that those in positions of attainment prevail as the primary clients of facilitators? Is this solely a factor of economic prowess?

Not really. Very often when someone reaches a pinnacle of success, that individual realizes that initial pursuits were shallow in purpose. The classically sought and illusive meaning of life is not found in success. Perplexity sets in and often overwhelms the individual. The questions dominate the mind: "What good is all of this?" "Is this what I really want?" "Do I want to spend the rest of my life like this?" "Have I been living a lie?" "What good am I doing in this mess of a world?" The questions compile, circulate and overload the brain.

It is at this very point in an individual's life that heliocentric astrology can be the most beneficial. The heliocentric horoscope strongly emphasizes the extended purpose in life. The map reveals roads to take to propel the seeker closer to a sense of meaning and fulfillment within the incarnation. The individual obtains and must utilize the expanded operating room of space in which one conducts the incarnation. Availability of purpose-related activities increase, enabling strong reinforcement aspects to one's destiny.

The strong significance of the heliocentric horoscope may lead to the question of how to know when it is time to look at the heliocentric chart. It could be confusing and overwhelming if the heliocentric chart is examined too early.

True, premature analysis of the heliocentric map holds the potential to demotivate the individual. Still, the determination of the timing for the initial look into the new world remains ultimately up to the owner of the chart. Any time the questions come up: "Why am I here?" "What am I doing in/with/through life?" "What good is all of this?" These are questions which require an initial heliocentric examination.

Astrological guidelines for delving into the realm of heliocentric astrology, which are less subjective than geocentric counterparts, do include the following familiar aspects in the geocentric horoscope:

1. Transits or progression to the lunar nodes by a major planet (Note: major planet is perceived to be Jupiter, Saturn, Uranus, Neptune or Pluto);
2. Transits or progressions to natal Saturn or Uranus by a major planet;
3. Saturn transiting, opposing natal Saturn;
4. Uranus transiting, opposing natal Uranus;
5. Any transit of Pluto by conjunction to planet or angle;
6. Any tense nodal axis orientation to itself;
7. Transits by Chiron to natal planets;
8. Transits by outer planets to Chiron, especially Saturn and Uranus.

Two other noted points in space contain strong aspect relevance and due to their great distances from us and the parallel affect of viewing hold the same geocentric and heliocentric positions. These points extend out in the realm of galactic phenomena and require long and laborious explanations to delineate. The purpose here is not to delineate these points, but to formulate a notation that natal contacts to these two points, when stimulated by transit or progression, virtually demand the shifting of gears into the heliocentric realm. The position for these commodities given is for 1985. The points precess at a rate of 1° every seventy-two years. This refers to a ten year motion of 8' and a five year motion of 4'. An orb of 1 by transit or progression exists.

The first of these points resides at 26° Sagittarius 37°. This point prevails as the center of the galaxy. Referred to as the Galactic Center, GC of Z, this point maintains centrality in the local portion of the Universe. An individual also rises to a sense of centrality, liking it or not, if a connection to this point exists in the natal horoscope. The destiny of knowledge and information resides in this focal point. It becomes the responsibility of the individual's destiny to act as a central figure, within the contextual sphere of his or her life, in the disbursement of new and progressive knowledge. Stimulation to the Galactic Center in the natal horoscope by transit or progression focuses the need to become collectively involved in the new information business.

The point 19° Capricorn 57' (1980 position) similarly holds a strong destiny implication for the major transition from the geocentric map to the heliocentric model. This degree of longitude refers to a point in nearby space known as SS433. SS433 consists of a neutron star (a star in the process of decay) and an ordinary yellow star locked in a binary orbit about each other. SS433 supports a strong inherent sense of destiny and purpose. Controversy surrounds this point as soon as the individual rumbles about the pursuit of destiny. Affiliations split and two distinctive and separate factions emerge; one supports the individual at all costs with resemblance to fanaticism and the other group opposes the individual with equal adamancy. Again, contacts to SS433 in the geocentric chart either by transit or progression, arouse the explicit need to engage in the heliocentric perspective of purpose.

Both mundane and natal events receive strong attention in heliocentric astrology. The purpose of orientation prevails through the interpretive significance from a greater, more evolutionary. Heliocentric charts of mundane events describe the *reason* for the event's occurrence. The actual physical dynamics of the event, especially for those plotting the tracks of disasters, do not appear with the clarity seen in the geocentric counterpart. Spiritual and psychological lessons manifest in the heliocentric view of the mundane. The geocentric mundane map speaks more accurately to the mental and physical concerns of the manifestation.

It is submitted that events not connected physically to the planet Earth need consideration from the heliocentric point of view. The most relevant application for such charts exists in astronomical phenomena, space travel and projects involving in-space defense, space stations, exploratory missions and the like. Consider the launching of the space shuttle, Challenger (1:30 p.m., EST, April 4, 1983, Cape Canaveral, Florida), when the partial purpose of the mission was to launch the first communications satellite from an orbiting platform. The motion of Mercury in Taurus at the launch was fast, not a detriment within itself, but was applying to a quincunx to Saturn in early Scorpio in conjunction with Pluto in Scorpio. Mercury also quincunxed Neptune in Sagittarius. The launch chart thus contained a Yod formation with Mercury creating the finger of the infamous Finger of God aspect. Mercury stood in application to the partile opposition to Jupiter in Sagittarius within 15' of an arc at the launch of the satellite from Challenger. Space history noted that the satellite tumbled through space, out of control, responding to no command (inconjunct to Saturn) signals (Mercury) for many hours. Control of the command signals was regained when the fast Mercury sped through the exact opposition to Jupiter and separated by an arc of 30 minutes! Quite an profound initial testimonial for heliocentric astrology in space began to form.

Now it remains up to you to apply this unexplored aspect of astrology and put it into motion in real life. Speculation, and good speculation at that, suggests that the interest and efforts in heliocentric astrology will bridge the existing gap between schools of astronomy and astrophysics and astrology. A new round of relating begins. It represents a realm in which astrology finally emerges from the medieval principles of space and the solar system and merges contemporarily into the dimension of accepted science. Perhaps heliocentric astrology contains the basis of interfacing again between astrology and astronomy. It will remain unknown unless applied.

Chapter Nine

The Eagle *Has Landed*

At 3:17:42 p.m., CDT, on July 20, 1969, the following words changed the entire world. "Tranquility Base here, the *Eagle* has landed." Those words spoken by the commander of the lunar module, *Eagle*, informed the planet Earth that the first manned probe intended to land upon the lunar surface had done just that. The *Eagle* set down at lunar latitude 0° 38' 50" and lunar longitude 23° 30' 17", some 102 hours, and 45 minutes after the launch from Cape Canaveral, Florida.

It is important to go back to the moment of the launch from the oceanside platform on the east coast of Florida to create astrological perspective for the lunar landing. The rocket engines ignited, pushing the trio of astronauts into space at 09:32 hours (a.m.), EDT, on July 16, 1969. An interesting and revealing study in the astrological analysis of events occurring off of the planet Earth begins here. (Refer to Horoscope 1a.)

Mercury, the planet of communication, rushed past the degrees of 22 Gemini 35, only five degrees past the planet's perihelion. The perihelion, in the eastern time zone translation, took place at 11:35 p.m. on July 14th. Although such an event takes place every eighty-eight days or so, the perihelion contact by Mercury does not usually fit into the t-square created with the square to Venus in Pisces and Pluto in Virgo. Venus makes the closest contact of the t-squaring trinity to the center of the galaxy, offering into the scenario all of the technological progress and advancement symbolism implied by a galactic center. This Sagittarian point bears tones of the ability to

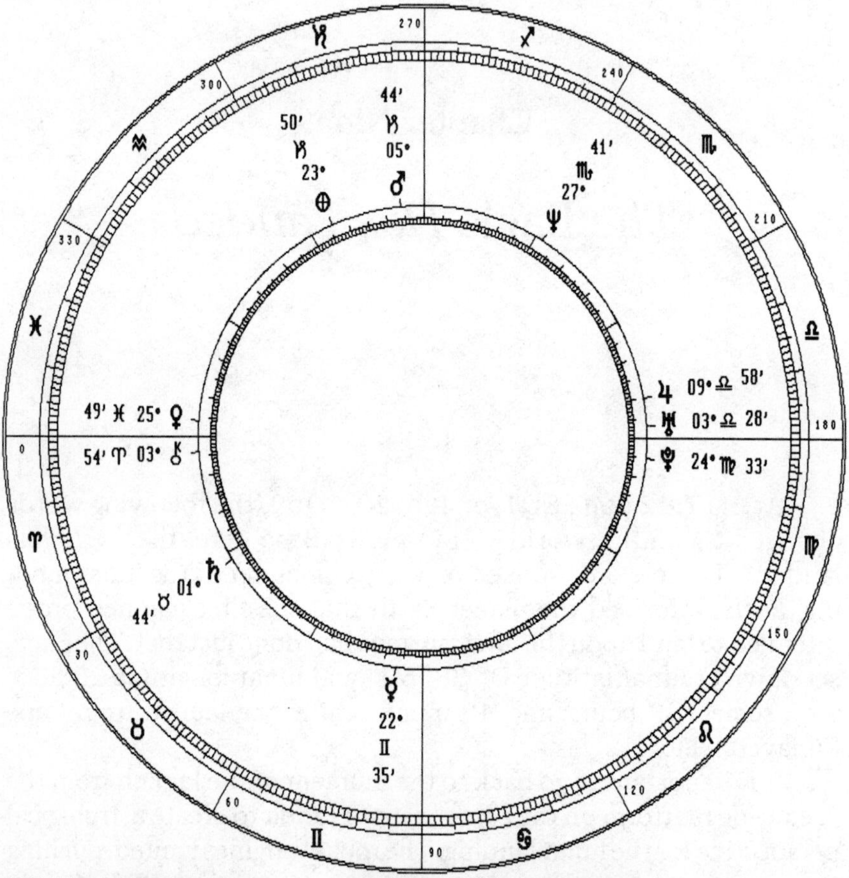

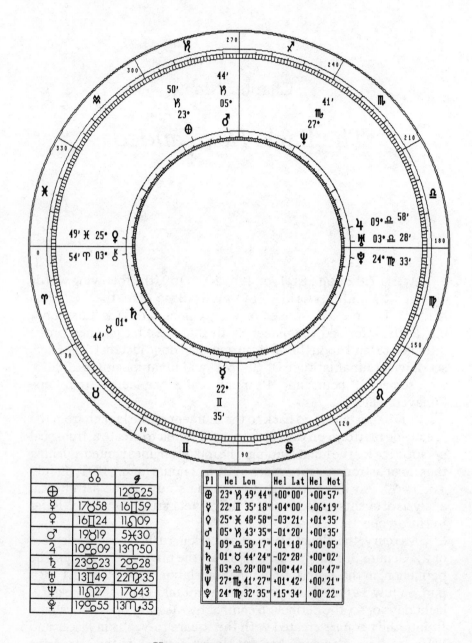

	☊	ℊ
⊕		12♋25
☿	17♉58	16♊59
♀	16♊24	11♌09
♂	19♉19	5♓30
♃	10♋09	13♈50
♄	23♋23	2♋28
♅	13♊49	22♍35
♆	11♌27	17♉43
♇	19♋55	13♏35

Pl	Hel Lon	Hel Lat	Hel Mot
⊕	23° ♑ 49' 44"	+00°00'	+00°57'
☿	22° ♊ 35' 18"	+04°00'	+06°19'
♀	25° ♓ 48' 58"	-03°21'	+01°35'
♂	05° ♑ 43' 35"	-01°20'	+00°35'
♃	09° ♎ 58' 17"	+01°18'	+00°05'
♄	01° ♉ 44' 24"	-02°28'	+00°02'
♅	03° ♎ 28' 00"	+00°44'	+00' 47"
♆	27° ♏ 41' 27"	+01°42'	+00' 21"
♇	24° ♍ 32' 35"	+15°34'	+00' 22"

Horoscope 1a. *Event: Launch*
July 16, 1969; 9:32 a.m. EDT
Heliocentric
(Cape Canaveral, Florida; 80W36/28N24)

capture great leaps and bounds of technological development through imagination and design. The Pluto integration through the square brought forth the pressure necessary to transform the old difficulties and technological inadequacies which previously precluded the program. Pluto also points out the competitiveness in the race for space between the United States and the USSR. Venus in Pisces contributed the creative resources which came into a fine tuned culmination as symbolized by the launch. Mercury delivered the communication necessary to bring plans, schedules and ideas together. The communications for the distant trip into space and return to Earth also came from Mercury's intrinsic urgency as it passed its own perihelion and the north node of Venus. Mercury pushed, pressed, checked and double checked all aspects of the flight. Last minute programming changes for the flight also fit into the Mercury to Venusian North Nodal in square to Venus (with generous orbs).

The launch chart implies that several last minute details and technological discrepancies received resolution. The t-square based upon Mercury contributes to this suggestion as does a last minute idea provided by Jupiter passing over the innovative and technological Uranus in April of 1969, a critical few months before launch. The Earth in Capricorn had passed over the energies of Mars at the end of May, providing the completion of the Jupiter/Uranian changes. The final checks took place just hours before the launch, allowing for some strong last minute tension in Florida and Houston. It was fortunate that Mercury had not yet moved into the inconjunct formation to Neptune. Space travel studies indicate that a quincunx involving Mercury provides much technological difficulty and significant communication discrepancies. Stability in the chart of the *Apollo 11* launch also comes from the trine of Saturn in early Taurus to Mars in Capricorn, allowing for extra insurance as to the safety and effectiveness of the journey.

Mars in the launch chart squared the nodes of Jupiter. The implication of this contact notes the differences in applied energy (such as technique, attitude and enthusiasm) directed towards the launch to create its success. This aspect again speaks of the high levels of competitiveness assumed to mean the race between the United States and the USSR to put men on the Moon. Mars squares, with a neat fit, the midpoint of Uranus and Jupiter in Libra. This Martian mode demanded the cooperation of a multitude of systems, procedures and people to produce the operational success of the

Apollo 11 mission. This aspect resembles inserting a square peg into a round hole and finding a fit of surprising ease.

The Earth's position in Capricorn tightly trined the Virgo location of Pluto. The transformation of the world stands as the theme of this aspect. Although this proclamation appears overstated, a massive change in consciousness resulted from the thrust of this mission. The preview of the lunar landing was set.

Worthy components to track through space as the *Apollo 11* craft tracked through the space between the Earth and Moon are the continuing transits of Mercury, Venus and Mars. Note also that from a symbolic point of view the *Apollo 11* mission wove the Moon and the Earth together, forever, supporting the integration of the Earth/Moon sub-system suggested in this work. The bridge had been crossed. The Pluto to Earth trine allowed for an accomplishment coveted for centuries, perhaps millennia.

Mercury passed over two significant contact points in the solar system as the lunar module trekked to its destination. It crossed over the North Node of Jupiter in Cancer and passed by the perihelion point of the Earth (also in Cancer) while *Apollo 11* was enroute to the lunar surface. These Mercurial communiques marked points of radical excitement as the orbital trajectory shifted to put the astronauts precisely on target. Mercury also opposed Mars during this process, making for additional modifications and redirections. As the fast moving Mercury sped over the perihelion of Earth, the proximity of space altered in the minds of those back on our sapphire colored planet. Mental consciousness began to shift as the module passed the halfway point and the accomplishment of target became obvious. Massive restrictions in the collective mind melted into oblivion and that which had once been a dream became a reality. The *Eagle*, as associated with the Scorpion energy, provided an accurate totem for all of mankind to perceive in realizing the potency, power and possibility of change and transformation. These aspects of Mercury drew the *Apollo 11* capsule closer to the Moon, within its gravitational pull, and prepared the stage for the descent onto the lunar surface.

Horoscope 1b depicts the event chart of the touchdown of the *Eagle* upon the cold, barren surface of the Moon. Neptune in Scorpio enters on the scene with its tight sextile to the Earth/Moon system in Capricorn. This Neptunian sextile provided a jubilant celebration of success and stimulated a synthesis of all people for the Capricorn-like achievement of the landing. The famous quote "a great step for mankind" symbolized this sensation. As a precursor to the event, though, the background (Scorpionic) inspiration, design idealism and engineering innovation come into culmination with an awareness of possibility. Neptune also exists in semi-square to Jupiter in Libra. This aspect again implies the competitiveness existing between the United States and the Soviet Union in the race to put men on the Moon. This event, as supported by Neptune, not only indicated a major event for the United States, but for the entire planet. The ideal application of this aspect creates a question of what results might have been produced with a cooperative effort between nations and technologies.

Jupiter stretches out to square Mars, also in Capricorn, once again verifying the competitiveness and a counterproductive isolationism stimulated through the landing. The Jupiter to Mars square similarly denotes the use of technological philosophies to direct a product capable of endurance, stress and new dimensions.

One of the more interesting sequences of aspects in the chart contains the conjunction of Venus and Chiron in Aries directly opposed Uranus in Libra. Those astrologers using a five degree orb note another event, the t-square in cardinal signs with the three bodies to Mars in Capricorn and its square to Jupiter in Libra. Chiron symbolizes the agreement of the soul to reside in body. Expanding this principle into the mundane, it states an agreement to exit the provided planet of existence. Chiron in Aries notes a "go-for-it" attitude in departing the planetary platform. The conjunction of Venus adds speculation as to all of the great things that could be explored by leaving the Earth. The opposition to Uranus summarizes the ability to finally break away and get beyond. Uranus, Chiron and Venus all form squares to the perihelion of Saturn in Cancer. Saturn further adds to the network by suggesting the perimeters of the home planet, Mother Earth, also holding perihelion in Cancer. Uranus forms the tightest of squares to the perihelion. Uranus actually conjuncts the midpoint of q/Q of Saturn. The motion of Saturn at this midpoint notes the quality of moving in retreat. The approach to the point of greatest distance further increases the impetus to depart the Earth physically. A great breakthrough in consciousness begins here. No longer must one die to leave the planet and be freed of its gravity. Gravity in this symbol relates to the heaviness perceived in dealing with the mundane. A symbol for the evolution of consciousness and of freedom, additionally symbolized as the *Eagle* totem of the vessel

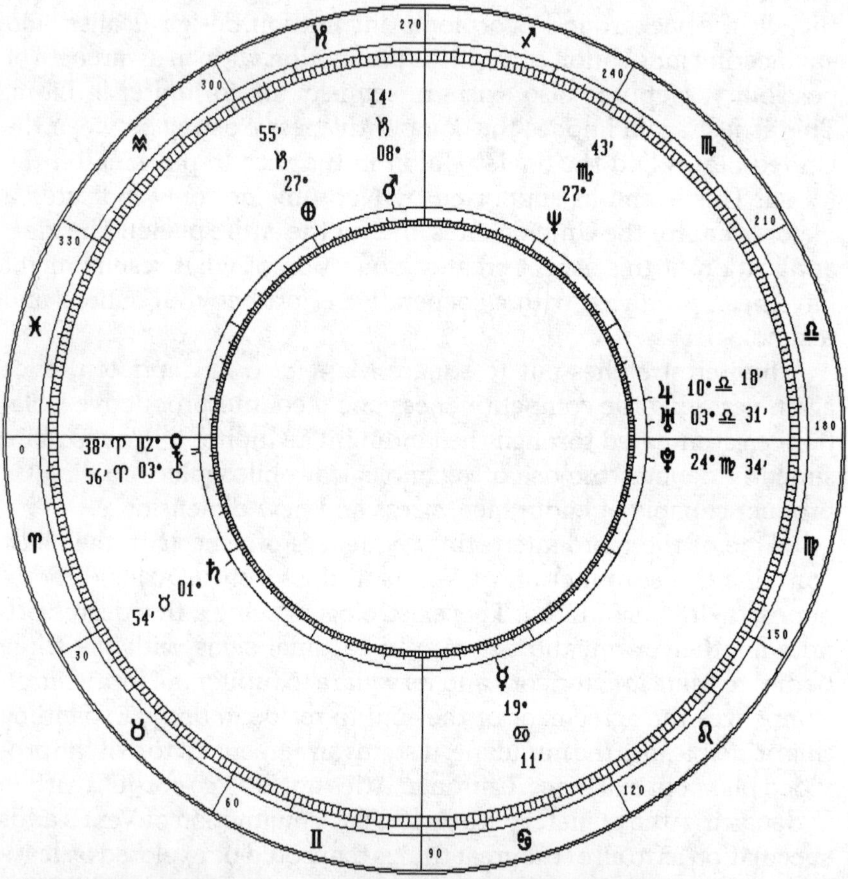

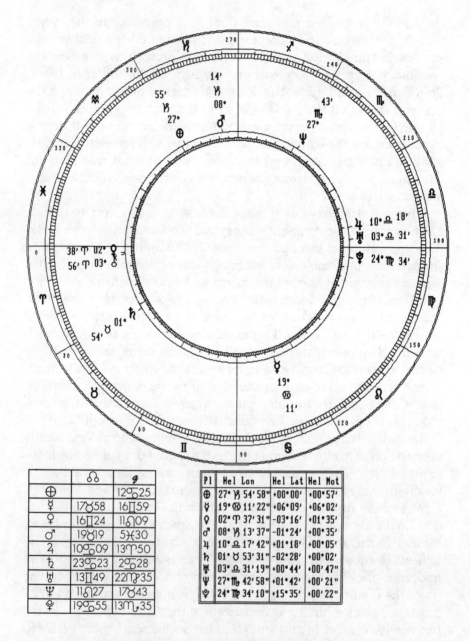

	☊	ℊ
⊕		12♋25
☿	17♉58	16♊59
♀	16♊24	11♌09
♂	19♉19	5♓30
♃	10♋09	13♈50
♄	23♋23	2♋28
♅	13♊49	22♍35
♆	11♌27	17♉43
♇	19♋55	13♏35

Pl	Hel Lon	Hel Lat	Hel Mot
⊕	27° ♑ 54′ 58″	+00°00′	+00°57′
☿	19° ♋ 11′ 22″	+06°09′	+06°02′
♀	02° ♈ 37′ 31″	-03°16′	+01°35′
♂	08° ♑ 13′ 37″	-01°24′	+00°35′
♃	10° ♎ 17′ 42″	+01°18′	+00°05′
♄	01° ♉ 53′ 31″	-02°28′	+00°02′
♅	03° ♎ 31′ 19″	+00°44′	+00′ 47″
♆	27° ♏ 42′ 58″	+01°42′	+00′ 21″
♇	24° ♍ 34′ 10″	+15°35′	+00′ 22″

Horoscope 1b. *Event: Lunar Landing*
July 20, 1969; 3:17:42 p.m. CDT
Heliocentric
(Houston, Texas; 95W22/29N46)

of exploration, etched its way into the personal and collective consciousness upon the Earth, back home (Cancer). The Venus and Chiron aspect to the perihelion of Saturn actually comes from their conjunction to the midpoint of Saturn's Q/q. This point indicates a re-acceleration back into the mundane platform known as home. The items—lunar rocks, photographs—that returned to Earth carried a new understanding of basic existence (Aries). Great value (Venus) in understanding the basic connection in our binary planet system of the Earth and Moon resulted, reinforcing the Chiron symbology. A push-pull relationship of history and progress merged through this lunar landing. This opposition sought to resolve the alienation suggested by the Jupiter to Mars square. Great unity occurred from the dramatic, clear representation of all nations being a part of one greater whole. Remember the impact of the first Earthrise pictures? Inevitably, these representatives of rising brought awareness of the greatness of the time.

Saturn contains the essence of tremendous creativity in this chart. The early Taurus implication demonstrates the need to redefine contact with resourcefulness, and receives amplification through two tight aspects. The Saturn quincunx to Uranus in Libra stresses numerous modifications and adjustments to ensure the cooperative participation between factions of diversified backgrounds. These relationships flexed under Saturn-Uranus were governmental, industrial, monetary, international, scientific—interdisciplinary. Venus being common by rulership to both signs involved in the inconjunct again supports an integrative need for pooling of resources upon all levels. Creative assistance to the project of cooperation came from the persuasiveness of Pluto in Virgo. Pluto provided transformation of detail, technology and implied that petty disturbances could be transmuted with the pure intent and motivation of the project. Those persons integrated (Virgo) within this major event required continual reminder of scope and effort. Pluto in Virgo worked well biquintile to Saturn to support this and received additional facilitation from its old buddy, Mercury. Mercury, although in no direct aspectual alignment with Saturn or Pluto, formed a conjunction to Pluto's North Node. This nodal contact generated strong discussion of the true Plutonian nature of the landing project. Mercury's influence here in Cancer pulled together, through communication, all factions and forces into one body capable of nurturing all of its components. Communication in the lunar landing project, obviously, remained essential. It is not likely that the public will ever know the full thrust of the background communications that produced the project's success. (Nor is it likely that the public will find out the full nature of all communications received after this lunar landing and for the duration of the flight.) Pluto again stimulates the technological breakthrough necessary for such a major shift in space travel through its placement by conjunction to the perihelion of Uranus in Virgo. Transformation occurred through changes, modifications, alterations, upgrades and improvements. Constant computer enhancement facilitated this work as Uranus and its Virgo orientation note. Course corrections in flight, for instance, secured the mission much in the way this connection relates. An understanding of the urgency of corrective action developed with this contact, allowing for a larger, more metaphorical understanding of the conditions necessary in response to crisis. This component of the chart also demonstrated the successful integration of completely new routines. (The Pluto to the perihelion of Uranus contact era brought great efforts in the progressive movements of mankind in more areas than space travel and lunar explorations.)

Completing the whole Saturn to Uranus and Pluto pattern, the semi-sextile of Venus in Aries to Saturn in Taurus generated one more sequence of mental input. Assertion of the individual contributed to the success of the project. Sitting back in ego form would not offer anything of ideas, creativity or worth.

Return to Mars in Capricorn for a moment and note the integration by conjunction of the planet to the Jupiter/Chiron midpoint. Mythologically, Zeus (Jupiter) placed the archer Chiron into the constellation of Sagittarius after the wounded archer requested that he pass along his immortality to relinquish his eternal pain. Jupiter, in effect, granted a pass to Chiron to leave the planet and prevail in the heavens. Mars in the landing chart energizes this symbolism.

Mars also conjoined the South Node of Jupiter and aligned directly with the perihelion of Earth. The Earth passed by aphelion on July 5th, just over two weeks prior to the landing. This Mars nature functioned at a highly symbolic level, dispelling many of the myths forever (Jupiter equates with myths). As absurd as it seems, the Earth revolves and is round, more or less, and the Moon is not made of green cheese. Let us expand this further, though, and note what Man on the Moon does exist. Numerous speculative works in publication claim that the lunar landings found evidence of life on the Moon, and contact with extraterrestrials presumably occurred. This Mars in Capricorn point works to safeguard any such information. The Mercury/Mars midpoint in Libra conjunct Jupiter indicates a similar effect based upon the belief that such an awareness would create turmoil amongst the general populace. The entire essence of these Martian effects stimulates a litany of philosophical reaction upon the Earth. The aphelion of Earth as connected with Mars realizes the need for retreat and proper treatment of information. A unique philosophy underwrites this (Jupiter's South Node Past), distinctly resembling the attitude of the ancient Chinese who forbade astrologers to communicate directly with the general population in order to prevent mass hysteria of upcoming events. Sometimes, the theory goes, precognition of the event amplifies the adverse potential of the event. Sometimes the reaction to precognition is the event.

Jupiter squares its own nodes, aligning with this midpoint and moving from North Node to South Node. Jupiter bisects the perihelion/aphelion axis of the Earth. Its influence on its nodes acts to modulate and negotiate between new philosophies based on new events and the old belief systems. Religion felt an enormous impact from this event. Thinking about the landing etched into the karmic memory of humanity a refutation of preconceived inaccessibility of those distant spheres in space. The fervor of human response (Jupiter) added to the collective impact. Jupiter eased the race in space toward this lunar conquest as implied by the Earth on the slow side of its orbit. Introspection, analysis and sharing information (Libra) should have developed out of the process. In theory, the United States openly shared its information of the lunar landing; at least lunar rocks were shared (Jupiter tying in with Mars in Capricorn).

The first step onto the surface of the Moon occurred at 109 hours, 24 minutes into the mission, some six hours and 39 minutes after landing. Mercury, the only planet significantly displaced across this time frame, advanced to a point past the North Node of Pluto and approached the North Node of Saturn. This implies "now that we have it, what do we do with it?" The obvious answer in this case was to play with it. The Plutonian level of transformation and change was done; now it was time to make something (as in Saturnian manifestations) of what occurred.

Mercury, additionally, moved into an exact inconjunct to the Mars/Chiron midpoint in Aquarius. This aspect actually expresses the ability to virtually be beside oneself. Mars and Chiron integrate to establish the energy needed to get beyond the restrictions of the physical body. Mercury enters as if on cue and adjusts to the lunar gravity, creating an animation of motion never before experienced by the human form. The entire spectrum of body mobility implied by the Mars/Chiron midpoint shifted.

The stay on the Moon lasted short of a day, with the astronauts spending an overnight on the lunar refuge. At 12:54 p.m., CDT, July 21, 1969, the rockets on the lunar module fired, lifting the capsule back up into lunar orbit for rendezvous with its comrade left in orbit while the other two astronauts fulfilled assignments below. The journey back to Earth had begun. Horoscope 1c represents the lift-off of the *Eagle* from the lunar landscape. Mercury moved into a tight sextile to Pluto, implying that the time for departure had arrived. Mercury further noted completion with the recent passage of the planet over the North Node of Saturn, indicating manifestation of assigned tasks. Mercury also just opposed the Earth's zodiacal initial launch position, further indicating that it was time to get on the road.

Mars added its two cents' worth by nearing a square to the original launch position of Jupiter, suggesting that it would be well to return prior to the current aspect (transiting square) of Mars and Jupiter. This square, as will be seen later, pulled into exactness a few short hours after the safe return of the astronauts to the Earth.

Venus passed through the opposition to Uranus during the stay upon the Moon, indicating the value of the experiments. The lunar samples were stored, data accumulated and electronic sensors (Uranus), not requiring human attention (Chiron, with the Venus conjunction), would be left behind to transmit signals and data back to Earth. The significance of the journey, again as Chiron in Aries supports, would continue long after the first men on the Moon were sleeping back upon the planet Earth.

The effect of the Earth trine Pluto faded as did the energy of Earth sextile Neptune. These waning effects contributed to a somewhat anticlimactic departure from the Moon and began to establish the momentum of new aspects that would mark the results of the return to Earth. The Earth itself stood on the verge of moving into the sign of Aquarius, bringing with it an entire new flavor of collective thought.

The trine of Mercury and Neptune in the lunar lift-off chart stimulated the effective communications and well being of the return to Earth. The return journey, like the nature of the trine, flowed. All aspects led to the anticipation of the return of the heroic astronauts.

195 hours and 18 minutes after launch from Cape Kennedy, the

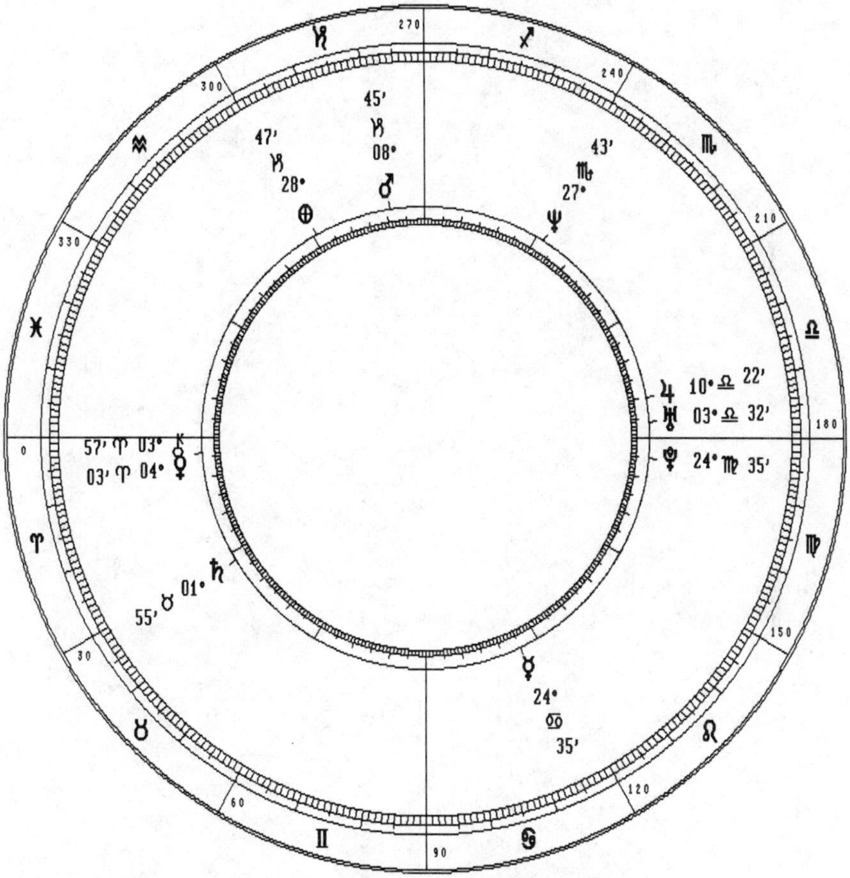

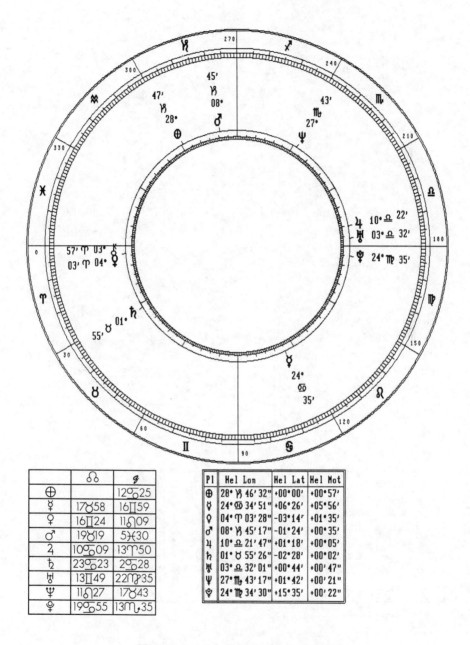

	☊	ɋ
⊕		12♋25
☿	17♉58	16♊59
♀	16♊24	11♌09
♂	19♉19	5♓30
♃	10♋09	13♈50
♄	23♋23	2♋28
♅	13♊49	22♍35
♆	11♌27	17♉43
♇	19♋55	13♏35

Pl	Hel Lon	Hel Lat	Hel Mot
⊕	28° ♑ 46' 32"	+00°00'	+00°57'
☿	24° ♋ 34' 51"	+06°26'	+05°56'
♀	04° ♈ 03' 28"	-03°14'	+01°35'
♂	08° ♑ 45' 17"	-01°24'	+00°35'
♃	10° ♎ 21' 47"	+01°18'	+00°05'
♄	01° ♉ 55' 26"	-02°28'	+00°02'
♅	03° ♎ 32' 01"	+00°44'	+00' 47"
♆	27° ♏ 43' 17"	+01°42'	+00' 21"
♇	24° ♍ 34' 30"	+15°35'	+00' 22"

Horoscope 1c. *Event: Lunar Launch*
July 21, 1969; 12:54 p.m. CDT
Heliocentric
(Houston, Texas; 95W22/29N46)

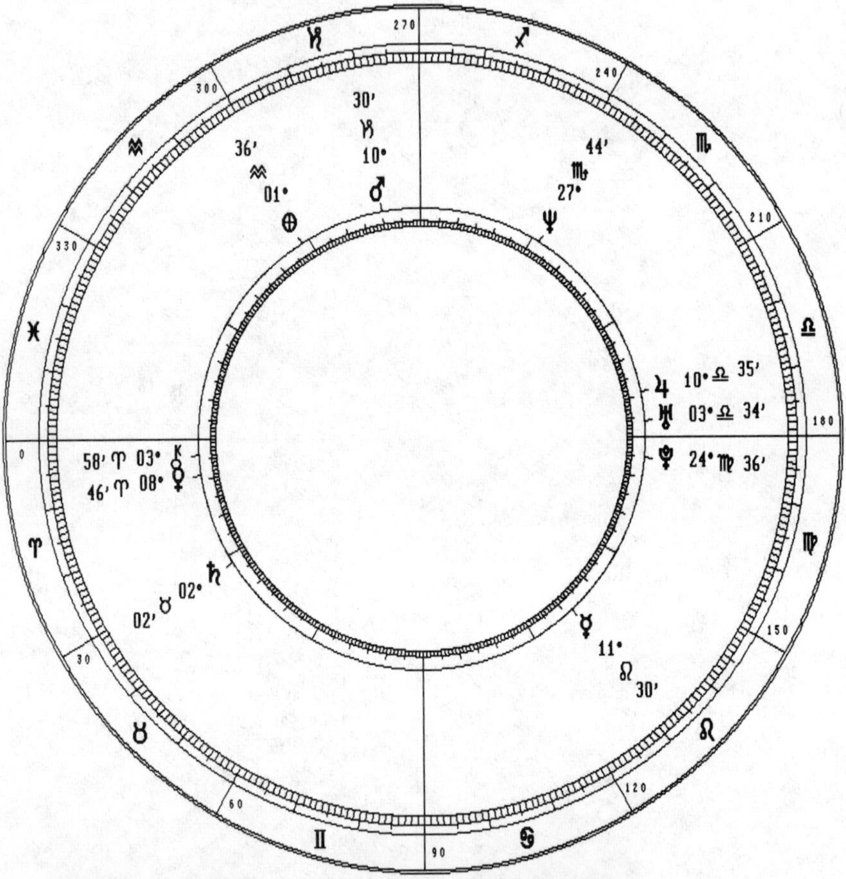

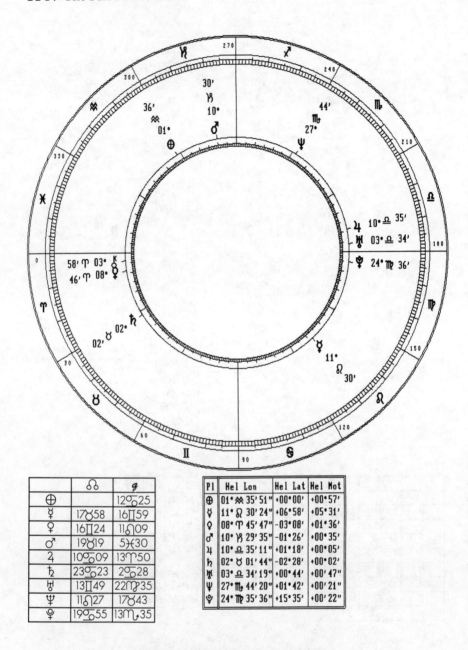

	☊	ℊ
⊕		12♋25
☿	17♉58	16♊59
♀	16♊24	11♌09
♂	19♉19	5♓30
♃	10♋09	13♈50
♄	23♋23	2♋28
♅	13♊49	22♍35
♆	11♌27	17♉43
♇	19♋55	13♏35

Pl	Hel Lon	Hel Lat	Hel Mot
⊕	01° ♒ 35′ 51″	+00°00′	+00°57′
☿	11° ♌ 30′ 24″	+06°58′	+05°31′
♀	08° ♈ 45′ 47″	-03°08′	+01°36′
♂	10° ♑ 29′ 35″	-01°26′	+00°35′
♃	10° ♎ 35′ 11″	+01°18′	+00°05′
♄	02° ♉ 01′ 44″	-02°28′	+00°02′
♅	03° ♎ 34′ 19″	+00°44′	+00′ 47″
♆	27° ♏ 44′ 20″	+01°42′	+00′ 21″
♇	24° ♍ 35′ 36″	+15°35′	+00′ 22″

Horoscope 1d. *Event: Splashdown*
July 24, 1969; 11:50 a.m. CDT
Heliocentric
(Houston, Texas; 95W22/29N46)

Apollo 11 team splashed down in the Pacific Ocean at 11:50 a.m., CDT, July 24, 1969. The first men to successfully set foot on another body in the solar system had returned home, safe and sound. Horoscope 1d represents the splashdown chart of the capsule with its team of astronauts and lunar rocks and samples.

Prior to this "splash heard around the world," during the return flight, Mercury opposed the Earth in changing signs. This Leo/Aquarius polarity set the stage of the dramatic celebrations to be held on behalf of the astronauts. The chart of the splashdown holds Mercury in Leo very tightly in conjunction with the North Node of Neptune and the perihelion of Venus. The collective Venus/Neptune combination contributed by these points brought every imaginable token of confetti, champagne, telegrams and glitter, even after an unimaginable journey. Perhaps celebration and celebrity status did not suit the entire crew. The Earth in Aquarius formed a tight square on approach to Saturn in Taurus. Maybe the astronauts would just want a little *space*—a somewhat ironic turn of events after all they endured.

It could be speculated that the return came none too soon. Granted the chart of the launch held a t-square (as did the landing chart), but the third time could be the charm. In considering of Earth's square to Saturn combining with the extremely tight Mars to Jupiter square, the square of Venus in Aries to the Capricorn Mars gained added tension. Mercury served both of the preceding t-squares (it fit into the lunar landing T-Square the day before the landing) and fell well out of direct support in the relationship of squares. Mercury in its Leo flair flashed an inconjunct in the direction of Mars. Mercury inconjuncts, as noted earlier, create difficulty in space travels at large (contributing to the blackout time that a craft encounters while re-entering the Earth's atmosphere).

Should one be interested in stretching orbs, a mystic rectangle could be created out of the *Apollo 11* return chart as follows: Earth in Aquarius sextile Venus in Aries, Venus in Aries trine Mercury in Leo, Mercury in Leo sextile Jupiter (Uranus) in Libra, finally, Uranus (Jupiter) in Libra trine Earth in Aquarius. These aspect patterns presumably contain strong occult and spiritual implication. Perhaps extra-terrestrial life, as speculated. Perhaps ESP experiments were conducted by our astronauts, as we have claimed the Russians do. Who knows? Will we ever know the full extent of what was discovered by our lunar voyages? One astrologer's speculation remains as good as another's.

This sequence of heliocentric horoscopes establishes the flow of the remainder of events to take place upon the Moon and within lunar exploration and potential colonization in the years to come. This initial lunar contact by mankind consummates the energy of establishing the technology of Earth upon its common gravitational mate. All subsequent events can be gauged against this nativity.

Another simple intrinsic beauty resides in the use of this heliocentric horoscope. This chart works as well on the Moon as it does upon the Earth. The geocentric horoscope for the landing, set for Washington D.C., plays up the President's reaction. The geocentric chart for Cape Canaveral evinces the exuberance demonstrated at the launch site. The Houston based geocentric chart reasonably contains far more tension than either of the preceding maps, since Houston controlled the mission after launch and maintained tight technical responsibility. Realize that the Washington, D.C., Florida and Texas geocentric charts all provide different angles. But an astrologer aboard the space capsule on the Moon could have used these heliocentric nativities to work with the effects of the mission, resolve personality crises, establish lunar based transmissions of communication and other application. The geocentric chart, quite simply, would fall flat.

Heliocentric astrology stands to be the astrology applied to any off-Earth function. Launch maps for space shuttles, construction of space stations, platforms and activities upon those shuttles and stations more properly come from the pages of the heliocentric ephemerides. This landing map marks a major turning point in space evolution. So does the launching of the first satellite, *Sputnik 1*, by the Soviets on October 4, 1957 at 7:21 p.m., GMT (beginning the Space Age). The launch location for this vessel remains uncertain but of no consequence to the heliocentric calculation. Yuri Gagarin, the first man in space, sets up another cycle of space evolution. His launch occurred on April 4, 1961 at 09:07 GMT a.m. Alan Shepard's suborbital flight of May 5, 1961 (9:34 a.m., Cape Canaveral time) marks the U.S. entry into the manned space race. John Glenn revealed the "right stuff" as he shot into orbit leaving the Earth at 9:48 a.m., EST, on February 20, 1962. Next, the first spacewalk took place by Russian cosmonauts at 11:30 a.m., Moscow time, on March 18, 1965, with a launch of an undisclosed time on the same day. For those interested in a more contemporary situation in space combining politics and science, the first woman on board a space shuttle,

Sally Ride, jetted off into the orbital plane on June 18, 1983 at 7:33 a.m., EDT, from Cape Canaveral, Florida. These bits of data are provided for follow-up use by the reader. A fascinating evolution of space developments emerges through the use of heliocentrics, with perhaps a higher level of applicability than geocentric maps.

The horoscope for the launch of the space shuttle containing Sally Ride follows (Horoscope 2). Consider the mundane ruler of femininity, Venus, in the horoscope. Venus forms the tightest (most dynamic) configuration between planets with a biquintile to Mars, the mundane ruler of the masculine. This aspect exists within an orb of two minutes by separation. Given that the biquintile bears the tone of the subconscious creative use of energy, talent and application, the integration of male and female upon this *Space Transportation System* (STS) project naturally and fluidly fell into place. Mars in Gemini resided in a conjunction to the North Node of Venus at the time of launch. The implication allowed by the nodal point of Venus indicates use (Mars energy) of female resources (Venus) with new and more diversified directions (North Node in Gemini). Mercury as associated with Gemini notes the full presence of both genders. All midpoint combinations of the Earth/Moon system and the motions of both Jupiter and Uranus in Sagittarius activated the South Node of Venus by conjunction. The Jupiter/Uranus/Sagittarius combination indicates the need to change (Uranus) the philosophy (Sagittarius) about models and roles in space travel (Jupiter). Mercury in Pisces squared the nodes of Venus, releasing the guilt trips, power trips and martyrdom forced upon women. Many claimed that Sally Ride's influence aboard *Columbia* resulted as pacific tokens towards women at large. The aspects in the launch chart indicate a profile of activity, suggesting the potential for sincere progress in an area of human interaction long abused. The Venus conjunction to the perihelion of Pluto, although wide, combined with the Venus placement upon the south nodes of both Mercury and Mars, implies transformation of the female gender. The wiring of this chart clearly speaks of an effort in the interest of resolution. The implication is that cooperation in space must exist (as supported in the *Apollo 11* lunar landing chart), between political, governmental, industrial, international and sexual factions.

Not only has the *Eagle* landed, a time of transformation in history now lands upon the direction and destiny of travel in space.

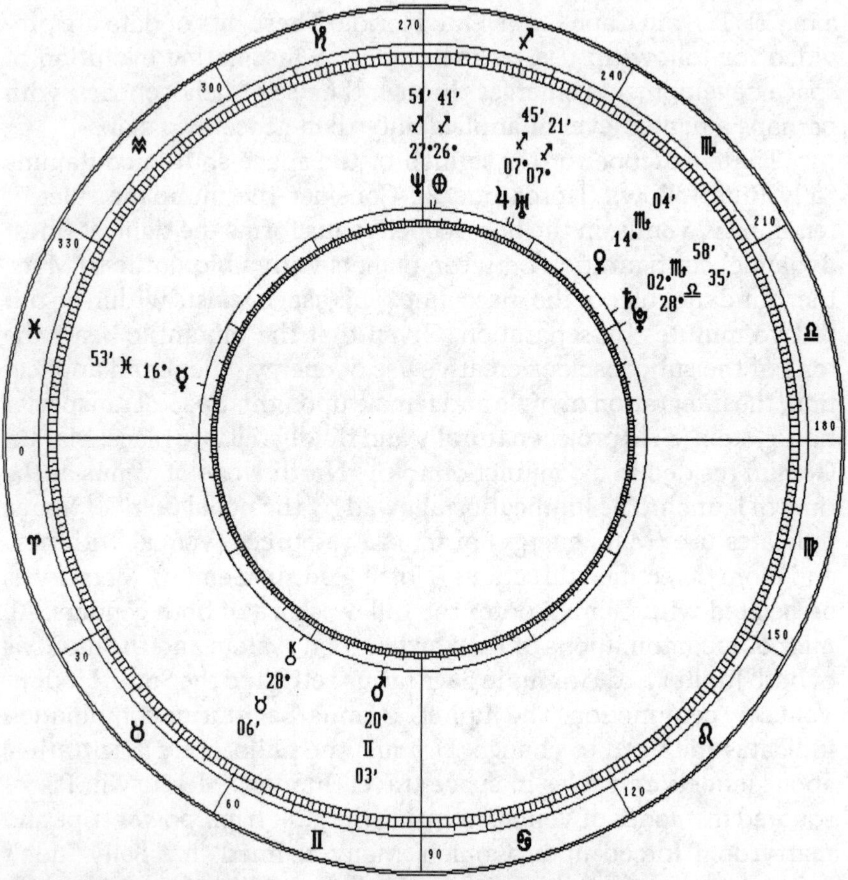

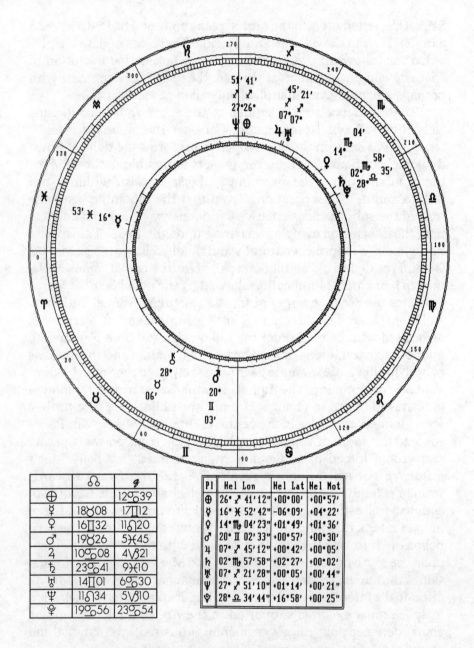

	☊	ℊ
⊕		12♋39
☿	18♉08	17♊12
♀	16♊32	11♌20
♂	19♉26	5♓45
♃	10♋08	4♑21
♄	23♋41	9♓10
♅	14♊01	6♋30
♆	11♌34	5♑10
♇	19♋56	23♋54

Pl	Hel Lon	Hel Lat	Hel Mot
⊕	26° ♐ 41' 12"	+00° 00'	+00° 57'
☿	16° ♓ 52' 42"	-06° 09'	+04° 22'
♀	14° ♏ 04' 23"	+01° 49'	+01° 36'
♂	20° ♊ 02' 33"	+00° 57'	+00° 30'
♃	07° ♐ 45' 12"	+00° 42'	+00° 05'
♄	02° ♏ 57' 58"	+02° 27'	+00° 02'
♅	07° ♐ 21' 28"	+00° 05'	+00' 44"
♆	27° ♐ 51' 10"	+01° 14'	+00' 21"
♇	28° ♎ 34' 44"	+16° 58'	+00' 25"

Horoscope 2. *Event: Sally Ride Shuttle Launch*
June 18, 1983; 7:33 a.m. EDT
Heliocentric
(Cape Canaveral, Florida; 80W36/28N24)

dynamic) configuration between planets with a biquintile to Mars, the mundane ruler of the masculine. This aspect exists within an orb of two minutes by separation. Given that the biquintile bears the tone of the subconscious creative use of energy, talent and application, the integration of male and female upon this *Space Transportation System* (STS) project naturally and fluidly fell into place. Mars in Gemini resided in a conjunction to the North Node of Venus at the time of launch. The implication allowed by the nodal point of Venus indicates use (Mars energy) of female resources (Venus) with new and more diversified directions (North Node in Gemini). Mercury as associated with Gemini notes the full presence of both genders. All midpoint combinations of the Earth/Moon system and the motions of both Jupiter and Uranus in Sagittarius activated the South Node of Venus by conjunction. The Jupiter/Uranus/Sagittarius combination indicates the need to change (Uranus) the philosophy (Sagittarius) about models and roles in space travel (Jupiter). Mercury in Pisces squared the nodes of Venus, releasing the guilt trips, power trips and martyrdom historically forced upon women. Many claimed that Sally Ride's influence aboard *Columbia* resulted as pacific tokens towards women at large. The aspects in the launch chart indicate a profile of activity, suggesting the potential for sincere progress in an area of human interaction long abused. The Venus conjunction to the perihelion of Pluto, although wide, combined with the Venus placement upon the south nodes of both Mercury and Mars, implies transformation of the female gender. The wiring of this chart clearly speaks of an effort in the interest of resolution. The implication is that cooperation in space must exist (as supported in the *Apollo 11* lunar landing chart), between political, governmental, industrial, international and sexual factions.

Not only has the *Eagle* landed, a time of transformation in history now lands upon the direction and destiny of travel in space.

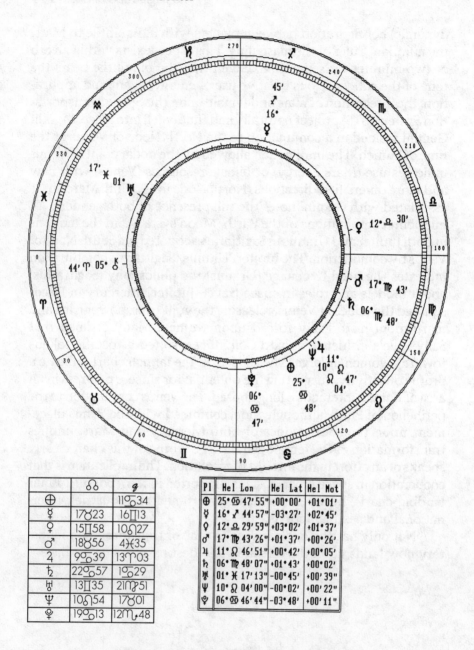

Horoscope 3. *Event: Start of Prohibition*
January 17, 1920; 12:01 a.m. EST
Heliocentric
(Washington, D.C.; 77W02/38N54)

Chapter Ten

A Ban on Booze

A new law took effect at 00:01 a.m. on Saturday, January 17, 1920, prohibiting alcoholic production and consumption, initiating a thirteen year period of rebellion, corruption and hedonism. Prohibition, as it came to be known, marks one of the clearest case histories in the mundane use of heliocentric astrology. Horoscope 3 depicts the heliocentric nativity for the commencement of the ban on booze.

Hypothesis would suggest a Neptune prevalence in the horoscope, Neptune ruling substances such as alcohol. Jupiter is separated from conjunction with Neptune in Leo 1° 43' away from exact. Neptune and Jupiter, by latitude, held a contraparallel configuration, supplementing this aspect. A unique combination of parity and disparity was set in motion through these contradictory aspects. Jupiter contains the moralistic imposition of society (religion, politics and every other group claiming to hold the answer to human corruption), contributing to the propagation of prohibition. This sense of correct behavior fueled a dramatic campaign to overcome the use of the nefarious substance. Ironically, the contraparallel of the two planets added to the natural double standard contained in Jupiter's mythological essence. Jupiter prevailed upon the Earth as a god of double standards. He judged those doing wrong and then did the same thing in the privacy of his presumably divine court. Jupiter indulged in everything and as one might suspect, indulged abundantly and exuberantly. The contraparallel adds the opposing flavor needed to set up the underground contradiction of the prohibition. The legislation

121

stood to be flaunted and held in contempt from the beginning second of that Saturday. The ban stimulated the influence of hedonism by creating an additionally lucrative appeal in alcohol. Alcohol's lack of availability caused a rise in addiction from a symbolic point of view. The shadow of Neptune seduced the collective with the decadence Jupiter promised. Jupiter/Neptune, archtypically representing smuggling and other associated forms of crime, provided the black market with alcohol and contributed to the collective corruption, far from eliminating it. Bathtub gin, moonshine and backyard stills appeared with greater regularity than the Model-T.

The Jupiter/Neptune conjunction sextiled Venus in Libra. The social status of drinking, contacts with those with alcohol sources, and clandestine speakeasies created a new mode of social relationship. Deviousness became a key Libran word of as lies regarding the use of alcohol contradicted reality. The ease of the sextile to Neptune facilitated the fabrications smoothly. Venus supplemented the Jupiter (and Neptune) sextile with a conjunction to the aphelion of Jupiter. The maximum aloofness of Jupiter prevailed within this Venus contact. This point of retreat added to the justification mode of the continued use of alcohol and raised questions about the government's right to regulate social behavior and personal choice. A primal seed of constitutional rights emerged within the barrage of justifications and excuses.

The Jupiter/Neptune conjunction in Leo conjoined with the North Node of Neptune. Neptune's node implies intended direction for the maximum evolution of humanity through spiritual application—best case. This nodal point does not include evolution through the use of spirits alone. Jupiter exaggerates the reasoning of the intended purpose of prohibition. Heated discussions prevail concerning the morality, rightness, intent and guiding purpose behind the law. The thinking behind prohibition seemed to indicate that the proponents of the illegalization of alcohol believed the law would actually stop use of alcohol. Another major breakdown of prohibition was in failing to note the motives for drinking. The Jupiter and Neptune conjunction meant that many drank to escape that which could not be justified or fit into place in life. Changes prior to the 1920s introduced unfamiliar and unknown things to which people needed to adjust rapidly. These changes included World War I and new economic considerations along, which resulted in automobiles and airplanes and much more. The influence of movies, a Neptune pursuit, strongly affected collective humanity and inspired alcohol use. Alcohol provided an escape-release, at least until prohibited. Given that a major reform had taken place during the 1920s, perhaps the negative effects of prohibition were diminished. Then again, consider the Neptunian personalities flaunting the substance to the temptable, using seduction to create addiction. All of this impact originated in Neptune's North Node guidance beam. Neptune stands alone of the most difficult planets to integrate. Neptune's nodes contain no greater ease of synthesis, partially due to the ambiguity and confusion surrounding Neptunian affairs.

Jupiter/Neptune conjuncts the Venus perihelion. Urgency of social issues prevails in this aspect. The need to control, regulate and authorize (Jupiter) the alcoholic flow in the country (Neptune) created the most pressing urge of the time. There was a basic misunderstanding of value systems. An astrologer looking at the heliocentric horoscope must wonder how the government could pass such a law at the time they did. A sense of moralistic supremacy must have submitted to excessive delusions of grandeur (Jupiter/Neptune). The sociability of Venus in Libra and the planet's perihelion in Leo stood to overwhelm the inferences of the moralism of the time. Prohibition proved again that moralism cannot be fed, forced or demanded of others through legislation.

Jupiter/Neptune aligns upon the Mars/Pluto midpoint, receiving reinforcement from the contact that the two planets make to the Q/q midpoint of Pluto (square Pluto's perihelion). The ultimate darkness of the prohibition era pervades through this point in space. The midpoint contains the quality of Pluto emerging from the darkness of space towards the light of the Sun. The integration comes from the acceleration of Pluto, which is required to effectively reach the ultimate essence of light. A crisis in transformation surfaces, falling back upon the Leonine implications of the contact. This Pluto crossroad requires that people act as individuals, counteracting the collective magnetism often compelled by Pluto and reinforced in this nativity with Venus in Libra. The era also marked the fortunate end of the involuntary imposition of collective will upon individual will. The people rejected a larger force in life indicating what they could and could not do. A major lesson took place despite the negativity and dark forces preying upon the subconscious during prohibition. This lesson now sets a precedent for other collective forces the the right ideas for everyone else. Like prohibition, other moralistic causes will submit to the consciousness of the general population on the planet. Moralism will only be tolerated until the undercurrent reaches up and pulls the force of control beneath the surface, suffocating the effort. Prohibition's aspects to this Pluto midpoint clearly stated such a case in point.

Sagittarius, the mundane ruler of moralism by sign, contains Mercury in the prohibition chart. Mercury squares Mars in Virgo, and forms a quintile to Uranus in Pisces (Neptune's sign). The extended communication of Mercury in Sagittarius proclaims another strong sense of self-righteousness. Mars in Virgo, representing activity, squares off against Mercury with verbal and action type conflicts. This aspect marks the wars between the groups of contraband alcohol manufacturers and distributors. It also demonstrates the violation of the purified law. Mercury's quintile to Uranus, while maintaining great creative potential, also contains a fear of the use of alcohol and the influence the substance may have upon one's faculties. Assuredly, those proclaiming prohibition the loudest held the lowest tolerances to alcohol and feared the shifts in their personalities perceived under the influence. The usually fleet-footed Mercury trudged through Sagittarius a mere eight hours and sixteen minutes after aphelion, also resting upon the South Node of Venus. The actual law intended to prescribe social standards to reduce stresses as implied by the Mercury contact with the Venereal South Node. These laws, however, were just words and, as the square to Mars relates, subject to conflict, rebuttal and ultimate refusal. A lack of mental agility characterized the procedure of declaring prohibition a law. Response to the law, in Mercury's bidirectional manner, slid to the unanticipated side of the outcome spectrum.

Mars in Virgo set the pace of the rebellion against prohibition, not only through Mercury as already seen, but with a barrage of other configurations. Mars quintiled Pluto in Cancer. This aspect of ingenuity activated the underworld, contraband, and secrecy. This aspect enhanced the abilities of bootleggers and their ilk. The ease of the effort again appears in the trine of Mars to the North Nodes of both Mars and Mercury. The cover-ups were good, the fronts were fast and the remainder succumbed to the bribe—as Taurus implies. Mars squared the nodes of Venus and, more widely, those of Uranus. Here comes the paradox in society. The crime element appeared as a malefic influence spreading corruption, death and money. It restored the choice to drink or not drink through providing the substance and stating that the controls held no control. The Uranian implication sustains some element of benefit even through all the negativity, although the value remains difficult to see. The Venus and Uranus nodal agitation from Mars sought to restore a balance of choice in life, social appropriateness and moderation in all things. Drinking just happened to be the mechanism of primary focus.

The communication emphasis of Mars fits in again to the event charting Mars square the perihelion of Mercury. Mars connected to the q/Q midpoint notes the deceleration of Mercury leading to subsequent retreat ultimately provided legislative reconsideration. Again, as the slow natal Mercury implied, this introspection would take time.

Uranus in Pisces biquintiles the Earth/Moon system in Cancer. This aspect of the subconscious levels of creativity seems to have the use of alcohol confused. The music and aesthetics of the speakeasies conducted as background to the alcoholic consumption sought to bring out the suppressed creativity at large. The subconscious mind yielding the basic insights and non-conformity associated with ultra-creative individuals seemed to seek collective nurturing. The urge of non-conformity with the law and personal statements of rebellion echoed through this aspect. Those involved in non-conforming activities acted like everyone else, merely pointing out the collective ultra-conformist nature, again supplied by Venus in Libra in the chart. The distortions created by the alcohol overlooked such effects.

The Earth/Moon system interlocked with Saturn indirectly as it found the North Node of Saturn straight ahead. The bureaucratic dogma loomed and for many this meant confrontation with the law. The higher ideal of the Saturnian North Node revealed here implies the protective nature of the Cancer South Node manifestated upon children. The worst case assumption of the node betrays that people do not maintain a strong enough sense of responsibility to conduct appropriate choices in life. This inaccuracy started all the trouble. Saturn sextiles Pluto from Virgo to Cancer. Saturn set down too much order for Pluto to absorb. Pluto, in effect, choked upon the smothering side of the nurturing dynamic. Pluto ties back into Saturn with a wide conjunction to Saturn's perihelion. Where Saturn perceived urgency, Pluto perceived suppression and surfaced by going underground in retaliation. The organization (Saturn) of the underworld (Pluto) responded to this configuration, urgently stating that the law would be illegally overruled.

Pluto also finds the North Node of Jupiter by conjunction. Pluto observes the philosophical direction intended and reacts. Principles again come through the horoscope loud and clear in this contact. Drinking may be detrimental to humans and often even catastrophic; still, no collective force can superimpose its moralism onto individuals. The strong Cancerian implication in the chart suggests good intentions. However, good intentions frequently fail in principle, precisely in Pluto's match to Jupiter here. Misguided principles rebounded with rebellion through a cause and effect relationship.

The lack of effective enforcement of prohibition stemmed from the Uranian conjunction to the perihelion of Mars in Pisces. The fixity of Uranus and the potential aloofness of Aquarius pushed the law into motion with a surprising lack of sensitivity. The obsessive energy (Mars contact in Pisces) with the drinking dilemma spurred on judgment without careful or complete contemplation. The results were erratic, unpredictable and upsetting to the entire emotional tone of the whole of society in the United States. Supplementing the nature of the perihelion of Mars, John Nelson of RCA's communication division researched a random sampling of his heliocentric charts relating to significant short wave radio disturbances and subsequent solar activity, revealing conjunctions to the perihelion of Mars in several of the charts. These conjunctions participate in the volatility of the time.

One other aspect from the chart of prohibition needs examination. The planetoid Chiron in Aries falls upon the Q/q midpoint of Saturn. This contact refers to the increase of speed of Saturn and the arrival of new structure. It refers to the collective reaction to the changing times leading up to 1920. Uncertainty, instability and inconsistency prevailed. The use of alcohol provided Chiron with the desired escape from the social condition of primal pursuit emerging large scale. Prohibition's need would have been greatly attenuated if the social services and government directed energy into the reform of society and the economy. The cause of prohibition does not lie entirely on those decadent souls preserving/destroying their livers in alcohol. The cause resides in blame (if there is such a thing), mutually and inclusively, on the governing forces in society and society's reaction to the governing forces.

Those individuals staying dry throughout the entire period of prohibition will tell you that thirteen years, ten months, fifteen days, seventeen hours and some thirty-one minutes transpired from the passage of the law of prohibition and its repeal. The repeal took effect at 5:32 p.m. EST. December 5, 1933 in Washington, D.C. (Horoscope 4). That Tuesday night in the nation's capitol many more serious issues than drinking occupied the minds of the law makers. The economy had fallen out of the window and the country struggled to prevent suicides, decrease panic and survive. Murmurs of large scale war flew through the east as China and Japan started kicking up hostility. The economy in Europe also slid into severe depression. Germany fell hard to the times. Inflation and crime in Germany ran that country ragged. Hostilities seemed imminent in Europe as well. The United States experienced rages of underworld crime. About the only positive thing came with the approach of Christmas and that next year the Yankees should look good in spring training. One more thing, Christmas cheer would be legal in 1933.

A strong synastry exists between the charts of the start and repeal of the prohibition era. That task remains to the readers as the interest here is to examine the repeal chart itself. Like the chart commencing prohibition, it could be surmised that both Jupiter (bearing moralism and principles) and Neptune (substance abuse) are strongly referenced within the map. This is born out.

Neptune in Virgo squares the Earth/Moon combination in Gemini (Neptune fits on Saturn of the prohibition chart) allowing for the perception of both points of view. This aspect provides permission and restores the element of decision. Much moralistic appeal for atonement results here within the proclamation of repeal. Under such aspects it would have been appropriate for the surgeon general, if there had been one, to have issued a warning on all containers filled with alcoholic beverage. Neptune's position arched away from Pluto in Cancer (approaching the Earth/Moon of the prohibition chart— transformation through an angle of 45 degrees, a semi-square. The inner tension of this acute angle brought no relief from the darker side of alcohol use. The crime fanned by the fires of prohibition did not cease. The disease known as alcoholism did not go away, instead it increased in proportion. Only the guilt based upon the illegality of guzzling the juice disappeared, as Neptune revealed. Many would have replaced sincere nurturing (Pluto in Cancer) with a bottle and perceived a strange sense of well-being while liquified. Therein, the social struggle with alcoholism intensified. The disorientation of value systems released those without money and seeking meager

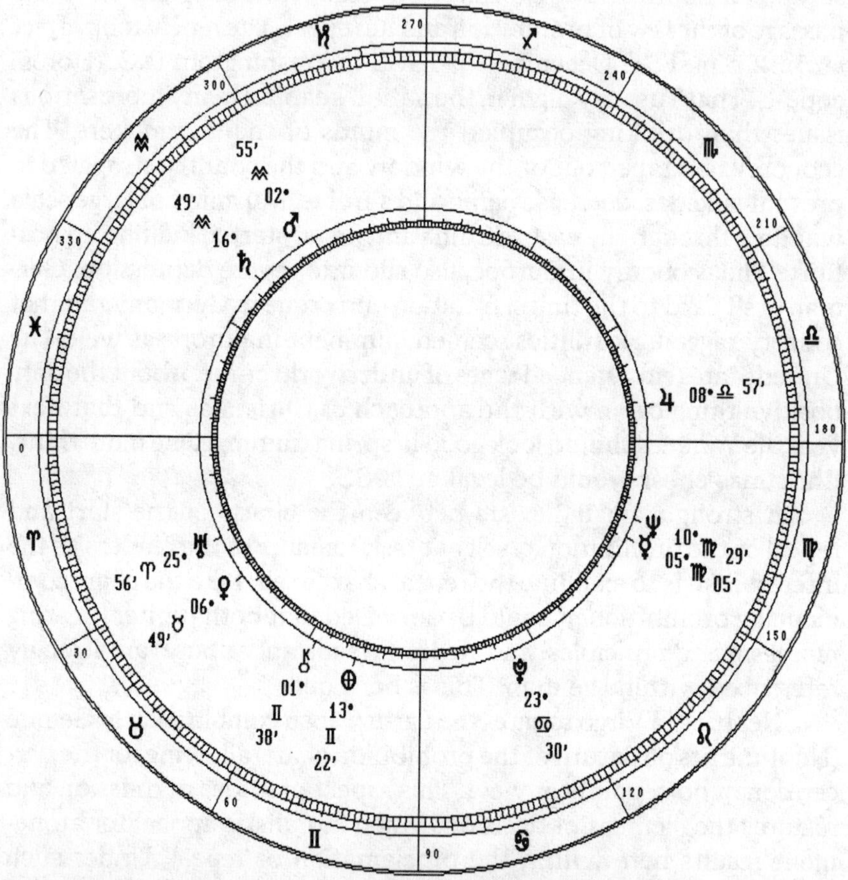

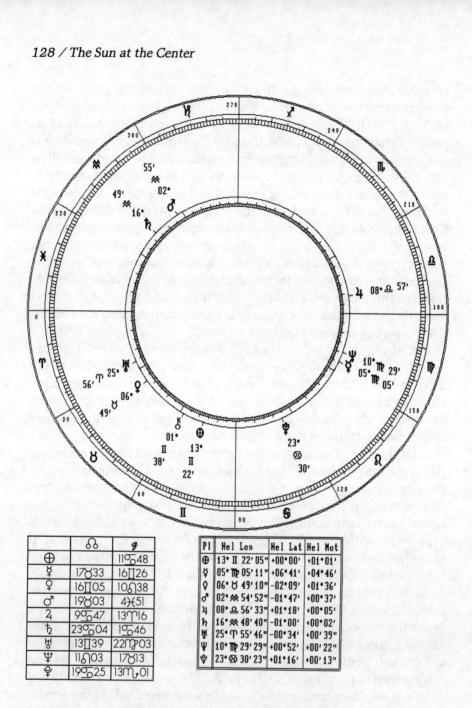

	☊	q
⊕		11♋48
☿	17♉33	16♊26
♀	16♊05	10♌38
♂	19♉03	4♓51
♃	9♋47	13♈16
♄	23♋04	1♋46
♅	13♊39	22♍03
♆	11♌03	17♉13
♇	19♋25	13♏01

Pl	Hel Lon	Hel Lat	Hel Mot
⊕	13° ♊ 22′ 05″	+00°00′	+01°01′
☿	05° ♍ 05′ 11″	+06°41′	+04°46′
♀	06° ♉ 49′ 10″	-02°09′	+01°36′
♂	02° ♒ 54′ 52″	-01°47′	+00°37′
♃	08° ♎ 56′ 33″	+01°18′	+00°05′
♄	16° ♒ 48′ 40″	-01°00′	+00°02′
♅	25° ♈ 55′ 46″	-00°34′	+00′ 39″
♆	10° ♍ 29′ 29″	+00°52′	+00′ 22″
♇	23° ♋ 30′ 23″	+01°16′	+00′ 13″

Horoscope 4. *Event: End of Prohibition*
December 5, 1933; 5:32 p.m. EST
Heliocentric
(Washington, D.C.; 77W02/38N54)

survival to winnow their funds on booze when food would serve a more substantial purpose. That trend still prevails consistently in the low income spectrum, inducing seduction to alcohol and ultimate ruin in the interest of Pluto's salvation—transformation.

Neptune met Jupiter in Libra through a semi-sextile, striving to generate a balanced idea of the use of alcohol. An imbalance of consumption was anticipated due to the widespread suppression of the past almost fourteen years. Then again, this energy created the belief that the use of drink actually created a sense of emotional balance. The biquintile of Neptune to physical Mars (Mars in wide trine to Jupiter) created a disillusionment of physical ease and mobility when in fact severe impairment of motor skills and cognitive sensory perceptions results. Back on the large scale, though, the Jupiter/Mars/Neptune activity restores the freedom of action (Mars) based upon belief systems (Jupiter) regarding the consumption of alcohol (Neptune).

Jupiter simultaneously quincunxed Venus from Libra to Taurus. The common denominator in this inconjunct is the Venus rulership of both signs. Social status and materialism is strongly reflected in this imbalance. Perhaps a counter-revolution took place, tempting non-drinkers to be drinkers. Advertisement soon followed, the theme of which was the belief (Jupiter) that one can demonstrate (Libra) social status (Venus, Libra) and affluence (Venus, Taurus) by spending one's money (Venus, Taurus) on alcohol (pulling on Neptune through a trine of over three degrees). Amazingly enough, this trend in social consciousness still receives support from advertisers of alcoholic products today.

Generally, the end of the prohibition era marks the increase of the use of booze, responsibly and irresponsibly. One may wonder if any real transformation resulted out of the prohibition phase of this country's growth. Pluto, the planetary representative of transformation, stands relatively barren of aspects, suggesting mundane realizations. The distant Pluto, at the time of this chart only three years old in cognition, connects with two midpoints. First, Pluto's Cancerian domicile conjuncts with the midpoint of Venus and Jupiter. Perhaps hope does exist. Pluto sought to bring a higher realization of the social relationships (Jupiter to Venus) created in the context of the environments of drinking. Realize that Pluto functions by going through the pits of darkness before emerging into light. This implies that individual awareness of the effects of alcohol may be recognized only after a fight with the evil, dark side of alcohol, directly or indirectly. Pluto can not think of a better way to learn (Jupiter) about our social vices (Venus feeding Pluto), which we perceive as good friends, good cheer and good feelings (Cancer). Pluto also connects to the point of intersection of Mercury to the Earth/Moon system. This midpoint discloses the need for open discussion of the background and real life experiences contained in the use of alcohol. The Earth/Moon binary loop forms an inconjunct from its actual position in Gemini to the perihelion of Pluto in Scorpio. The dangers of the game of drinking and social interacting come through in this configuration. Pluto speaks of the proximity to danger and the Gemini point, at best, seeks to solicit both perspectives, and at worst, simply justifies. The threshold of entrapment appears as thin, precarious and highly imperceptible through the blend of these energies. Pluto deposits its flux upon the North Node of Saturn, picking up the inertia established by the Earth's connection to that node at the start of prohibition. This transformative thrust of Pluto persuades the legalization, implied through the nodal direction of Saturn, to change in shape and form and clearly marked the inevitability of the repeal. By the time Pluto exactly rested upon that node, in mid-July of 1933, the absoluteness of the repeal would have been known. To deny or delay the repeal would have invited another form of inner turmoil not needed by the country. The implementation of drinking ages replaced the exclusiveness of the prohibition law, keeping Saturn in the drinking scenario.

To digress for a moment, in late 1983 as Saturn moved to within five degrees of the perihelion of Pluto in Scorpio, legislators in the northeastern United States proposed establishing uniformity (Saturn) of the drinking ages in the states to prevent the interstate drinking activities of underaged individuals. The pre-legal aged youth drive over the state lines to fill up on liquor and to party and drive back very inebriated, creating risks for themselves and others. The late Libra transits of both Pluto and Saturn, to follow this lineage further, squaring the nodal axis of Saturn in Cancer, induced many states to intensify the penalties for driving under the influence of alcohol. The organization MADD, Mothers Against Drunk Drivers, formed in the western United States, producing a strong influence upon the legislators. MADD calls upon the Cancerian implication of Saturn's North Node to protect the children. Many of the organizers of MADD had lost children to drunk drivers in alcohol connected fatal traffic accidents. The death implication of Pluto's square to the nodes took physical form and the Saturn square imposed structure. California responded by increasing the severity of its drunk driving penalties to include jail sentences. California drivers on the highways also see a variety of billboards from the California Highway Patrol, MADD and other concerned organizations.

Saturn's activity in the repeal horoscope adds tremendous impact. The ringed body links with another ringed body, Uranus, through a quintile between the signs Aquarius and Aries. This aspect actually contains the makings of strong research efforts upon the effects of alcohol on the physical body. The quintile produced a greater awareness of alcohol. We sought to comprehend the entire psychology of drinking. Saturn's Aquarius space in the map squared the nodes of Mercury, the nodes of Mars, perihelion of Pluto and the perihelion of Neptune. The latter two perihelion contacts put Saturn upon the q/Q midpoint of Pluto and the Q/q midpoint of Neptune. The energies into the communication of the effects of alcohol again appear with the addition of the nodes of Mars and Mercury. These nodal notes also indicate, at another level, the advertising and promotion of pro-alcohol factions. The Mercury and Mars nodes pull through the polarity of the signs Taurus and Scorpio, establishing the dilemma of delicate balancing between the extremism of the signs. The use, non-use, abuse confrontation exists within these parameters, brought into manifestation by Saturn. Neptune's connection of motion to Saturn, the Q/q midpoint, represents pulling from the depths of space (warming out of the subconscious) and heading towards closest contact to the Sun. Neptune's energy increases with this Saturn amplification. This brings one of two options: Either the motive of use becomes clear or the unconscious fabricates creative reasons for drinking. A Neptunian comes into mind with this phrase, "Oh this? It's for medicinal purposes only." Normally this expression receives only laughter. Embarrassment stands as the mechanism of laughter for both parties. The mode of embarrassment introduces Saturn's conjunction to the q/Q midpoint of Pluto. Saturn aligns with the point of Pluto's orbital plane, wherein the planet scoots back into the far reaches of space, reassuming its most distant domicile. The understanding of the dark depths of the unconscious prevails within the powers of Pluto. Such understanding notes that a scam exists in the justification of the use of alcohol. Pluto knows at this point that no justification need exist. Further, Pluto knows that justification declares the lack of need of the substance. The subtle permeation of Pluto's perceptiveness into the back of the consciousness induces embarrassment and with Saturn, manifests the cover-up. Justifications at all levels of consciousness, personal and collective, stem from this retreat of Pluto back into the darkness.

Final connections with Saturn include a square of Uranus in Aries to its nodes and Mars at inconjunct to the nodal orientation plane from an Aquarius point of view. The Aquarian energy forces adjustment through the inconjunct. Blending with the nonconformity of Uranus, squeezed by a square from Saturn's nodal structures, all cooperatively combine enough resources to sustain the successful rebellion of prohibition, inducing the repeal.

The entire sustenance of Uranus in the horoscope was tension. Uranus in Aries semi-squared the Earth/Moon in Gemini, asked questions and provoked thoughts relating back to the wishes of the self. A sesquiquadrate of Uranus to Neptune's Virgo integration tested the purity of intent, questioned deceit, stressed the structural rules and pondered the belief system in force. Uranus square Pluto in Cancer pushed self-interest into oblique confrontation with the forces of support ("governmental" control) and leaned upon the realism (or lack of realism, i.e. truth) behind the whole of the mechanism of prohibition. The unsatisfactory responses generated by Uranus with regard to prohibition noted the inconsistencies. Uranus then used these inconsistencies to proclaim the need for modification, change and progress. The conjunction of the Earth/Moon to the north node of Uranus rallied to support the planetary persuasions when Uranus spelled out its case. The direction of change received support from the consensus, providing the undeniable momentum of popular support. The popular consensus brought by the systemic influence of the Earth/Moon also connected by conjunction of the north node of Venus and the perihelion of Mercury. Once established as an Aquarian truth, courtesy of Uranus, the communicative urgency created by the perihelion of Mercury entered, insisting upon the reformation of social issues prescribed by the North Node of Venus. The nature of this array of aspects remains suspect; it appears unclear as to the level of thought quality applied to the insistence upon repeal, somewhat similar to the lack of mental continuity invoking the prohibition law.

Mercury in Virgo trine Venus links back to the Earth/Moon connections to the contacts of Mercury and Venus. The ease of communication actually adds to the fervor of the communicative efforts, possibly with application of morals and social stands, whether individually felt or not. Principles, correctness in the Virgo sense, stand corrected. Mercury quincunxes Mars in Aquarius, demanding that action (Mars) for the good of the people (Aquarius) be initiated. The entire chart theme of the repeal notes a highly critical segment in collective consciousness. The mid-July time referred to earlier had the undercurrents of a potential mass uprising. The chart could have functioned in one of two ways—with repeal or with revolt.

Moralism again wrote the bottom line of the entire prohibitive movement from beginning to end. Jupiter in Libra squared its nodal axis of Cancer/Capricorn. The collective philosophy concerning social issues as implied by Venus standing directly at odds with the historical memory of legalization. It appears that part of the resistance came out of the collective karmic memory of humanity from past suppressions by legalization, dogma or doctrine per the South Node of Jupiter in Capricorn. The North Node sought to gain a sense of non-interfering support in the socialization of the masses. The foundation of this configuration stressed the imposed philosophy to the breaking point, so that its effect diminished into nonexistence. The only question of rhetoric remaining in this aspect plane is: Did an effective replacement philosophy move in to fill the void created by the removal of the antiquated beliefs?

That question remains an issue. The question can be seen on billboards nationally, in editorials, in psychological journals and in the increasing number of alcohol rehabilitation centers throughout the United States. One very fundamental postulate emerges out of the study of the prohibition charts: regardless of proclaimed reason, excuse or justification, alcohol abuse develops out of a basic lack of belief in support of or for the self. An individual who cultivates a lack of faith in others leans toward surrogate nurturing.

Astrologers conducting extensive research on alcoholics declare that no clear signatures emerge. They further indicate that as many reasons exist for drinking and abusing alcohol as there are individuals in the condition of abuse of alcohol. The hypothesis to be tested here implies that individuals abusing alcohol demonstrate contacts in the heliocentric horoscope to the points of Jupiter's orbital motion (perihelion, aphelion), to the nodes of Jupiter, or hold heliocentric Jupiter in strong (tense) aspect orientation in the nativity. An indisposition could appear dramatically demarcated in the heliocentric horoscope through its thematic node. This statement applies to any motivation of any grouping under research analysis. The hypothesis now awaits testing, analysis and either confirmation or rejection.

The horoscopes of prohibition reference events dealing with alcohol consumption in the United States. Currently the repeal chart holds more relevance. New laws appear under aspects to the heliocentric energies. Programs and rehabilitation efforts would do well to work with these heliocentric patterns and cycles. Above all, to guarantee success, scope and purpose, referring to a higher side of Jupiterian application, require complete integration into the context of events and programs. Perhaps a ban on booze and even drugs may never demand implementation if the reasons of abuse and purposes of use become understood.

Chapter Eleven

The Heart of Don Juan

A series of books started appearing on bookshelves in the late 1960s involving the education of a man by the Yaqui Indians in Mexico. The teachings which this man received fell into the realm of the highly unorthodox and sought to create understanding of the dimensions of consciousness. This student underwent a series of drug induced psychedelic experiences geared to enhance his consciousness. The student frequently felt perplexed by his Yaqui guide, Don Juan. In his path to mastery he received questions for answers and continually confronted the experiential without explanation. The writer of this series of books, Carlos Castenada, receives attention through heliocentric astrological analysis in this personality portrait. The chart of Castenada (Horoscope 5) represents the solar system at 1:45 p.m., December 25, 1925.

The drug induced experiences so often mentioned in his writing generally encourages astrologers to have a look at his Neptune. Neptune falls in Leo strongly aspecting Mars in Scorpio by quintile, Uranus in Pisces by quincunx and Chiron in Aries by trine. Phenomena involving Neptune include a conjunction of Saturn in Scorpio to the aphelion of Neptune and a square of Mars in Scorpio to Neptune's nodes. An interesting point of contrast of geocentric to heliocentric astrology appears in the first aspect noted above, a quintile. The quintile is an aspect of creativity, innovation and dexterity in connected mind and action. The process of writing shows itself in key places four times in this heliocentric map. Geocentrically, two of the quintiles appear, both with respect to angles based upon Earth motion.

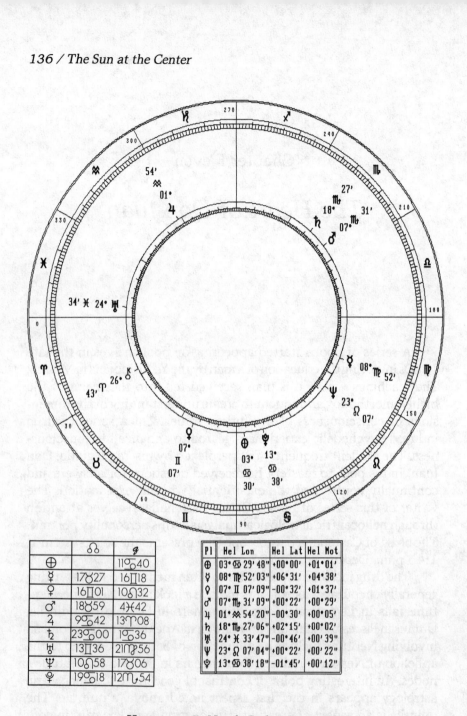

	☊	♌
⊕		11♋40
☿	17♉27	16Ⅱ18
♀	16Ⅱ01	10♌32
♂	18♉59	4♓42
♃	9♋42	13♈08
♄	23♋00	1♋36
♅	13Ⅱ36	21♍56
♆	10♌58	17♉06
♇	19♋18	12♏54

Pl	Hel Lon	Hel Lat	Hel Mot
⊕	03° ♋ 29' 48"	+00° 00'	+01° 01'
☿	08° ♍ 52' 03"	+06° 31'	+04° 38'
♀	07° Ⅱ 07' 09"	−00° 32'	+01° 37'
♂	07° ♏ 31' 09"	+00° 22'	+00° 29"
♃	01° ♒ 54' 20"	−00° 30'	+00° 05"
♄	18° ♏ 27' 06"	+02° 15'	+00° 02"
♅	24° ♓ 33' 47"	−00° 46'	+00' 39"
♆	23° ♌ 07' 04"	+00° 22'	+00' 22"
♇	13° ♋ 38' 18"	−01° 45'	+00' 12"

Horoscope 5. *Natal: Carlos Castenada*
December 25, 1925; 1:45 p.m. EST
Heliocentric
(Cajamarca, Peru; 78W31/7S10)

The quintilian nature of Castenada's heliocentric nativity carries twice the creative force perceived in the geocentric map.

Neptune in Leo, at a cursory glance, in quincunx to Uranus in Pisces, might believe in the use of drugs to shift perceptions of reality in the interest of self-discovery. The perceived shift in reality subsequent to the use of the drugs extends from an altered condition of autonomous perception occurring with an out-of-body type experience. The modification of awareness stemming from such a detached and objective perception of the soul within the body provides a high understanding of will and the conditions of agreement within an incarnation. Sensitivity and an ability to perceive power extend from this use of Chiron blending with Uranus to Neptune. Neptune rests upon the Venus/Mars midpoint using the energy of Chiron to generate a sense of the presence of both genders while in an altered condition. Neptune's greatest retreat, the aphelion, finds contact with Saturn in Scorpio. Never once was the indiscriminate or undisciplined use of drugs recommended throughout Castenada's writing. The demonic implication of drug use appeared but in Neptunian relation to the demons inside the mind and body. The aphelion implies retreat, objective pause, aloofness and blending of the impersonal into the personal. This improves total self-awareness. Much of this developed out of Scorpio energies involving the intense, the dark and the possessive. The drugs were perceived with Scorpionic regard and gender-referenced the Venus/Mars midpoint. Mars in Scorpio, intensified by co-rulership, squares the nodes of Neptune. This aspect speaks quite clearly throughout the books regarding use and abuse of drugs. Mars points out (through Don Juan) that certain applications of substances produce effective shifts in consciousness, initiating the process of growth in those individuals resisting the natural processes about them. Further, Mars stimulates one of the first references to power and the reverence of power, quite fitting for this aspect. Mars cooperates with Neptune to point out the nature of stagnation, imperceptibility and premature persistence.

The drug usage in the tales of the Yaqui Indians implies, at one level, the release from an embodiment upon the planet Earth. Ironically, the substances used, such as peyote, come directly from the Earth. What implications from the Earth/Moon placement in the horoscope feed more information into the evolution of the student? The Earth in Cancer quincunxes Jupiter in Aquarius, trines (widely) Mars in Scorpio, and sesquiquadrates Saturn, also in Scorpio. The Earth/Moon/

Pluto midpoint falls upon the North Node of Jupiter. Pluto conjoins the perihelion of Earth. A tremendous nurturing potential falls into perspective here. The trials of Don Juan's pupil were guided with expertise by a reluctant guide, mystic or, if you prefer, a master. However, this shaman invoked the very high side of the Cancer polarity, fully aware of the hazards of over nurturing and interfering. The reluctance on the part of the shaman served the student well for arrival at a clear understanding of support. The student encountered very unpleasant experiences during his growth experience and, as the master related, many events bordered upon the precarious. This is Mars trine the Earth—rapid acceleration into the mundane through the ease of the trine. Saturn attracts some discipline from its Scorpionic cave in the sesquiquadrate. An element of wizardry comes out of this angle to the Earth, with the teacher being represented through the solid authority of Saturn on Earth. The perihelion of Saturn undermines the Earth, granting urgency and control to the discipline necessary for the transformation to occur for the good and not into an abasement of evil. The quincunx of Earth to Jupiter again calls upon adjustment and symbolizes the radically shifted point of view when everything is perceived in total sensory response. The shaman encouraged the complete use of all the senses and recommended the use of the senses applied to each other. For instance, hearing what would normally be seen. The Earth/Pluto relationship to the Cancerian North Node of Jupiter speaks of the nurturing required of the master to student, regardless of how it looks. A tough drill instructor in the Marines may actually render support and growth to the unseasoned recruit even though it appears that he is relentlessly picking on the young Marine. Ultimately, the drill instructor may have saved the recruit's life through an initiation to the training. The same instance arises here. Discipline and nurturing do not bear the molds seen in many cultures regarding protective parent to child relationships. This push in the chart designs a new, north node view of mechanisms containing pure support and unconditional love. Pluto finds the Earth indirectly in a conjunction to the Earth's perihelion. This creates an urgency of discovery of the resources of the Earth. Don Juan is taught to respect, understand and perceive the Earth, its resources and its power. Power is lucid explained through this configuration. But power, it is explained, remains inert in quality. The use of power upon the planet creates the evil or divine manifestation. Demons frequently appear on the plane and divas fill the desert with apparitions of the dark for the student to grasp it experientially. *Tales of Power*, bases its theme upon this Pluto/Earth principle.

Pluto, to continue the power theme, trines its own perihelion in Scorpio, creating a natural bond of expression while squaring the perihelion of Jupiter. This q/Q connection reveals that Jupiter at this point would slow down and go into seclusion. Pluto reveals the need for quiet, inner contemplation and inner peace. The trine to Pluto's closest point to the Sun works well with this principle, enabling comfort to be felt in a realm of usual discomfort. To a shaman, the depth is natural. To a student, the solitude and isolation implied arouses fear and panic. The Pluto relationships provide a quelling calm, allowing initial entry into the depths of ultra-consciousness.

Discipline and respect for natural authority, Saturn concepts, are found throughout the books. Saturn, as one might expect, finds strong connection in the heliocentric phenomena. Jupiter in Aquarius stresses the perihelion of Saturn through a tight inconjunct. Saturn falls on Mercury's South Node, the South Node of Mars, the aphelion of Neptune. Finally, the Saturn/Mars midpoint hits the perihelion of Pluto. The breakdown of dogma affords a new level of discipline and application implied by the quincunx of Jupiter to the perihelion of Saturn. The shaman, working with Saturn's speed, executed the changes with great speed and skill. The South Node of Mercury again implies the alteration of sensory responses and communicative efforts. A key point in this would be to be still, quiet and listen. The hustle of the city from which the student came precluded such silence. The shaman insisted upon the discipline of silence. Saturn's South Node connection of Mars and Mercury alters responses. The theme was not to act when fearful. Pause in the moment, to become aware of your energy, the feelings and the reasons. The aphelion of Neptune observes that sometimes one must artificially induce the state of awareness first, thus the use of peyote and other substances.

Mercury, the key to communications, neared the point in space where its speed shifts from fast to slow. The Virgo Mercury maintained motion just on the fast side in the nativity of Castenada. The fleeting Mercury squared Venus in Gemini, sextiled Mars in Scorpio, biquintiled Jupiter in Aquarius and quintiled Saturn. Further, Mercury called up the aphelion of Uranus. Detachment from the normal modes of communication means expression, verbally and non-verbally. Castenada understood through this alignment that communication also contains the effect of listening. So it was that Don Juan taught him how to listen. The alteration of communication led the shaman to teach the ease of using energy when receptive (Mercury sextile Mars). The biquintile to Jupiter notes that new things can be constructed out of thoughts and perceptions. This Aquarius to Virgo realization typically goes by the name of magic. Manifestation increases with the quintile of Mercury to Saturn. The powerful Saturn in the chart, through listening and the use of latent power, becomes fully developed. The result is a truly magical being with an alchemical consciousness.

It appears clear that Castenada felt that most people waste energies on trivialities in life and never get to the real stuff. The inconjunct of Venus in Gemini to Mars in Scorpio refers to impotency of energies when dual in awareness cannot be held. Misdirection (Gemini worst case) of power (Mars in Scorpio) developed as a massive theme. Further, the Venus to Mercury square notes that much of this energy of atrophy stems from poor communication and sensory skills. Castenada wrote through the Venus to Mars square to develop these points. The Venus quintile to Uranus in Pisces blended the value of the awareness and sensitivity together. The mutable theme of thoughts along with their use and abuse fell into direct contrast with Uranus. This brought an ultimate integration of energies of apparently divergent forms, assisted by the sesquiquadrate of Mars to Uranus.

Castenada's heliocentric chart carries an emphasis of the second quadrant, the matter of expression of space. This "if, then" dynamic is strong. Castenada speaks directly and indirectly of the availability of all things right in one's own place of existence. He notes that the "if, then" crisis comes from basic inattentiveness and, moreover, an unwillingness to be clear about the acceptance of the power of effects.

Castenada's chart does not yield indications of great drug cult leadership. The curious resistance to his writings by many stems from the very issues he describes on his pages. The dichotomy of Earth-bound existence, as his Earth/Moon system understands, states that incarnation does not represent prison, unless the mind creates a prison within. His themes speak of transformation, power, principle and ultimate reason. This reasoning quality relates to the application and interpretive dynamic of similar to the concept of the use of the heliocentric chart. It describes the awareness of what is and the purpose of use and application of what is.

Chapter Twelve

Our Ancestral Father

During his lifetime, Nicolaus Copernicus brought the consciousness of humanity to the perceptions of the long lost heliocentric model of the solar system. A tribute to this heliocentric personality would only be appropriate to understand more of the heliocentric heritage. The analysis of the birth chart of Copernicus has an initial problem regardless of astrological system used. Disparity in the Copernicus' date of birth of exists depending upon the book of reference. Astrologer Lois Rodden in the book, *The American Book of Charts* (Astro Computing Services, San Diego, Ca.) quotes a reference indicating that Copernicus was born on February 23, 1473 at 4:48 p.m., in Torun, Poland. Other sources indicate a date of birth as February 19th, 1473 in Thorn, Poland (now known as Torun) with no time given.[1] Both charts can be found herein (Horoscopes 6 and 7, respectively). The chart of February 19th is set for noon and the lack of time creates no major difficulty in the heliocentric observations. Comparisons of Nicolaus Copernicus' natal chart, to the date he received his copy of his monumental work, *De Revolutionibus*, to the charts of Kepler and Galileo, to two charts of Inquisition events which effected his theories and to the commencement chart of writing this book will be made here. All of these events or people had an influence on him. The conclusion reached here is that the chart of February 19th maintains greater connection and activity to these dates and people, thus will be the chart explored in this investigation.

---

[1] Pannekock, A., *A History of Astronomy*.

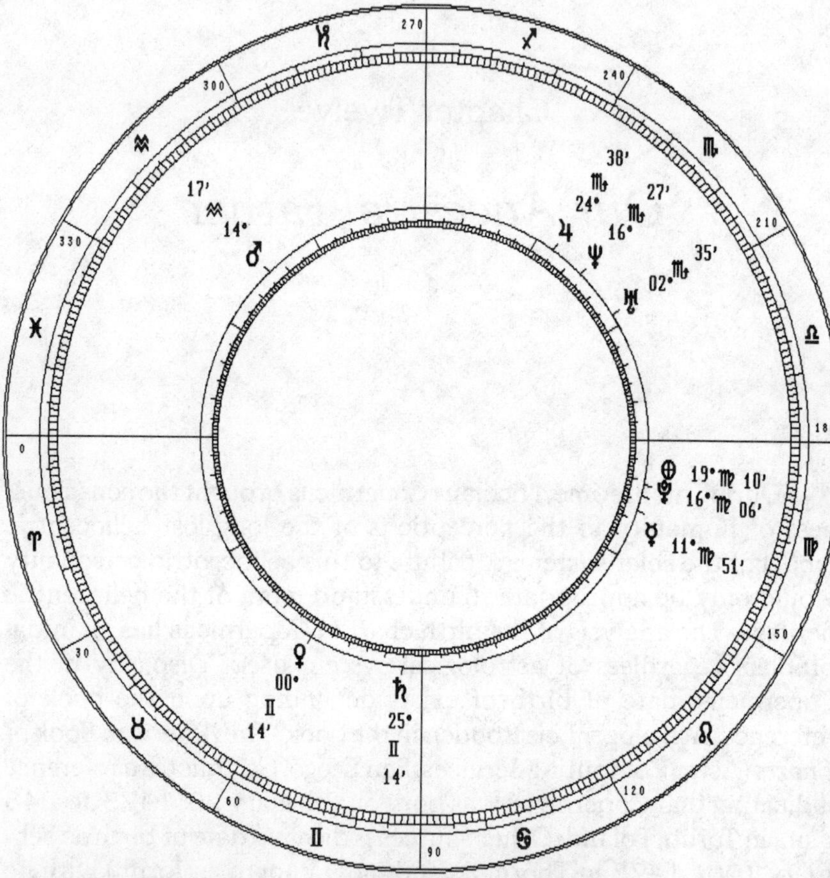

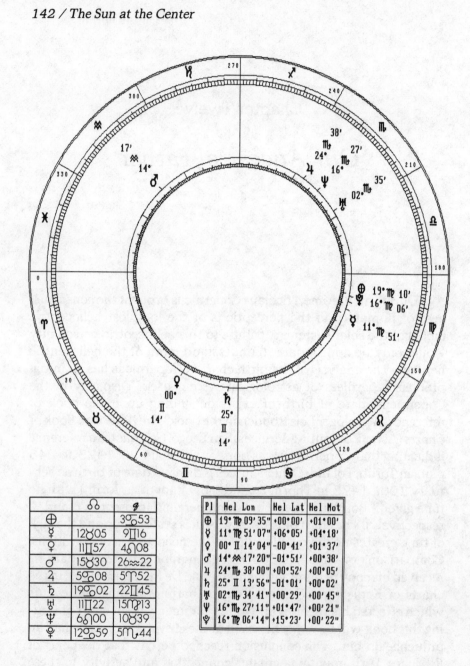

	☊	☋
⊕		3♋53
☿	12♉05	9♊16
♀	11♊57	4♌08
♂	15♉30	26♒22
♃	5♋08	5♈52
♄	19♋02	22♊45
♅	11♊22	15♍13
♆	6♌00	10♉39
♇	12♋59	5♏44

Pl	Hel Lon	Hel Lat	Hel Mot
⊕	19° ♍ 09′ 35″	+00°00′	+01°00′
☿	11° ♍ 51′ 07″	+06°05′	+04°18′
♀	00° ♊ 14′ 04″	-00°41′	+01°37′
♂	14° ♒ 17′ 20″	-01°51′	+00°38′
♃	24° ♏ 38′ 00″	+00°52′	+00°05′
♄	25° ♊ 13′ 56″	-01°01′	+00°02′
♅	02° ♏ 34′ 41″	+00°29′	+00′ 45″
♆	16° ♏ 27′ 11″	+01°47′	+00′ 21″
♇	16° ♍ 06′ 14″	+15°23′	+00′ 22″

Horoscope 6. *Natal: Copernicus*
February 28, 1473 (Julian); 4:48 p.m. LMT
Heliocentric
(Torun, Poland; 18E35/53NO2)

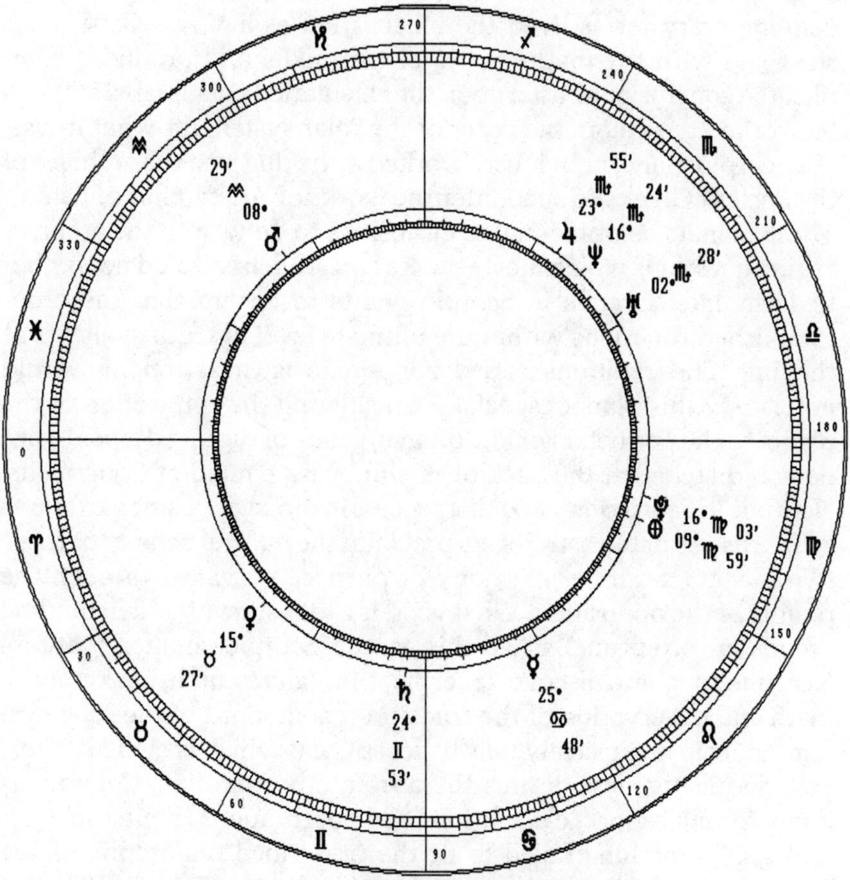

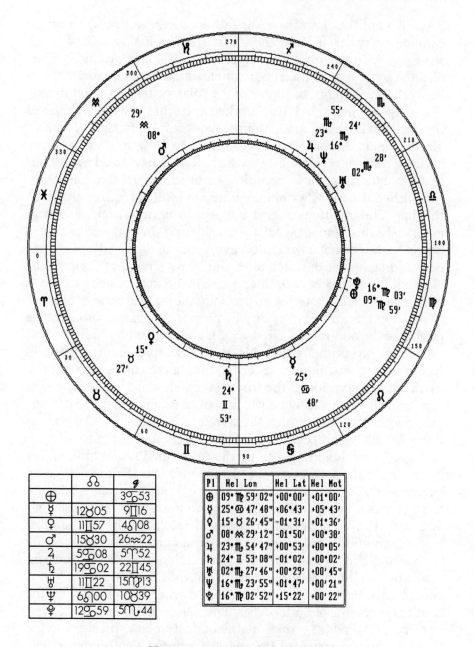

	☊	q
⊕		3♋53
☿	12♉05	9♊16
♀	11♊57	4♌08
♂	15♉30	26♒22
♃	5♋08	5♈52
♄	19♋02	22♊45
♅	11♊22	15♑13
♆	6♌00	10♉39
♇	12♋59	5♏44

Pl	Hel Lon	Hel Lat	Hel Mot
⊕	09° ♍ 59′ 02″	+00°00′	+01°00′
☿	25° ♋ 47′ 48″	+06°43′	+05°43′
♀	15° ♉ 26′ 45″	-01°31′	+01°36′
♂	08° ♒ 29′ 12″	-01°50′	+00°38′
♃	23° ♏ 54′ 47″	+00°53′	+00°05′
♄	24° ♊ 53′ 08″	-01°02′	+00°02′
♅	02° ♏ 27′ 46″	+00°29′	+00′ 45″
♆	16° ♏ 23′ 55″	+01°47′	+00′ 21″
♇	16° ♍ 02′ 52″	+15°22′	+00′ 22″

Horoscope 7. *Natal: Copernicus*
February 19, 1473 (Julian); 12:00 p.m. LMT
Heliocentric
(Torun, Poland; 18E35/53N02)

Regardless of the chart used, the father of heliocentric astrology in contemporary terms lived the incarnation as a Virgo. Copernicus struggled with the mathematics of his model and produced complicated conclusions based upon the calculations of his labors. Truly, he worked to explore the order of the solar system for what it was. His Scorpio planets obviously worked as he dug into the archives of the ancient Greeks to encounter the works of Aristarchus of Samos. These planets combine innate curiosities to delve into the archives asking questions which most readers and students would not bother to formulate. Uranus in Scorpio wants to ensure that the order established functions within the ultimate level of truth available at the time. The traditions passed from age to age in astronomy would not satisfy this planet especially considering the connection of the planet to the perihelion of Pluto. An urgency of digging deeper to understand etched at the back of the innovative mind of Copernicus. Neptune in Scorpio assisted this process in direct opposition to Venus in Taurus. As many astrologers proclaim the natural octaves of these two planets, an inner harmony of purpose prevailed through the pulling of the opposition. What good is the system of understanding (Venus into Neptune) asked this aspect (Scorpionic interrogation). Neptune sought to discover (Scorpio) through research, background, math and observation of the true and real motions of the solar system. Scorpio intrinsically fails to accept that which is evident. Scorpio's inquisitiveness desires the absolute bottom line. Copernicus knew from his work, calculations and observations (Jupiter in Scorpio) that something failed to fit the prescribed philosophy of the dynamics of the solar system. Neptune pulled on Pluto in Virgo by sextile while Venus reached out through a trine to the powerful Pluto to resolve the discrepancies. The Virgoan implication of the distant and potent Pluto provided the basis of resolution by the labor of calculation and uncovering of old astronomical data provided by Aristarchus and his followers. The Venus/Neptune polarization continues by picking up the nodal axes of both Mercury and Mars. Venus occupies the north nodes of both planets while Neptune sits on the south node points of both bodies. The Venus to north node of Mercury contact creates strong mathematical ability, precisely what Copernicus demonstrated through his laborious calculations. The labors come from the Venus to north node of Mars stimulation allowing for the energies of effort to prevail within his work. Ironically, as Neptune on the respective south nodes notes, the calculations of

Copernicus offered little if any improvement to the work done by the ancient Greeks. It does appear, though, that the Neptunian implication of the opposition network provided levels of pure insight and intuition required to arrive at the Copernicus' conclusions.

Mars in Aquarius squares off of all of the Scorpionic energy in the chart. Mars, most specifically squares the midpoint of Uranus and Neptune. Mars made direct contact to the south node of Neptune, squared the perihelion of Neptune with direct connection to the Q/q midpoint, finally squaring the perihelion of Pluto with conjunction to the q/Q midpoint of the Pluto trajectory. Again Neptune enters the chart with strong flavor, this time with collective implication. Copernicus devised a organization for the solar system which seemed rather Piscean to his contemporaries. They would scratch their heads, shrug or wonder if the mathematician submitted to some strong forms of medication. Still, as the contact in Pluto's orbit implied, Copernicus paused, going from q to Q with Pluto, to look, listen and perceive. Neptune's orbital push induced Copernicus to begin to be innovative (as in acceleration from Q to q), to conceive and speculate. He reviewed (Neptune's South Node) all past studies of the structure of the solar system. More importantly, he learned from review that the collective theories were incorrect.

So, with Mars in Aquarius he dared be different. He put the theories and figures together to support his designs of the solar system. He did so with an Aquarian reverence (dedicating the *De Revolutionibus* to Pope Paul, III) and with the firmness of conviction which comes from fixity (Mars in Aquarius, Venus in Taurus and the Scorpionic trinity).

Copernicus, by his own system of astronomy transposed upon astrology, becomes a Virgo. The Earth-Moon system in his chart sextiled the Uranus/Neptune midpoint while quincunxing the position of Mars in the ingenious Aquarius. This subsystem of bodies squared the nodes of both Venus and Uranus at nativity while also squaring the perihelion of Mercury. This Mercurial motion contact occurred on the q/Q midpoint of the fast planet's orbit. Mercury in the chart of Copernicus maintained a daily motion of 5° 43′ 15″ easily qualifying as a fast Mercury. The Mercurial modification of motion comes from the link-up with the orbit to the Earth/Moon system. Copernicus revealed in the introduction to *De Revolutionibus* that the manuscript represented thirty-six years of work! It remained as a very deliberate effort following the prescription of fast Mercury placements.

Copernicus used the Earth/Moon square to the nodes of Venus and Uranus to measure and modify the pictures of the solar system held in his time. His Jupiter in Scorpio aligned with the midpoint Q/q of Mars. His philosophies caused quite an uproar with his contemporaries. Martian aggravation of the Copernican beliefs surfaced prior to the publication of *De Revolutionibus*. Martin Luther, the leader of the Protestant Reformation, defiantly proclaimed in his Earth in Taurus manner that, "the fool will upset the whole science of astronomy, but as the Holy Scripture shows, it was the sun and not the earth which Joshua ordered to stand still".[2] John Calvin, another leader spearheading the Reformation, after quoting the ninety-third Psalm noted that "the earth is also stablished (sic) that it cannot be moved who will venture to place the authority of Copernicus above that of the Holy Spirit?"[3] Despite the dedication to Pope Paul III, the Lutheran minister Osiander wrote in the preface to Copernicus' work that the information was merely speculative, theoretical and convenient for the purposes of mathematical calculations. This flurry of comments established a trend not reversed until 1979 when the Catholic Church finally pardoned Galileo for purporting the Copernican Doctrine. This decision was later rescinded in 1988 to protect the infallibility of the Pope!! Galileo, during the Spanish Inquisition, submitted to extreme abuse and judgments of heresy.

The Jupiter in Scorpio to Saturn in Gemini quincunx in the natal map of Copernicus brings tremendous amounts of determination and diversification. This blend of Jupiter and Saturn in this aspectual relationship encourages the individual to develop strong, persevering aspects of the personality. An inherent push-pull relationship of cosmic checks and balances became one of the many gifts of the astronomer/mathematician. This aspect afforded Copernicus the ability to see both sides and formulate alternative considerations once the Scorpionic nature of investigation set the stage for the Gemini divergence.

Pluto figures strongly within the chart. The emphasis of Pluto not only sextiles Neptune, but trines Venus in Taurus and forms an inconjunct with Chiron in Aries. The Chiron in Aries portion of the aspect matrix contributed the emphasis of needing to step outside of the self, in particular, one's perceptual faculties. Although this aspect

---

[2] Dreyer, J.L.E., *A History of Astronomy from Thales to Kepler*, p.352.

[3] Kuhn, Thomas S., *The Copernican Revolution—Planetary Astronomy in the Development of Western Thought*.

occurred somewhat generationally, few integrated with the ease that Copernicus did through the utilization of his trine of Venus in Taurus. That Venus contact isolated the generational aspect down to about a ten day period of time. Pluto, further, made direct alignment with the perihelion of Uranus. This persuasion encouraged our heliocentric ancestral father to persevere to complete his works, findings and to publish his conclusions. A sense of urgency regarding the manifestation of the heliocentric system must have pervaded the consciousness of Copernicus. The commitment and dedication biographically described about this man suggest that he felt that the publication of *De Revolutionibus*, with its transformative implications stood to provide him with freedom from the physical world. The aspect of adjustment, the inconjunct to Chiron, supports this assumption. Chiron, symbolizing the release of the soul from body or the integration of soul and body, notes the portending death of Copernicus upon publication of the manuscript. The destiny became fulfilled and on May 24, 1543, Copernicus knew so.

Legend tells us that Copernicus received the first and only tangible evidence of his massive work in the pages of *De Revolutionibus* on May 24, 1543. This was also the day of his death. The chart (Horoscope 8) for the expiration of the astronomer represents the birth of consciousness of heliocentric theory in the world. This publication began a movement of counterculture proportions as well as adamant resistance to the perpetration of the speculations upon the pages of the treatise. The correspondences of the publication chart to that of the nativity of Copernicus will be left to the reader.

The Sagittarian Earth/Moon system of the publication chart figures strongly into the collective urges with the bearing of this new thing called heliocentricism. The sesquiquadrate of the Earth/Moon to Venus in Cancer and the semisquare to Jupiter in Libra generate enough social response to upset the traditional belief systems of astronomy. The difficulty with the work resided in the manner of writing which included a need to review one's position on beliefs, acceptance of fact and teachings. The Earth/Moon system also formed an adjusting quincunx to the perihelion point of Neptune pushing for modification of perception regarding those matters contained in the universal implications of Neptune. The Taurean implication of Neptune's zodiacal position points abruptly to the brash teaching technique of the time combined with the natural acceptance of mental the age by encouraging students to consider that there might be

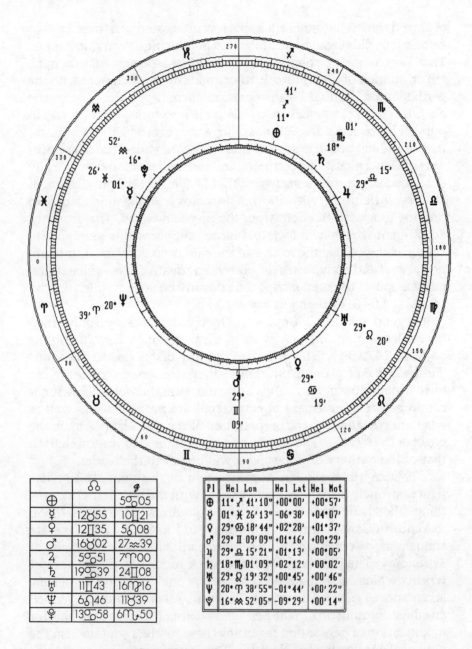

Horoscope 8. *Event:* ***De Revolutionibus***
May 24, 1543 (Julian); 12:00 p.m. LMT
Heliocentric
(Torun, Poland; 18E35/53N02)

another answer. Further, the Earth met by conjunction the aphelion of Mercury. This point of mental and intellectual distance called for retreat in order to prevent narrow vision and to open the spectrum to other considerations. Slowness, inherent in Mercury at this point, observed the response patterns of the thinkers of the time. Some extensive consideration and contemplation had to precede the acceptance of such a brash theory and speculation. Thus, the initial momentum of heliocentric acceptability took time. The Earth/Moon system also connected with the southern nodes of Venus and Uranus. Venus in this case implies the historical acceptance of society regarding astronomical matters. All that has been established stood firmly in the protection of social pressure placed upon those daring to sway outside the norm (the inference of Uranus by South Node). Still, the Uranian principle applied here called out for free thinking individuals to reach for more understanding. It is ironic that the religious reformers of the time, also calling out for free thinking, opposed the free thinking of Copernicus. This subjective bias originated out of the Mercury aphelion in almost retarded proportion. The breakthrough came about through the vehicle of social interaction, when those in positions of authority used the principle of creative license and influence in life to sway others.

Saturn in the publication chart added tremendous potential to the acceptance of the heliocentric doctrine. The event's Saturn squared Pluto in Aquarius from its position in Scorpio while quincunxing Neptune. Perceptual adjustment of existing structures provided an ultimate massive change from the implication of the quincunx, while the suggestion of change received support from the natural tension of the square to Pluto, ensuring the momentum towards ultimate transformation and innovation (Aquarius). The ferocious retention of the geocentric model of the solar system drew strongly upon the Saturn conjunction to the South Node of Mars. This Scorpion connection inspired redundant efforts at keeping the previous energies enforced. Traditional preservation, as contrasted to progressive implementation, set the tone of this collective urge to the printing. Fortunately, two other Uranian aspects occurred with enough emphasis to encourage ultimate advancement.

Uranus formed the midpoint from its position in Leo to Jupiter's trine from Libra to Mars in Gemini. Venus in late Cancer semi-sextiled Uranus as well. Uranus also opposed Mercury in Pisces through an incompatible elemental opposition, making the opposition intrinsically more separated. Still, Uranus formed the pivot point of a kite formation, linking the grand trine of Mercury to Mars to Jupiter, with Mercury being odd in element standing (in water instead of air). Venus also quincunxed Mercury in this configuration, but from a common element, reducing the stress of the suggested adjustment. The inspiration of the trine received focus from the fire based Uranus, noting the need for expansion, freedom of thought and sensitivity to what existed beyond just apparent perceptions. Mercury, Venus and Mars, linked within the aspect system circuit, all refer to the utilization of basic senses and the resulting process of observation. The relative quality of the apparent view set forth by the deception of the physical senses required the use of the non-physical Uranus, exaggerated by the influence of Jupiter, to ensure that an accurate look could occur. Uranus in the network collectively links to the aphelion of Mars, inducing a slow down of reflectiveness long enough to bypass his blatant interest in the legacy of heliocentric understanding.

Other interesting links of Kepler (Horoscope 9) to the book's chart and the chart of Copernicus can readily be found. Kepler's Mercury in Capricorn sought out the physical substantiation for the new model. This slowly moving planet conjoined the South Node of Saturn, representing the old astronomical model and also fell upon the South Node of Pluto, promising transformation of the old. Kepler realized that this could only be done through the vehicle of Mercury; thus he produced the equations and dictated the mechanics of operation of the planetary orbits. This, in turn, substantiated the model with Capricornian order, structure and format.

The Venus of Kepler in Aquarius tightly squared the structure of Saturn in Scorpio. Venus simultaneously squared the nodes of both Mercury and Mars. This combination of influences noted the system's retention of power (Saturn in Scorpio), again calling for a Mercurial solution to the problem of proof. The South Node of Mercury used traditionally established math to disrupt (Mars) the energies directed into an old, outdated system. The aggravation level induced by Kepler must have been horrendous, yet the Venus placement in Aquarius directed the major disruptions elsewhere (as in Brahe's Denmark and Galileo's Italy). Venus fell directly upon the South Node of Neptune, again calling loudly for the revision of the old visions. Finally, Venus pursued its own South Node by conjunction, allowing immunity from the social conditioning which so often con-

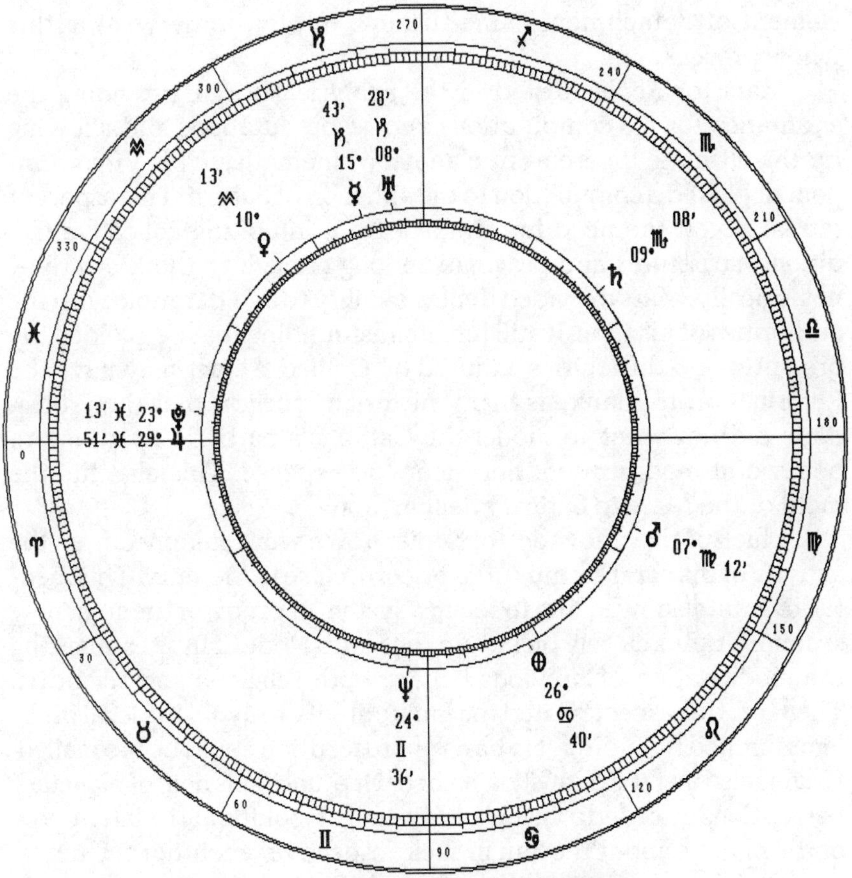

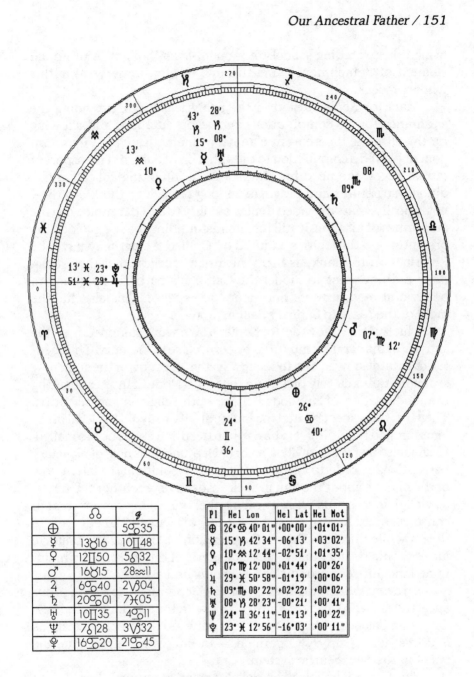

	☊	q
⊕		5♋35
☿	13♉16	10♊48
♀	12♊50	5♌32
♂	16♉15	28♒11
♃	6♋40	2♑04
♄	20♋01	7♓05
♅	10♊35	4♋11
♆	7♌28	3♑32
♇	16♋20	21♋45

Pl	Hel Lon	Hel Lat	Hel Mot
⊕	26° ♋ 40' 01"	+00°00'	+01°01'
☿	15° ♑ 42' 34"	-06°13'	+03°02'
♀	10° ♒ 12' 44"	-02°51'	+01°35'
♂	07° ♍ 12' 00"	+01°44'	+00°26'
♃	29° ♓ 50' 58"	-01°19'	+00°06'
♄	09° ♏ 08' 22"	+02°22'	+00°02'
♅	08° ♑ 28' 23"	-00°21'	+00' 41"
♆	24° Ⅱ 36' 11"	-01°13'	+00' 22"
♇	23° ♓ 12' 56"	-16°03'	+00' 11"

Horoscope 9. *Natal: Kepler*
January 7, 1572 (Julian); 2:30 p.m. LMT
Heliocentric
(Weil der Stadt, Germany; 8E52/48N45)

firmed the preceding schools of thought-sans-thought. A profound element of detachment came through Kepler, underwriting this whole process.

Mars for Kepler rested in the analytical Virgo, providing the endurance for his computations and recomputations and allowing for the ultimate theorems of planetary kinematics. This Virgo component picked a conjunction to the aphelion of Saturn. This aspect of retreat noted the need for removal from inhibiting collective traditions, structures and pragmatism long enough to think clearly—not logically. Mars provided Kepler's ability to avoid trouble with the authorities of his time. It still remains astounding that he avoided the pressures and difficulties endured by Galileo. Kepler may have the Reformation to thank, as many historians suggest that the Protestants did not want to model the Catholic's barbaric approach to behavioral modification, nor incur the expense. This also fits the mold of the Mars to Saturn phenomenon.

Much of the innovation of Kepler's own work stemmed from the activity of his natal Uranus in Capricorn, close to Mercury. This mental ingenuity allowed him to set up a system of proof for the great new system. Uranus closely picked up the South Node of Jupiter, marking the modification of previous beliefs, both religious and scientific. Then too, this aspect related the innate ability to avoid the legal problems implied by Jupiter. No basis of prosecution could be reconciled. Uranus also met the perihelion point of Neptune. This note of planetary perceptions afforded a vision and system of looking at the latent flow of the planets about the Sun in their respective revolutions. Uranus, as well, joined hands with its own aphelion, calling for a retreat in consciousness. Kepler must have used his Pisces planets well to dream while in connection to the aphelion of Uranus. The creative juices within the mentality (consciousness) of this astronomer maintained magnificent proportions of genius and artistry.

An event worthy of note concerning Copernicus (to return to our ancestral father's legacy) came in 1581 with the adoption of the new Gregorian Calendar. This new calendar drew its basis from calculations and theories set up by Copernicus—an interesting effect, due the belief in the heliocentric system.

The flow of heliocentric development continued. Kepler and Galileo exchanged letters in 1597, leading up to the time when the great rejection of heliocentricism took place by the Catholic Church. Unfortunately, Galileo received the brunt of the rejection. The

Catholics placed him under house arrest, forced him to reject his theories and to renounce his mother. This all took place under the persuasive threat of torture. On February 24, 1616, the conferees of the Inquisition met and determined that the previously established theory of the Earth at the center of the solar system was correct. They dismissed the Copernican doctrine as simply being "false and absurd." This event (Horoscope 10) set the stage for repression of the helio-centric model.

The above event contained a series of nodal aspects, demon-strating tendencies to draw upon the past, as well as a series of ambiguous nodal aspects noting that the event could have swung in either direction. This suggestion implies that the leaders of the Catholic Church knew of the truth of the system and could not make it fit in the context of their religious thought. This brought about the rejection of the system with a force implied by the square of Mars in Aquarius to the nodal axis of Mars implied. The Martian push towards the South Node in Scorpio not only reset the past philoso-phies but implied the torture, dungeons and killing which took place in an effort to produce conformity with the theology of the past. It had to be Aquarian energy to permit such an irony. Jupiter formed a strong case for justification, with its Sagittarian conjunctions to the aphelion of Mercury and the South Nodes of Venus and Uranus. This aspect clearly pointed out that the Church (Jupiter) had the answers and direction (Sagittarius) and no changes, or socially avant garde reconsiderations of the theories of the Church would be permitted (summarizing the aphelion and South Nodes). Virtually no choice existed.

The value of the heliocentric system, shown by the response of the Catholic Church in Venus in Libra, rejected any possible validity, noting that the system was developed by those without base or social cause (Venus square the nodes of Saturn). Further implications of potential change, symbolized the position of Uranus in Cancer, negated all potential for change with an impeding square to the North node of Jupiter. The Church again reiterated a policy of Divine guidance and knowledge to which there was no contest. Uranus met the midpoint of the motion effects of Jupiter, aligning with its q/Q. This reduction of speed sought to squelch the inertia to the Church doctrine created by the heliocentricism crisis. It further implied the direction of isolation, i.e. imprisonment, for those supporting the system. Justice, as in Jupiter, simply did not exist. Supression of the

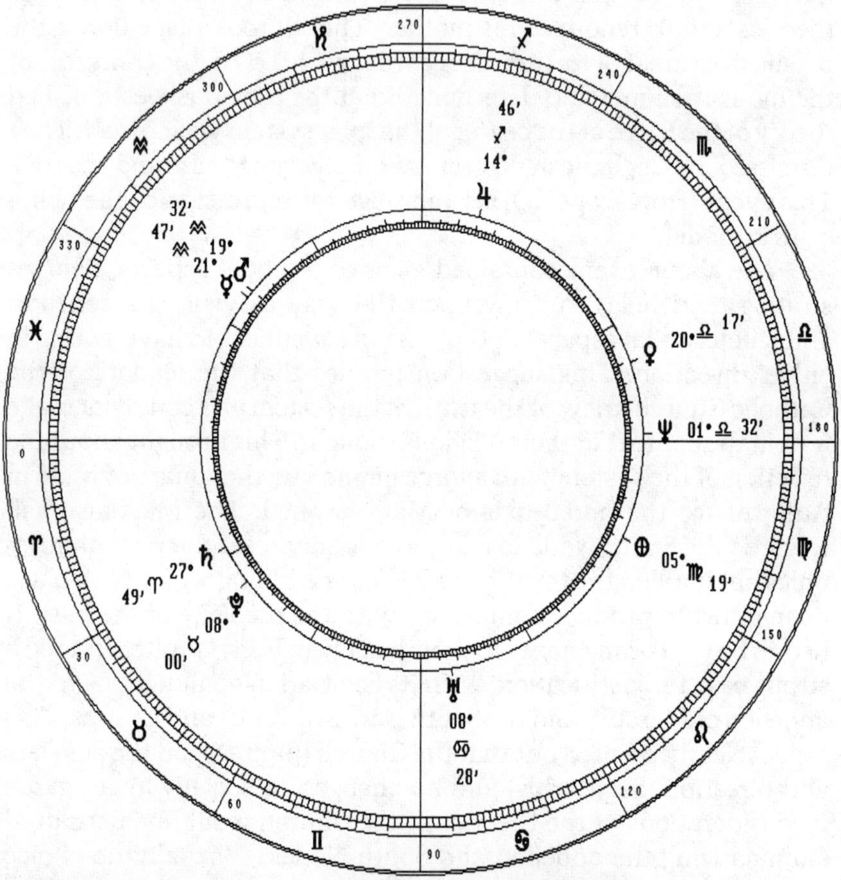

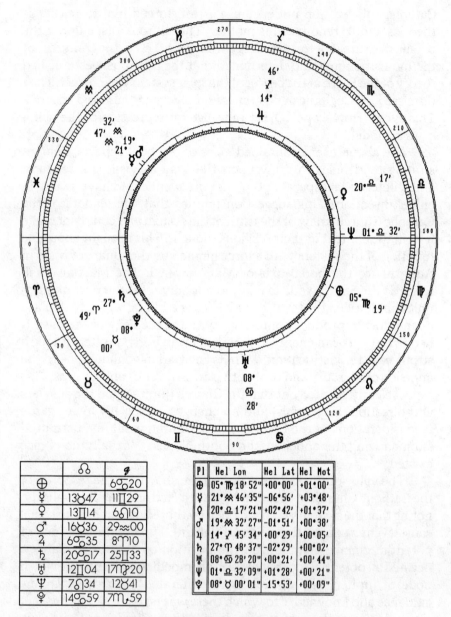

	☊	q
⊕		6♋20
☿	13♉47	11♊29
♀	13♊14	6♌10
♂	16♉36	29♒00
♃	6♋35	8♈10
♄	20♋17	25♊33
♅	12♊04	17♍20
♆	7♌34	12♉41
♇	14♋59	7♏59

Pl	Hel Lon	Hel Lat	Hel Mot
⊕	05° ♍ 18′ 52″	+00°00′	+01°00′
☿	21° ♒ 46′ 35″	-06°56′	+03°48′
♀	20° ♎ 17′ 21″	+02°42′	+01°37′
♂	19° ♒ 32′ 27″	-01°51′	+00°38′
♃	14° ♐ 45′ 34″	+00°29′	+00°05′
♄	27° ♈ 48′ 37″	-02°29′	+00°02′
♅	08° ♋ 28′ 20″	+00°21′	+00′ 44″
♆	01° ♎ 32′ 09″	+01°28′	+00′ 21″
♇	08° ♉ 00′ 01″	-15°53′	+00′ 09″

Horoscope 10.

Event: Copernican Doctrine Declared "False and Absurd"

February 24, 1616; 12:00 p.m. LMT

Heliocentric

(Rome, Italy; 12E29/41N54)

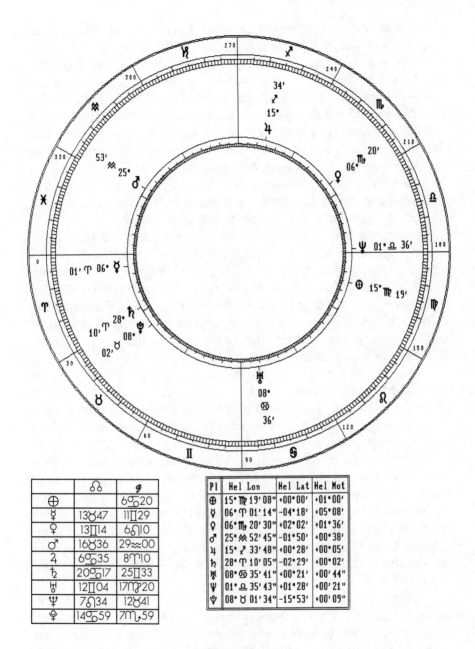

Horoscope 11.
Event: Church's Blanket Censure of Heliocentricism
March 5, 1616; 12:00 p.m. LMT
Heliocentric
(Rome, Italy; 12E29/41N54)

forces of evolution maximized. The planetoid Chiron in Pisces spoke clearly of both the principles of the Church and the impending death of those rebutting any Church policy. This referral comes from the inconjunct of Chiron to Venus in Libra (it also incorporated social pressure for spying on friends and neighbors). Chiron aligned with the aphelion of Uranus. The implication refered to the Uranus principle, via the promulgation of the heliocentric system, submitting to an unwilling adjustment of Chiron to Venus; either the vital organs would be removed, which relates to reproduction, or the life would be taken and the soul released from the body. A campaign of massive slaughter and tortuous death was fanned by the fires of agitation caused by the heliocentric model of the solar system.

Pluto, suggesting change and transformation, fell in Taurus, occupying a retardant square to the nodes of the perceptive Neptune. Simply, Pluto precluded perception. Pluto aligned with its own aphelion, noting that inferior forces claimed superiority by moving into power, which established an arena of repression. Pluto met the Q/q midpoint of Venus, accelerating and exaggerating the merits of the heliocentric model. The value of the system underwent subversion as only Pluto can provide.

Less than ten days after the initial decree, the Catholic Church increased its ban on heliocentric involvement. On March 5, 1616 (Horoscope 11), any book by Copernicus or any book on the subject of heliocentric theory was forbidden. Worthy of note in this chart were the Mercury (ruling communication and words) aspects. Mercury configured a tight quincunx to Venus from Aries to Scorpio. The common Mars and Pluto bond of the signs notes the anger, physical violence and an undercurrent of suppression operating out of the worst case of both signs. Mercury squared Uranus in Cancer, allowing little chance for innovative expression. Mercury opposed Neptune in the early degrees of Libra, allowing no freedom of perception to exist there. Mercury semi-squared Pluto in Taurus to complete the matrix of religious dominance.

Mercury of the proclamation chart resided upon the perihelion of Jupiter, ruler of publication. The urgency of the publications became apparent but the need to censor and dictate acceptable printed matter, in this Jupiter imposition upon Mercury's dynamic, overruled truth. Jupiter overtook the South Node of Mercury in the event chart. This aspect stated again that the information of the past was relevant, shall be printed and nothing more. The Earth/Moon system aggravated Mercury's influence from a square out of Virgo to the nodal axis of the messenger. No messages would be generated out of this aspect except for those fitting the Virgo and listing appropriate words generated by the Church. Although the lid was sealed from the Catholic point of view, the word about heliocentricism crept out into the world. Slowly the evolution continued.

In 1620, the Catholic Church allowed a reprinting of *De Revolutionibus*, censored, of course. Simultaneously, they forbade, "all books teaching the same thing." The Church increased pressure in 1633, three years after the death of Kepler. Not until 1822 did the Catholic Church condone the printing of books relating to the heliocentric model of the solar system. This was long after the work of Sir Isaac Newton had proven the model. This did not mean that the work would be accepted. In 1873 a former president of the American Lutheran Teachers condemned not only Copernicus, but Newton too! Finally, in 1979, Galileo received a pardon for his sins of heresy involving the use, support and proclamation of the heliocentric model. This decree, as noted earlier, was reversed in 1988 in the interest of preserving the infallibility of Papal authority. This implies contemporary resistance to heliocentric astrology.

The path paved by Copernicus has been a long one indeed. The time is ripe for complete activation of the true perceptions of the solar system. Those not following this path seem to contribute to the already redundant resistance to heliocentricism. Perhaps we await the activation of the Scorpio planets of Copernicus and the Saturn in Scorpio of *De Revolutionibus* combined with the perihelion of Pluto, as Pluto transits Scorpio, to propel heliocentricism into its own. Our ancestral father may then rest in peace.

Chapter Thirteen

A Real Live
Normal (Sort of) Person

With the consideration of the heliocentric charts of the two events and two historical figures, it seems appropriate to include a natal analysis for a "normal" person who fits the criteria of seeking knowledge about the meaning and purpose of life. The individual in this discussion began incarnation on May 22, 1953 at 8:15 PM, CST, Chicago, Illinois, USA, Earth (Horoscope 12). For reference purposes a copy of the geocentric horoscope (Horoscope 13) is provided but will not be read in comparison or contrast to the heliocentric chart.

This individual followed a normal path of life, as one is supposed to live it, for a number of years. She married a physician, had two children, did social and philanthropic work and assumed the roles of super-mom and super-mate. All the while she wrote freelance articles for magazines and assorted periodicals. Still, something seemed to be missing.

In 1987 a divorce was initiated, followed by a series of moves, the last of which was a major move to California in 1989 to persue her ultimate aspiration . . . to become a screenwriter and novelist. The transits and progressions for all of this activity fit the timing of both the heliocentric and geocentric horoscopes.

First, a look at her natal pattern is required. Being a geocentric Gemini, she now maintains an Earth/Moon pairing in Sagittarius. Venus in Aries is traded in for a Venus in Sagittarius and Mercury insistently holds its ground in Taurus. The chart holds a third quarter dominance of planetary positions, yielding the theme of application

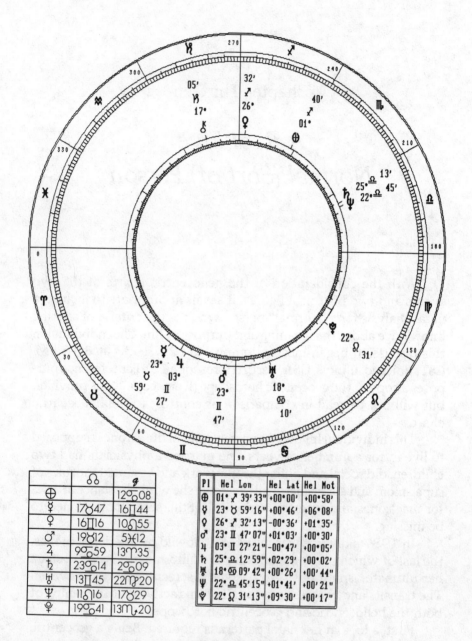

	☊	♃
⊕		12♋08
☿	17♉47	16♊44
♀	16♊16	10♌55
♂	19♉12	5♓12
♃	9♋59	13♈35
♄	23♋14	2♋09
♅	13♊45	22♍20
♆	11♌16	17♉29
♇	19♋41	13♏20

Pl	Hel Lon	Hel Lat	Hel Mot
⊕	01° ♐ 39' 33"	+00°00'	+00°58'
☿	23° ♉ 59'16"	+00°46'	+06°08'
♀	26° ♐ 32'13"	−00°36'	+01°35'
♂	23° ♊ 47'07"	+01°03'	+00°30'
♃	03° ♊ 27'21"	−00°47'	+00°05'
♄	25° ♎ 12'59"	+02°29'	+00°02'
♅	18° ♋ 09'42"	+00°26'	+00'44"
♆	22° ♎ 45'15"	+01°41'	+00'21"
♇	22° ♌ 31'13"	+09°30'	+00'17"

Horoscope 12.
Heliocentric Natal: A Real Live Normal (Sort of) Person
May 22, 1953; 8:15 p.m. CST
(Chicago, Illinois; 87W39/41N52)

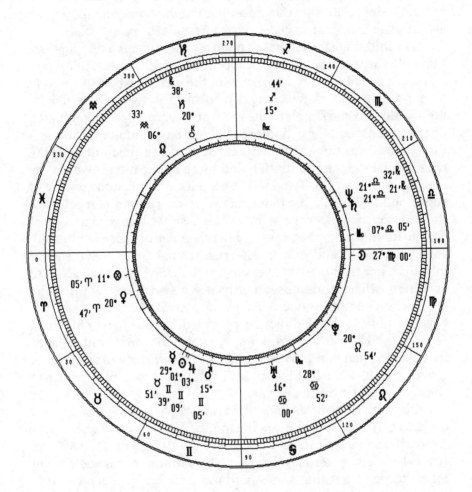

Horoscope 13.
Geocentric Natal: A Real Live Normal (Sort of) Person
May 22, 1953; 8:15 p.m. CST
(Chicago, Illinois; 87W39/41N52)

of self. Mercury nears perihelion and is categorized as fast with a daily motion of six degrees and some eight minutes, nearly maximum. According to the criteria of Astro Computing Services, located in San Diego, California, the geocentric nativity contains sixty natal aspects. The heliocentric chart possesses only thirty aspects.

The initial suggestion based upon aspect number alone suggests that with the transition to the heliocentric consciousness, this woman stands to reduce the complexity of the web of aspects woven to lunar phenomena and house angles by planetary angles. Quite simply, life should become simpler. The geocentric horoscope is dominated by the trine aspect; the heliocentric counterpart contains mostly sextiles. In the transition to the heliocentric model the inspiration of the trine receives greater definition and more application towards the real, pragmatic world. Two instant benefits, providing the energy of superconductive ease, are immediately noted. Her initial reaction to the heliocentric horoscope stands to be positive, but perhaps one of perplexity at the implied ease of life when her purpose is pursued. Given her move and efforts towards her path, her move should introduce her talents to the blessings of the Universe as she seeks to enlighten others and subsequently herself with her words. The geocentric Gemini individuality already created manifests in the guise of philosophical direction provided by the Earth/Moon in Sagittarius. The early degrees imply that her words contain seed thoughts to open minds to other points of view. Her words need not strive to be the ultimate philosophy. A Johnny Appleseed approach to consciousness-spreading begins.

Our publishing protagonist holds most of her planets in the third quadrant. This quadrant bears the tone of application of self. In this sector the individual intrinsically knows the attributes of the self and strives to receive external validation. This externalization seeks to get others to point out that she is not insane for having such destiny-oriented thoughts about herself. Those thoughts have been with her forever, since day one in this lifetime. So, she solicits the opinion of others, the academia, other literary professionals. Opinions of her talents are rendered with very high marks and praise. Then she wonders if these people are being honest with her—a Venus in Sagittarius question. A better question might be, "Why would they have any reason to lie to her?" Perhaps she knows that her natural ability to inspire others is based upon encouraging people to do what they want instead of what they should do. Perhaps she feels that they could never say, "keep your day job." Still, when the validation comes her way, it is her karmic responsibility to reject the input with doubt, suspicion and great internal interrogation. The point is that she must rely upon her own instincts of herself, knowing that she can do it, that she is powerful and, most certainly, motivated.

A series of interesting aspect patterns can be seen in the chart. Foremost is the fickle finger of God aspect—the *Yod*—comprising Mercury in Taurus quincunx to Neptune and Saturn in Libra, sextile Venus in Sagittarius, quincunx Mercury, completing the cosmic Y. The key point of the *Yod* is a fast Mercury, highly editing and internalized, perfect for a writer. The obsession of writing brings out the Taurus need for something to be substantive in order for it to be a worthwhile endeavor. Writing is good, but does it say anything important? The quincunx to the Libran dynamic indicates messages involving relationships, especially about women with reputations for being less than cooperative. This of course stems from the patriarchal Saturn in Libra confusing the perception of women (Neptune) and subsequent suppression or incarceration by virtue of living a life without choice. These Libran energies, sextile Venus in Sagittarius, need to explain the intelligence of women and the truth about relationships as they have been in the past. Her first two major writing projects deal with a woman in a condescending relationship with a husband and about polygamy in the late 19th and early 20th century Mormon societies—perfect manifestation of this *Yod*.

Two strong oppositions exist in the chart. These are Jupiter in Gemini opposed Earth/Moon in Sagittarius and Uranus in Cancer opposed Chiron in Capricorn.

The Chiron/Uranus polarity carries the relationship of the grandfather (Uranus) to the grandson (Chiron). Chiron's nature requires the essence of healing to prevail in life. The healing notes the need to ease the pain of the family. It is interesting to note that the maternal grandfather was the product of a polygamous relationship. Although this aspect is generational, both planets connect to a number of other planetary energies, including the more personalized planets. The literary efforts describing polygamy originate in Mercury, which widely sextiles Uranus and trines Chiron. Healing this family genealogy heals not only her personal relationships, but addresses the contemporary social trends of multiple relationships and affairs. The theory of Mormon polygamy stressed having all that you want and all that you could support. Her personal message for healing from this opposition encourages her to take on as much as she can and to endure the levels of personal pleasure intended for her enjoyment without fear of indulgence and decadence.

Jupiter opposing Earth/Moon requires that a philosophy of strong mental orientation preset any acceptance of nurturing. She has embarked upon a highly stylized, pragmatic approach to metaphysics, striving to create a support system of personal endorsement. This opposition, containing one of the planets in the third quadrant, supports the rediscovery and application of self.

A t-square begun by the Chiron to Uranus opposition continues with both outer bodies square Saturn and Neptune. This trinity sextiles Venus in Sagittarius and Pluto in Leo; Venus and Pluto trine each other. Pluto sextiles Mars in Gemini which trines the Libran conjunction. Mercury sextiles Uranus, squares Pluto and semi-sextiles Mars. Mars semi-sextiles Uranus which semi-sextiles Pluto which forms a quincunx to Chiron.

A primary vertebra in this aspect backbone originates with Mercury square Pluto. Supported by Venus in Sagittarius, this square insists and demands that the truth be told. Yet the *Yod* induces Mercury to be shy and coy on its own behalf. Saturn dissects the previously described relationship of grandfather (Uranus) and grandson (Chiron) entering the essence of father. Here the male domination syndrome begins perceiving men as being in the position of authority over women (Libra), an illusion to be sure (Neptune), but a strong inhibition for not being the wrong kind of girl. "I'm a nice girl," she often proclaims. So, that still did not win the approval of the paternal. In fact, in personal relationships it only caused individualized suppression to overcome intensifying her need to explain the truth about all of this struggle.

The intricate Mercury aspects energetically (Mars in Gemini) connect with the need for change (Uranus) to achieve personal power (Pluto), allowing for a healthy image of one's feminine energy—male or female, Saturn or Neptune—without perceiving the self as a screaming, insatiable person. This eases the perception of self into a healed, honest well being (Venus in Sagittarius). Mars trine to the Libran trio allows for the energy (Mars) and discipline (Saturn) if the vision (Neptune) of the need to express is held high above personal vendettas and concerns. Venus trine Pluto allows for relentless pursuit of the cause to support its twin trine. Mars and Pluto, co-rulers of Scorpio, direct intensity and perseverance into the cause.

Of interest is the last name change that our study initiated after her divorce. She changed her last name to her animal totem on the last day of the Scorpio Sun sign.

Two quadrature type aspects also bear delineation. These are Jupiter semi-square Uranus and Uranus sesquiquadrate Earth/Moon. With a strongly Uranian tone to the chart, individuality bears strong noting. Jupiter carries the requirement of the strong philosophical underwriting to make life a success. The deficiencies of the given philosophy are first noted. Then she must be wronged (or make herself wrong) about the beliefs to allow for their elimination and replacement with more substantial thoughts. The Uranus contact to the Earth/Moon system brings practical energies. Her essential drive asks the question, "If it was good for me to go through, could anyone else benefit from the message?"

Change is transformative. We would expect that thought from a member of the generational grouping with Uranus conjunct the North Node of Pluto. Of course change is transformative, but bear in mind that it must be supported and gentle (without being protected) to accommodate the most effective healing. With the aspect matrix involving Uranus, she is intended to communicate her transformative process, with some objectivity and personal distancing to ensure that the words are not personal retaliation.

Jupiter squares the perihelion of Mars, just approaching culmination of a volatile energy. Concern for action and non-action may induce immobility. Being concerned about going too fast slows her to a stand still. Worrying about not doing enough stimulates work—rewrites and edits—highly frustrating and de-motivating worry about incompleteness. The solution resides in Jupiter's essential doctrine. Create a philosophy that works. Flow with biological energy cycles and go at the pace the Universe provides, not the pace directed by fear, panic or anxiety about perfection, acceptance and rightness. If it is there, it is right.

Neptune fits along with its Libran companion, Saturn, in a conjunction to Saturn's nodal axis. A balancing act with the rules of a male dominated, paternal society results. Not all of the social structure and relationship rules are wrong. Keep what is valid, discard what is not, and adopt new images and parameters to replace what was deleted. Perhaps it is the interpretation (Neptune). Perhaps it is drinking, or worse yet the psychological medication of personality disorder. Consider as a parallel analogue, a woman sedated by a doctor spouse into control and submission. Inspiration and creativity must be accepted by society at large. Art, love and creative prowess are what we live for; the pragmatic only provides the vehicle of support. Being physically patronized without being psychologically or emotionally patronized is the summation of this social tightrope which it is now her duty to explain. This must be done without a negative edge. Neptune makes specific contact to the midpoint of Pluto's nodal axis. Feminine goddess power emerges. She is indeed powerful and a goddess. Prior to age thirty-five, her absolute power intimidated the men in her life into efforts of control (fearing her dark seductiveness). But was it her seductiveness or their reaction to the essence of feminine power?

Examine the relationship of natal heliocentric Venus in Sagittarius sesquiquadrate to both the North Node of Neptune and the perihelion of Venus. The urgency of self-acceptance of women and the direction of the images of the feminine/spiritual to society as a whole are implied. Past life connections (Neptune's South Node) to powerful female societies are suggested. Fear of persecution—a witch's complex—for having and holding power emerge. These thoughts range from trite lack of acceptance to fear for her life when her power violates the masculine principle about her. The essence of the power teaches the need to influence without coercion, only coming from clarity of intent and purity of heart. The feminine power is transformed, healed and unstoppable.

The sextile of Mercury to the North Node of Saturn in Cancer provides a vehicle for using words in a nurturing, supportive manner. Mercury's mischievous trickery might even make those involved laugh at themselves to breathe and heal. Her words are funny, her images convoluted and comical, and the reality profound.

Chiron trines the North Node of Mercury, noting that the healing is hers (and of her age generation) for the talking, writing and expression. Speak up and be healed. How simple. How elegant!

A series of heliocentric midpoints makes conjunctions to the space contacts of planets. These are briefly summarized to add extra adjectives and adverbs into her purpose personality.

The Earth-Moon/Saturn midpoint connects with the perihelion of Pluto. No authority, regardless of how supportive and assisting it professes to be, can usurp her power. Sometimes being patronized is not worth the resignation of self. No hooks can be attached to support. No controls can be put on giving.

The Mars/Pluto midpoints embrace Saturn's nodal axis, reiterating another version of this same theme. You may love me, but don't even think about controlling me. I am my own authority. Accept me without changing me or telling me how great I'll be after transformation—or don't accept me.

The Earth-Moon/Pluto midpoint contacts by conjunction the perihelion of Jupiter. Knowledge is power. Knowledge is not a function of education. Knowledge is a factor of experience, learning and the insightfulness of inner voice. Perhaps, she would think, education is a conspiracy to create homogeneous thought in society. Instead, perhaps everyone should think individually.

The Mars/Jupiter intersection greets the North Node of Uranus in Gemini. Diversity of concept, knowledge and action allows for optimum changes. Action and thought require open response to all input in order to determine direction. Direction may not be set with pre-determined opinion. Rightness and wrongness become a personal issue and reaction to opinion intensifies. Healing in this configuration pulls off the above midpoint of knowledge and power. Justification is not required for that which feels right.

The divorce in this woman's life began at the transit of heliocentric Uranus conjunct Venus in late Sagittarius. The reality and completion of the divorce process followed as Saturn pushed over Venus to do the legal paperwork and fight about the money. Her husband left on January 20, 1988, with Uranus one degree separating from Venus, and Saturn three degrees away in application. As Saturn completed the conjunction, she was awarded a support and financial settlement, freeing (Sagittarius) her to manifest her female message (Venus, especially in the philosophical Sagittarius). Along a similar polarity axis, as Jupiter crossed in opposition from Gemini to that same Venus, in September, 1989, final plans to move to Los Angeles to pursue destiny formed and separated her from her past links and ties. Soon, Saturn, Uranus and Neptune will aspect the natal square of Uranus to Neptune and Saturn, squaring Chiron. At this point, beginning in February, 1990 (as Saturn forms a conjunction to Chiron), through May of 1996 (when Neptune squares Saturn, the last aspect of this pattern), at least fifteen manifestations of her destiny (one for each aspect of transiting Saturn, Uranus and Neptune to natal heliocentric Chiron, Uranus, Neptune and Saturn) occur to heal not only herself but the world.

The peak benefit of her words occurs in April, 1993, when a

major award for her work should be won (Pluto opposing Mercury's transmission source in Taurus). Money, honor and self-worth will prevail. The healing of expression at that point will be complete. Thus, the works after mid-1993 manifest with greater ease and sense of purpose than ever before.

This discussion is intended to be only a slight introduction to how the heliocentric interpretation integrates the soul and purpose oriented personality. The chart needs to be read from above an ego level and directed in the pursuit of one's highest good.

In this case we find a woman clearly defined on her path, headed towards destiny. On track and on target, much will be heard from this woman who has claimed her identity and purpose from family, society, heredity and the Universe.

Chapter Fourteen

Heliology

A major drawback that exists in virtually any system of astrological reference originates in the tendency to overlook the basis of the system. Traditional geocentric astrology tends to neglect the planet of reference, the Earth. Such an unfortunate oversight limits one's ability to perceive the true intent and purpose of the horoscope under examination. The intention behind this section of this treatise is to include the plane of reference of heliocentric astrology in order to ensure a total integration of the solar system in astrological considerations.

Helio refers to sun or solar influence and *ology* relates to the knowledge of that which precedes the suffix. Thus, heliology denotes the knowledge of the Sun. The Sun must be kept in mind as a source or causal force in order to manifest heliocentric astrology with insight and intelligence. Some basic views of the astrophysics of the Sun combined with astrological precepts will serve to round out the perception of an astrologer generating an accurate solar consciousness.

The Sun of the solar system in which the Earth exists falls into the category of a rather ordinary main sequence of stars. The star is further characterized by the fact that it is a quasi-periodic, magnetically variable star.

The solar experience of a person on the planet Earth, or any other plane for that matter, is one of historical nature. Earthbound observations of the Sun note events which resulted some 500 seconds before—roughly eight and a third minutes. The Earth and its inhabitants are subject to the solar effects of earlier events. Obviously, we receive the light and heat from the Sun on this planet in solar based orbit, but that is only a small part of the spectrum. The Earth is also bombarded by x-rays, ultraviolet (UV), infrared (IFR), magnetic fields and the solar wind.

The Sun consists of a core of nuclear energy much like a massive nuclear furnace. The core comprises about one-fourth of the solar radius and this furnace is the powerhouse and generating station of basic solar energy. The thermonuclear process pushes energy outward into the intermediate interior of the Sun. The nuclear energy proceeds through the intermediate interior, becoming diffused radiation. The diffused radiation continues until past the perimeter of the interior (which extends out to approximately eight six percent of the Sun's radius). The energy enters the turbulent convection zone, extending out to just 500 kilometers short of the whole of the solar radius. The convection zone, although occupying some thirty percent of the solar volume, only contains one to two percent of the solar mass (due to low surface density). The convection zone produces the super granular cells which account for the grain-like appearance of the Sun in many photographs and reinforces the theory that the Sun operates with a relatively cool photosphere.

The photosphere comprises the last 500 kilometers of the solar radius. This portion of the Sun allows for the escape of radiation and establishes the Sun's energy flow outward into space. This emitted energy takes the form of sound, gravity, and electro-magnetic radiation combined with the solar wind. These ejections, when combined with other surface effects of the Sun, contribute to the stimulation of the atmosphere of all planets in this solar system.

Synthesizing an array of solar information and theory, Robert W. Noyes, in his contribution *New Developments in Solar Research*, states:

> The weight of the evidence, plus other data relating to coronal holes to times of high geomagnetic activity (known to be related to solar wind fluctuations), strongly suggests that coronal holes do have a profound influence on the solar wind and therefore on geophysical phenomena.[1]

Noyes continues:

> The suggestion is particularly interesting because independent studies indicate circumstantial evidence for a relation between

---

Averett, Eugene H., Editor, *Frontiers of Astrophysics*, p. 69.

solar wind, related interplanetary magnetic field structures and terrestrial weather, in the sense that changes in the inter-planetary field are correlated with changes in the 'vorticity' of the earth's atmosphere (Wilcox, et al., 1974; Hines, 1974).[2]

The Sun demonstrates a bipolar magnetic field that reverses polarity every eleven years and completes polar shifts with a twenty-two and a half year periodicity. This magnetism affects the infamous solar phenomenon of sun spots. Sun spots are cold regions of the sur-face of the solar body varying the electrical current flows in the Sun. Every eleven years sun spots begin to peak in numbers, ranging to typically thirty degrees north and south of the solar equator. As time goes by, the number of sun spots declines and their height drops nearer to the equator. The sun spots nearly disappear by the end of the eleven years, awaiting the next magnetic shift to interrupt the heat distribution on the solar surface. E. W. Maunder, in 1904, plotted the sun spots with respect to solar latitude and time to derive a diagram which resembles a butterfly. The Maunder Butterfly has become an accepted representation of sun spot activity.

Other external solar phenomena are the chromosphere and corona. The chromosphere extends outward some 2,500 kilometers from the true solar radial surface. Dramatic jets originate in the chromo-sphere and are known as spicules. These jets thrust into the sur-rounding space at velocities of up to twenty kilometers per second.

The corona surrounds the chromosphere. It is the outermost extremity of the solar body and consists of optically thin gas (making it difficult to see in light of the chromosphere). The corona is visible during total solar eclipses when the other, brighter components of the Sun become obscured.

The reversal of the Sun's magnetic field maintains several subtle cycles worthy of note. These cycles further define the nature of solar dynamics. Studies done for the National Aeronautics and Space Administration suggest a solar-planetary coupling mechanism. This indicates that planetary cycles directly correlate into solar phenomena. These cycles modify the model of the Sun to include quadrapole magnetic characteristics and a rigid rotating core with a mean syn-odic rotation period of twenty-seven days.

The cycles originate due to the resonant sidereal periods of the inner planets and the synodic resonances of the four major planets

---

[2] Averett, Eugene H., *Op Cit.*

(Jupiter, Saturn, Uranus and Neptune). The inner planets create a cyclic dynamic of about 180 years.

As H. P. Sleeper, Jr. reports to NASA:

> ... it is anticipated that planetary gravitational or dynamic effects can produce sensible effects in the sun's chromosphere, which in turn have a significant effect on gravity waves in the photosphere.[3]

Earlier, in his introduction, Sleeper notes, "The galactic cosmic-ray intensity is correlated inversely with helio-magnetic fluctuations associated with the solar activity cycle."[4] He continues, "Finally, some recent information indicates that secular variations of the Earth's non-dipole magnetic field, changes in mean rotation rate, and active seismic periods may be correlated with the 22-year solar activity cycle."[5]

The resonances of the inner planets noted to be effective are:

46	sidereal periods of Mercury	11.079 yrs.
18	sidereal periods of Venus	11.074 yrs.
137	synodic revolutions of the Moon	11.077 yrs.
11	sidereal revolutions of the Earth	11.000 yrs.
6	sidereal revolutions of Mars	11.286 yrs.

Coronal holes constitute an area on the solar surface essentially void of x-ray emanation and appear to be relatively cool. Coronal holes offer contrast to other areas on the solar surface from which violent eruptions of energy and radiation plunge into space. These active regions represent rapid changes in the magnetic solar flux. Soft x-rays, SUV and UV radiation most typically result from these disruptions. Magnetic knots and x-ray loops often form with grotesque twisting patterns. Solar flares represent the most dramatic and violent of the solar ejections. The flares result from an acceleration of energy rapidly ejected and distributing electrons at nearly the speed of relativity (speeds approaching the velocity of light).

A condition known as metastability precedes the solar flare. Metastability exists when the magnetic field maintains the potential to retreat to a lower, more quiescent energy condition and does not

---

[3] Sleeper, H. P. Jr., *Planetary Resonances, Bi-Stable Oscillation Modes, and Solar Activity Cycles*, p. 2-1.

[4] *Ibid.*, p. 1-1.

[5] *Ibid.*, p. 1-1

stabilize. An anomalistic trigger appears on the scene and the surface explodes, sending electrons into space, swirling around the magnetic flux lines and generating gyrosynchrotron radiation that bombards the region with radio (microwave) frequencies. X-rays also fly from the flare, adding their intense vibrations to the event. Rapidly moving electrons known as Type III radio bursts penetrate successive layers in the atmosphere, exciting the surrounding particles. This action produces a "ringing" effect that oscillates through the atmosphere.

So it is that the Earth and all the other planets are not only subject to the obvious effects of sunlight and warmth, but also fall under the domain of the solar ejections. The solar wind strives to push the planets away from its body. Yet, the Sun *is* 99.8% of all the physical matter in the solar system. Subsequently, the Sun demonstrates more weight, gravitational influence and centeredness. The pull of the solar gravity grasps all the planets into its domain through the exertion of the gravitational influence. A push-pull effect develops, combining the natural solar forces of wind and gravity.

Solar energy, as viewed from the Earth, is totally ambiguous. The lower reception of solar life forces deprives regions of vitality, yielding cold, desolate waste lands. Conversely, the abundant reception of solar goodness burns out an area, generating a hot region of waste. A combination of several solar stimulations results in a vitality/survivability polarity.

Frank H. Shu, Professor of Astronomy at the University of California, Berkeley, points out several relevant considerations in his fabulous text, *The Physical Universe, An Introduction to Astronomy*. Shu states that it is the quantity and quality of solar emanation which creates the optimum living environment. Shu also notes that the Sun does not provide the absolute in energy to the Earth. If it did, the Earth would heat up with the continued reception of solar energy. In fact, the Earth returns one erg (a unit of energy measure) of IFR energy into space for each erg of sunshine received. Actually, the Earth sends back a bit more energy due to the hot core of the planet. A key point Shu makes is that the energy crisis is an inaccurate label. His suggestion is that it is not an energy crisis, but an entropy crisis.[6]

---

[6] Shu, Frank H., *The Physical Universe, An Introduction to Astronomy*.

Entropy is defined by the Random House Dictionary as:

1. (thermodynamics) a quantity, expressed as a function of the temperature pressure and density of a system that is a measure of the amount of energy unavailable for work during a natural process. For a system undergoing a spontaneous change, this quantity increases. 2. the measure of the frequency with which an event occurs within a system; measure of probability in a close or isolated system. 3. degree of sameness or similarity. 4. homogeneity, uniformity, or lack of distinction or differentiation.[7]

Shu's observations, as well as a synthesized blend of solar astronomy, create a dramatic foundation for compehending the ability of an individual on the planet Earth to transfer from the geocentric horoscope to the heliocentric horoscope. It is the conjecture in this book that the heliocentric horoscope will stand to be of little value until the owner of the horoscope has manifested a true solar consciousness or actually *becomes* his or her Sun sign. The natural preoccupation with the Sun sign perpetuated by the astrological newspaper syndications stands as an unconscious effort to focus attention on the will or vitality/survivability axis already established but withdrawn from awareness.

---

[7] Stein, Jess, Editor, *The Random House Dictionary of the English Language Unabridged Edition.*

Chapter Fifteen

Cycles

Most astrologers become aware of cycles at a very early point in their involvement with astrology. Recognition of the annual cycle of the solar return and the returns of Venus and Mercury occurring roughly once a year come with relative ease. Highly touted cycles such as the Jupiter/Saturn conjunction cycle of nearly twenty years also readily fit into early astrological awareness. Speculations of cycles and their effects are based upon a historical review of what types of events occurred in the past at the time of manifestation at the cyclic peaks.

Many problems exist during the typical analysis of cycles in astrology. Often astrologers speak in incredibly broad terms about cycles that maintain collective influences, relating the planetary configuration to an isolated individual or event. For instance, frequently an astrologer delineates the meaning of Saturn opposed Uranus in the chart of a well known personality while neglecting the fact that the aspect, within a reasonable orb, exists for many weeks and affects many people. This type of reference contributes to the accusations that astrology is an inexact system of personality analysis. It remains important under such conditions to retain a sense of the relationship of the frequency of occurrence and the duration of effect for any astrological influence.

So often astrologers lack the astronomical basics that give so much background information to the effects they seek to illuminate. The Mercury retrograde effect provides a clear example. Astrologers learn very quickly that Mercury goes into retrogression three times a year. Few astrologers consciously acknowledge the relative motion of the planet with respect to Earth, let alone the true source of the Mercury retrograde effect. Heliocentrically, within the true perspective of the solar system, Mercury always moves in a prograde direction. The effect of Mercury retrograde results because of the planet's inferior conjunction with the Earth. This effect results every 115.88 days. Comparing the geocentric observations of Mercury to the heliocentric observations, an astrologer sees that Mercury conjoins the Earth, heliocentrically, about halfway through the era of the infamous and dreaded Mercury retrograde. The entire meaning of the Mercury retrograde cycle undergoes a change with assistance from the heliocentric input. Mercury, in its true communication nature, strives, with added intent, to align with the Earth during Mercury retrograde. This suggests that collectively an additional emphasis on Earthly or mundane considerations prevails. Mercury conjunction to the Earth prevails upon cognitive understanding of the total spectrum of communication by both parties. Expression regarding values, priorities, economics, contribution (of the self to the whole) and negotiation seeks to be resolved. Mercury conjunct the Earth now bears a totally different concept than the backwards impressions yielded by geocentric notation. Do copy machines, typewriters and communication equipment break down under Mercury retrograde? Yes, they do. However, now we perceive that the breakdowns occur from overloads on those objects based upon the intensity of the existing communication drive in progress with the Earth and Mercury alignment.

The flavor of Venus retrograde also undergoes a similar transformation. This cycle occurs when Venus forms a similar inferior conjunction with the Earth. Mars, during its retrogradation period, also experiences an inferior conjunction of the Earth. Earthlings prefer to note this as Mars at greatest elongation. Geocentric observation sees this configuration as an opposition of the Sun and Mars, or heliocentrically, the Earth/Mars conjunction. The Mars effect—it feels like Mars is in a particular sign forever when retrograde—comes about within the Mars/Earth conjunction cycle or once every 780 days.

With an understanding of the true nature of astronomical effects, an astrologer's participation in geocentric astrology improves. Still, heliocentric analysis offers perceptions of astronomical correspondence which will induce higher levels of astrological acceptance. Correspondences in real life cycles result which fit neither return patterns nor the conjunction cycles (see Appendix E.) Those outside look at the discipline as failing to fit the models of nature and the order of the events upon the planet Earth. It is at this point that new systems of cycles enter upon the horizon.

Astrological researcher Thomas Shanks, following the innovative astrological work of Dr. Theodor Landschiedt, noted the effects of planetary cycles with respect to the Galactic Center (26 Sagittarius 38, epoch 1985)[1]. The theory is that the central point of revolution within the entire galactic structure maintains a profound effect upon the Sun and subsequently the entire solar system. Landschiedt suggests, through work strongly supported by statistics, that solar flare activity occurs with greater frequency when the Sun transits the hemisphere facing the Galactic Center, with the Galactic Center as midpoint. This midsection of the hemisphere would be the zodiacal longitude of the Galactic Center (Z or GC), or 26 Sagittarius 38 for 1985, with range out to ninety degrees either side beginning with 26 Virgo 38 and ending with 26 Pisces 38.

Landschiedt reports that the midpoint of Jupiter and Pluto with respect to his hemispheric demarcation yields a close correspondence to the successive appearance of flare activity. Such a midpoint is the arithmetic average of the longitudes of the two planets. The track of the midpoint will not occupy the hemisphere away from GC (the Gemini based side) but will return to repeat its effects when the midpoint reaches the separating square. This means that as a midpoint reaches the point of Pisces in the square, that the point flips sides, ending up at the Virgo square to GC, initiating the cycle again.

Prior to entering into an analysis of compound cycles to the GC, consider the simpler effect of a single planet transiting the Virgo midpoint through Sagittarius to Pisces hemisphere described by the centrality of Z. Jupiter's period of duration through this hemisphere would equal one half of its entire solar revolution interval. Since the revolution of Jupiter is 11.86 years, this period equals 11.86 years divided by two, or 5.93 years. Numerous mundane effects fit into a 5.93 year cycle, including pig iron prices, grouse population, and copper prices.[2]

Examination of the planetary conjunction cycles reveals no interval even close to this period. The listing below contains the half-

---

[1] Shanks, Thomas, *Journal of Geocosmic Research.*

[2] *Ibid.*

revolution period of all planets (allowing for the cyclic interpretation of the Galactic Center based hemisphere). Beginning and ending points of the cycle would be longitudinally determined from an ephemeris and must be figured into the cyclic considerations.

Planet	Half of Solar Revolution Period
Mercury	43.98 d
Venus	112.35 d
Earth (Sun)	182.65 d
Mars	343.50 d
Jupiter	5.93 y
Saturn	14.73 y
Uranus	42.01 y
Neptune	82.39 y
Pluto	124.21 y

The quarter cycles (one-fourth of the sidereal planetary period) and other numerical derivatives (1/8, etc.) may also be computed to reveal significant planetary periods.

Compound cycles such as the Jupiter/Pluto midpoint can be computed. Cycles involving more than two planets may also be calculated (as revealed in the equations provided by Shanks in his article.[3])

Consider some of the mundane effects taken for granted which represent the natural rhythm of cycles. Mercury, in its basic return cycle heliocentrically, provides such an example. The Mercury return occurs roughly every 88 days. This interval closely approximates three months and the nature of the Mercury return refers to the quarterly report. The 115.88 day period of the Mercury to Earth conjunction cycle bears correspondence in stock transactions. This usually stems from an announcement (Mercury) made by a company regarding an upcoming business plan (leaning into the Earth).

Women are dramatically aware of the cycles that are intrinsic in the solar system. Best known is the period of twenty-seven and a half days, the synodic period of the Moon. This cycle is downplayed a little in heliocentric analysis. It is replaced by the rotation of the solar core, which completes one rotation in 27.04 days.

---

[3] Shanks, Thomas, *Op Cit.*

Other cyclic phenomena: A major war cycle hinges upon an interval of roughly thirty-three years, close to the Saturn/Pluto conjunction cycle. Economists note that major swings in the political/ economic structure take place at intervals of about every fifty years, or one Chiron revolution about the Sun. Additionally, the fifty year cycle now refers to a point in life where many upper echelon managers find themselves without work. Job employment organizations now cater to such a grouping of individuals.

Division of cycles also take place. The famous seven year itch ties in with the energies of Saturn and more neatly with Uranus. The curse of a broken mirror also fits this pattern. Although not scientific in nature, these correspondences imply a collective primal awareness of the natural resonance of cycles.

The overlay of cycles must also be considered. Many possible combinations of planetary resonances can be computed by relating the synodic and sidereal periods of planets with respect to one another. The conclusions of the previous chapters on planets carried the natural resonances of the blends of planetary combinations and the relationship back to the source, the Sun.

To refresh you on the definitions: a sidereal period refers to the repetition of a planetary cycle to the same point (referenced to the "fixed" stars); the synodic period is a conjunction cycle between two (or more) astronomical entities. Synodic relationships can be described between any two objects in the solar system regardless of the intimacy of their relationship. The synodic meaning of the Earth/ Moon pairing obviously maintains a level of astrological significance, as does the Jupiter/Saturn conjunction cycle (due to the planet's size and gravitational dominance). The synodic period of Mercury and Pluto, may also be used irrespective of the apparent lack of symbiosis between the wanderers. The sidereal period, subsequently, represents more of a phasic nature and can infer the nature of development of the conditions contained within the meaning of the planet involved. Synodic relationships require integrative link-ups in delineation of the natural implications of the planets involved. The synodic relationship need not be restricted to a two planets. Synodic definitions of three, four or more planets compile the accumulated influences of the planets. Scott Sleeper astutely notes that the basic synodic or sidereal period may not complete the understanding of the planetary relationships.[4] Sleeper marked both synodic and side-

---

[4] Sleeper, H. P. Jr., *Op Cit.*, p. 2-4.

sidereal relationships based upon multiplicities of the prime intervals. It was in this manner that he managed to obtain the correspondences of planetary resonances to natural cycles of solar activity. A cursory consideration of cycles does not unlock the essence of the repetition.

The inner planets, obviously, determine the short period activity cycle of 11.08 years (plus or minus a time orb). The slower moving planets conform to a synodic norm though mild mathematical gymnastics: 178.55 years (also plus or minus a time orb).

Short Term Resonances (11.08 yrs.)

46 sidereal revolutions of Mercury	11.079 yrs. (tropical)
137 sidereal revolutions of Venus	11.074 yrs.
18 synodic revolutions of the Moon	11.077 yrs.
11 sidereal revolutions of Earth	11.000 yrs.
6 sidereal revolutions of Mars	11.286 yrs.[5]

Long Term Resonances (178.55 yrs.)

6 sidereal revolutions of Saturn	176.746 yrs.
18 sidereal revolutions of Jupiter	177.933 yrs.
9 synodic periods, Jupiter-Saturn	178.734 yrs.
14 synodic periods, Jupiter-Neptune	178.923 yrs
13 synodic periods, Jupiter-Uranus	179.562 yrs.
5 synodic periods, Saturn-Neptune	179.385 yrs.
4 synodic preiods, Saturn-Uranus	181.455 yrs.

With regard to the short term cycle, note that:

10 synodic periods, Earth-Mars	10.919 yrs.
40 synodic periods, Mercury-Mars	11.061 yrs.[6]

Also reported by Sleeper was a twenty-two year cycle concerning the reversal of the bi-stable magnetic polarity of the Sun.

The key point of this look at cycles is to remind astrologers that traditional astrological points of view in cyclic analysis may not suffice for requirements of modern understanding. The study of multiplicities of the sidereal and synodic periods of planets is in its comprehensive set of tables that sets out the synodic and sidereal

---

[5] Time orb = 1.02% or 10.808 yrs. to 11.132 yrs.

[6] These two figures were derived from Appendix B and were not included in the NASA report by Sleeper.

periods for each combination of whole number multiples up to twenty-five. Still, that effort would merely be the tip of the proverbial iceberg. The study required to apply cycles of this magnitude involves the cooperative commitment of virtually all astrologers involved in all levels of astrological application. The noble product of such work might be the publication of an encyclopedia of cyclic times, observed effects and cross-referenced correlations. Cycles may also be expanded into large magnitudes. An obvious cycle based upon the longitudinal precession of the Earth's equinoctal effect generates the transition of the great zodiacal ages. This effect runs roughly 26,000 years (with fine-tuned estimated figures of 25,868 years, 25,600 years, and 25,920). This approximate range generates an astrological age approximately every 2,160 years.

Perhaps an even greater cycle extends from the heliocentic extrapolation of this geocentric phenomenon. Consider the cycle of the Sun in space about the Galactic Center—approximately once every 250 million years. This produces a Solar Age of 20.833 million years. A Galactic Center based age moves one degree every 694,-433.33 years, a mere trifle of time in the cosmic scheme of things. Within a precessed age cycle of a mean 26,000 years, this means that 26.7 complete precession cycles transpire within a motion of one degree on the galactic plane!

Consider the microcosmic level of quantum physics. Do quarks, charm particles, mesons, besons and the like operate with cyclic regularity parallel to the extended macrocosm? Scientific studies striving to substantiate such things as biorhythms found that certain life forms respond dramatically to shifts in the environment that interrupt natural cycles. Could the subatomic realm be linked with these cyclic effects as well? Does DNA have a cycle? Does the splitting of an amoeba fit any given periodic regularity? Incisive interpretation of cycles and a subtle understanding of the innate rhythms of the universe on all scales might provide answers.

This treatise does not profess to provide hard core scientific substantiations for the ramifications of cycles. Phase relationships of all possible combinations must be considered for accurate understanding. This work only sets the stage for research to follow. The publication of this book begins a new cycle. The heliocentric model must continue to be unveiled. The use of cycles represents the most cogent means to that end.

Chapter Sixteen

Concluding Comments

The old equation set forth by ancient civilizations that the Sun equals God held forth in the times of Nicolas Copernicus. Copernicus was a Neoplatonist, following the quasi-theology set in motion by Plato. Copernicus also set forth a major paradigm shift in astronomical thought and theory, to which astrology has not yet adhered. For astrology to follow a natural evolution, for it even to survive, this shift of the perception paradigm must take place.

Astrological like-mindedness now ironically creates one of the major stumbling blocks. As long as support and congruency in thought in astrological models prevail, astrology will retain an archaic single model of geocentricism. Those pursuing the realm of heliocentric astrology will certainly for now lack the support of their peers. Astrology will persist within the stagnant thinking of the middle ages. Perhaps these are harsh words to direct at a system that works. Yes, geocentric astrology works. But without the widespread addition of a new heliocentric model, astrology may not reach optimum proportions. If we have the apparent viewpoint we must all have the true perspective. That which is apparent is relative. That which is relative depends upon something else. That which is dependent is subjective. That which is subjective is not objective. The veracity of the solar system is misunderstood.

Heliocentric astrology, as noted, supports the evolution and growth of the soul. Such evolution aligns in principle with the suggestion of an Age of Aquarius. Polarized through Leo and the Sun, Aquarius strives to shine forth in a new vehicle, in a new way of life.

Those who often refer to the end of the world, note the end of the world *as we know it*, not the complete obliteration of the planet. The implementation of heliocentric astrology on a widespread level suggests such an alteration. This new way of life brings the New Age. Knowing one's soul is an individualized contribution to the implementation of the New Age and to the collective evolution of humanity via the personal level. Each person discovering the heliocentric self moves the planet closer to the real time invocation of the Age of Aquarius.

Another asset of heliocentric astrology is that the system provides a second right answer. This second point of view of the nativity yields not a perception less accurate or more vague than another but an additional mechanism for discussing the nature of a given entity or event. This alternate point of view acts in an integrative manner rather than a confusing one. There is no double-bind. Rather, heliocentric astrology always provides a second level of consideration, creating choice and the understanding that life contains a series of answers. No longer must one perceive life as a condition of circumstances in which there is no choice. Actually the term *no choice* refers to a perception that only one choice exists. When a client says *no choice*, simply read the geocentric and heliocentric charts in tandem. (But do not mix components specific to each particular horoscopes).

The heliocentric horoscope offers a more universal point of view. A greater sense of purpose and individualized relevance of any person or event emerges from heliocentric observation. Principles known to work in astronomy, astrophysics and quantum physics fit more effectively and fluidly into the heliocentric system. A widespread use of heliocentricism should grab the lackadaisical attention of the scientific community. Heliocentric astrology works toward re-integration of astrological and scientific groups.

So now is the time for re-integrating into the mainstream of the Universe. Now the resources exist to conduct effective and accurate heliocentric astrology through the computer and the publication of precise ephemerides. An astrologer unwilling to examine the dimension of heliocentrics must offer a different reason other than a lack of resources. Now is the time for the initial investigation of heliocentric astrology to gain momentum. It may not be that the system will click-on in the collective astrological mind. But heliocentricism stands to be the astrology of the future. Perhaps Pluto at perihelion in 1989 induced a majority to integrate the heliocentric model.

Truly, in the solar light of heliocentric astrology, the use or non-use of the system will always remain an issue of individual choice. So, now with the basics considered, the rest is up to you.

Appendix A

Heliocentric Horoscope Example Calculation

It is assumed that the reader has never calculated a heliocentric horoscope. Although the heliocentric ephemeris operates in the same manner as its geocentric counterpart, some differences do exist. Most notably, the planets Jupiter through Pluto appear in five day intervals instead of daily. Astrologers will find that logarithmic ratio extrapolation functions with great ease in the interpolation of a planet within a five day period.

First, the selection of the time and date (and to a lesser degree location) enters into erecting a heliocentric horoscope. To set a time/ space relationship for an example chart in the spirit of exactitude, the U.S. Naval Observatory clock was employed. The call took place at 16:21:05 EST, December 19, 1983. The point of origin of the call was Massapequa Park, New York. The U.S. Naval observatory cesium (atomic) clock can be called for the nominal fee of fifty cents at (900) 410-TIME (8463). Or call Coordinated Universal Time at (303) 499-7111; time is stated once each minute, with ticks for seconds in between until the next minute. These time sources give much higher levels of accuracy for those working with great precision.

Next comes the calculation of the intervals of time differential from the reference point of the ephemeris. The planets Mercury through Mars are referenced daily (to midnight GMT). Jupiter through Pluto appear in five day increments (also referenced to midnight GMT). A calculator with a memory capacity will help greatly in this process.

The daily time interval represents the time into the day, GMT, for the time of the horoscope under construction, in terms of a decimal percentage of the whole. This ratio is best determined working only with minutes. One day of twenty-four hours contains 1440 minutes (24 hrs. x 60 min./hr.). This establishes the denominator of all daily ratios. It is the decimal percentage of 1440 that we seek. The numerator comes from the GMT in minutes.

Per our horoscope example, based upon the corrected time to GMT:

Step 1. Determine GMT by adding EST time correction:

$$16:21:05$$
$$+ \quad 5:00:00 \quad \text{EST correction to GMT}$$
$$21:21:05 \quad \text{GMT}$$

Step 2. Convert this figure to minutes:

  a. Multiply hours by 60 min./hr.:

$$21 \text{ hrs.}$$
$$\times \quad 60 \text{ min./hr.}$$
$$1260 \text{ min.}$$

$$1260 \text{ min.}$$
$$+ \quad 21 \text{ min.}$$
$$1281 \text{ min.}$$

  b. Divide sec. by 60 sec./min.:

$$\frac{05 \text{ sec.}}{60 \text{ sec./min.}} = .083 \text{ min. (60 sec./min.)}$$

  c. Add hours and seconds converted to minutes:

$$1281 \text{ min.}$$
$$+ \quad 0.083 \text{ min.}$$
$$1281.083 \text{ min.}$$

Step 3. Determine this figure's percentage of 1440:

$$\frac{1281.083 \text{ min.}}{1440 \quad \text{min.}} =$$

Answer: $0.8896409 = t_1$

The ratio t_1 represents the time interval of the day referenced to GMT for midnight. This instance relates that the day had elapsed through a portion of 0.8896409 (where 1.0 is 100%). Store this figure in the memory of a calculator for use on the planets Mercury through Mars.

The second time ratio to be established is the interval of a five-day ephemeris reference period. The ephemeris in December of 1983 uses the dates December 17 and December 22. Our period of reference here, up to December 19, contains two full twenty-four hour intervals plus the daily portion calculated above. The following calculation (t_1) merely contains the new reference sum in minutes divided by the new reference interval in minutes.

Step 1. Determine number of minutes into five-day ephemeris reference period.

December 17:	1440	min.
December 18:	1440	min.
December 19 (portion): +	1281.083	min.
Total:	4161.083	min.

Step 2. Determine number of minutes in entire five-day period:

$$\begin{array}{r} 1440 \\ \times \quad 5 \\ \hline 7200 \text{ min.} \end{array}$$

Step 3. Determine the percentage (portion) of the five-day reference period for December 19, 1983, 16:21:05 EST:

$$\frac{4161.083 \text{ min.}}{7200 \quad \text{min.}} = 0.5779281 = t_2$$

Store the figure t_2 in calculator memory for the figuring of the longitudes of Jupiter through Pluto. The individual planets may now be calculated with relative ease. For each planet the following procedure is used.

1) Store t_1 or t_2 in the memory of the calculator.
2) Subtract the zodiacal longitudes for the day of calculation from that of the *following* day.

3) Convert the difference into minutes. Multiply by the stored time differential (figure in calculator memory); convert back to degrees and minutes if necessary.

4) Add this figure to the lesser of the zodiacal longitudes. This figure corresponds to the ephemeris longitude for the date of the chart. Example planetary calculations follow for t_1 and t_2:

t_1 *Example.* Subtract ephemeris position for date of event from position for following day:

$$
\begin{array}{ll}
\text{Mercury:} & \quad 29 \text{ Aries } 40 \quad (12/20) \\
& \underline{-\ 24 \text{ Aries } 07} \quad (12/19) \\
& \qquad 5° \qquad 33' \quad \text{longitude difference}
\end{array}
$$

Multiply degrees by 60 to obtain minutes (60 min./ degree)

$$5 \times 60 = 300$$

Add minutes:

$$300 + 33 = 333 \text{ minutes daily interval}$$

Multiply by t_1, portion of day

$$
\begin{array}{r}
333 \\
\times\ 0.8896409 \\
\hline
296.25041
\end{array}
$$

Divide by 60 min./° to determine degrees:

$$\frac{296.25041 \text{ min.}}{60 \quad \text{min./°}} = 4.938°$$

Convert decimal to minutes (60 min./°), multiplying by 60:

$$
\begin{array}{r}
0.938 \\
\times\ 60 \text{ min./°} \\
\hline
56.28 \text{ min. or, rounding off, 56 min.}
\end{array}
$$

Mercury moved 4° 56′ in the interval of the event-day, so

$$
\begin{array}{r}
24 \text{ Aries } 07 \\
+\ \ 4 \qquad 56 \\
\hline
\end{array}
$$

28 Aries 63, or 29 Aries 03 is Mercury's exact position.

t₂ Example. Subtract ephemeris position for date of event from position for following day:

    Jupiter: 22 Sagittarius 33.9 (12/22)

            −22 Sagittarius 09.8 (12/17)

              0°   24.1′

Multiply by t_2, portion of day:

  24.1′

×   0.5779281

   13.93′ = 13.9′ (rounding off).

Add to ephemeris position of event-day:

22 Sagittarius 09.8

+   13.9

22 Sagittarius 22.7 = 22 Sagittarius 23, exact Jupiter position for the event.

Appendix B

Kepler's Laws of Planetary Motion

Johannes Kepler (January 7, 1572, 2:30 pm LMT, Weil Der Stadt, Germany), the German astronomer who followed the works of Copernicus and was in communication with both Galileo and Tycho Brahe regarding heliocentricism, contributed some of the first tangibility to heliocentric perception. Kepler's contributions include his three laws of planetary motion. These laws still apply with great accuracy today and serve to open the gates to clear understanding of how the Earth exists in a heliocentric solar system in the first place. Reach back into your memory banks to high school science to recall and review these laws of planetary motion.

The First Law: A planetary orbit is an ellipse with the Sun at one of its foci (plural of focus). Refer to Figure One and note the squashed circular shape of the ellipse. The position of the Sun is a focus point for the equation describing the ellipse; the other focus point results from the same relationship to aphelion that the Sun has to perihelion.

The Second Law: A straught line from the Sun to a planet will sweep out equal areas in space in equal periods of time as the planet travels through its orbit. Or stated more formally, the radius vector (RV) of a planet in elliptical orbit sweeps out equal areas in equal periods of time. Refer to Figure Two on page 194. For example, if the time of planetary motion is the same between point 1 and point 2 as between point 2 to point 3, then the shaded areas described by the RVs of these two motions are equal in size.

The Third Law: For all planets, the ratio of the cube of a planet's average distance from the Sun to the square of the time it takes that planet to complete one revolution of the Sun is the same. So, if

r = average distance from the Sun, and

p = period (time to complete one revolution)

$$\frac{(r_1)^3}{(p_1)^2} \quad = \quad \frac{(r_2)^3}{(p_2)^2} \quad = \quad \frac{(r_3)^3}{(p_3)^2} \quad = \quad \text{etc.}$$

Planet 1 **Planet 2** **Planet 3**

For instance, the arbitrary period (p) of the Earth is 1 year, with a mean radius (r) of 1 AU (astronomical unit). Mars has a period of 1.88 yrs. and a mean radius of 1.52 AU. Inserting the adjusted cubes and squares into the equation (where Earth = Planet 1 and Mars = Planet 2):

$$\frac{1^3}{1^2} \quad = \quad \frac{1.52^3}{1.88^2}$$

Is that true? Here's how it works out. The left side works out to 1. The right side works out to:

$$\frac{3.511808}{3.5344}, \text{ or}$$

.9936079—very close to 1.

Although a minor discrepancy may result, the equation is purposeful for calculating planetary characteristics that would otherwise have been unknown in the time of Kepler.

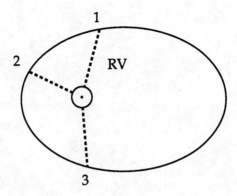

Figure 1. An Elliptical Orbit

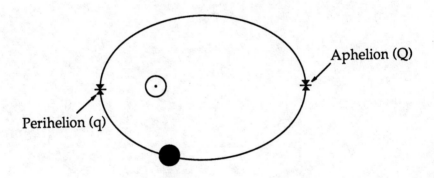

Figure 2. Kepler's Second Law

Appendix C

An Introduction to
The American Heliocentric Ephemeris, 1901-2000
(compiled, programmed and copyright by Neil F. Michelsen, d. 1990)
(printed courtesy of ACS Publications)

by Robert Hand*

Why this Ephemeris?

Heliocentric planetary positions are those determined using the *heliocenter*, or Sun's center, as the point of observation. That is, a heliocentric chart reveals how the planets are arranged as viewed from the Sun. In contrast, the majority of astrology (and thus of astrological references) is *geocentric*, or viewed from the center of the Earth.

Yet, of all the astrological research conducted over the last 30 years, heliocentric astrology has been one of the most fruitful in demonstrating a correlation between celestial and terrestrial phenomena. Evidence exists, with various degrees of reliability, showing the potentially great value of heliocentric astrology not only in natal (behavioral) analysis, but also in predictions of mass uprisings, or geophysical phenomena such as radio interference and weather conditions, of stock market and other economic fluctuations, etc.

This ephemeris was created in response to a major demand from the astrological community for a complete heliocentric ephemeris, to allow more detailed and extensive research into this promising area. Previously there have been few sources for this information. Computer firms such as Astro Computing Services have made heliocentric horoscopes available for some time now. Otherwise, one was generally limited to government ephemerides, such as *The American*

---

* *Editor's Note:* Hand's piece stands on its own merits as quite a bit more than a simple "apology" for a ground-breaking astrological system and the ephemeris specific to it. This essay is remarkable as a biographical statement of the genesis of Michelsen's important work and also as a statement from one of this century's very best astrologers of the uses and importance of the heliocentric system.

JANUARY 1901

DAY	☿ LONG	☿ LAT	♀ LONG	♀ LAT	⊕ LONG	♂ LONG	♂ LAT
	° '	° '	° '	° '	° '	° '	° '
1 Tu	0♐56	1S41	29♎11	2N28	9♋55	9♌59	1N50
2 W	3 43	2 0	0♏47	2 24	10 56	10 26	1 50
3 Th	6 29	2 20	2 24	2 20	11 57	10 53	1 50
4 F	9 14	2 39	4 0	2 16	12 58	11 19	1 50
5 S	11 59	2 57	5 36	2 11	13 59	11 46	1 50
6 Su	14 44	3 15	7 12	2 7	15 0	12 13	1 50
7 M	17 28	3 33	8 48	2 3	16 2	12 39	1 50
8 Tu	20 13	3 50	10 25	1 58	17 3	13 6	1 50
9 W	22 58	4 7	12 1	1 53	18 4	13 32	1 51
10 Th	25 44	4 23	13 37	1 49	19 5	13 59	1 51
11 F	28 31	4 38	15 13	1 44	20 6	14 25	1 51
12 S	1♑19	4 53	16 49	1 39	21 7	14 52	1 51
13 Su	4 8	5 8	18 24	1 34	22 8	15 18	1 51
14 M	6 59	5 22	20 0	1 29	23 9	15 45	1 51
15 Tu	9 51	5 35	21 36	1 24	24 11	16 11	1 51
16 W	12 45	5 47	23 12	1 18	25 12	16 38	1 51
17 Th	15 42	5 59	24 47	1 13	26 13	17 4	1 51
18 F	18 41	6 10	26 23	1 8	27 14	17 31	1 51
19 S	21 42	6 20	27 59	1 2	28 15	17 57	1 51
20 Su	24 46	6 29	29 34	0 57	29 16	18 24	1 51
21 M	27 54	6 37	1♐10	0 51	0♌17	18 50	1 51
22 Tu	1♒ 5	6 44	2 45	0 46	1 18	19 16	1 51
23 W	4 20	6 50	4 21	0 40	2 19	19 43	1 51
24 Th	7 39	6 54	5 56	0 35	3 20	20 9	1 51
25 F	11 2	6 58	7 32	0 29	4 21	20 35	1 51
26 S	14 30	7 0	9 7	0 24	5 22	21 2	1 51
27 Su	18 3	7 0	10 42	0 18	6 23	21 28	1 51
28 M	21 41	6 59	12 18	0 12	7 24	21 55	1 51
29 Tu	25 25	6 56	13 53	0 7	8 25	22 21	1 51
30 W	29 16	6 51	15 28	0 1	9 26	22 47	1 51
31 Th	3♓12	6S44	17♐ 3	0S 4	10♌27	23♌13	1N51

FEBRUARY 1901

DAY	☿ LONG	☿ LAT	♀ LONG	♀ LAT	⊕ LONG	♂ LONG	♂ LAT
	° '	° '	° '	° '	° '	° '	° '
1 F	7♓16	6S35	18♐39	0S10	11♌28	23♌40	1N51
2 S	11 27	6 23	20 14	0 16	12 29	24 6	1 51
3 Su	15 45	6 9	21 49	0 21	13 30	24 32	1 50
4 M	20 12	5 53	23 24	0 27	14 31	24 59	1 50
5 Tu	24 47	5 33	24 59	0 33	15 31	25 25	1 50
6 W	29 30	5 11	26 34	0 38	16 32	25 51	1 50
7 Th	4♈22	4 46	28 9	0 44	17 33	26 17	1 50
8 F	9 23	4 18	29 44	0 49	18 34	26 44	1 50
9 S	14 33	3 47	1♑19	0 55	19 34	27 10	1 50
10 Su	19 53	3 13	2 54	1 0	20 35	27 36	1 50
11 M	25 21	2 37	4 29	1 5	21 36	28 2	1 50
12 Tu	0♉58	1 58	6 4	1 11	22 36	28 29	1 49
13 W	6 44	1 16	7 39	1 16	23 37	28 55	1 49
14 Th	12 37	0 33	9 14	1 21	24 38	29 21	1 49
15 F	18 38	0N11	10 49	1 26	25 38	29 47	1 49
16 S	24 45	0 56	12 24	1 31	26 39	0♍14	1 49
17 Su	0♊56	1 41	13 58	1 36	27 39	0 40	1 49
18 M	7 12	2 25	15 33	1 41	28 40	1 6	1 48
19 Tu	13 30	3 7	17 8	1 46	29 41	1 32	1 48
20 W	19 50	3 48	18 43	1 51	0♍41	1 58	1 48
21 Th	26 8	4 25	20 18	1 55	1 42	2 25	1 48
22 F	2♋25	4 59	21 53	2 0	2 42	2 51	1 48
23 S	8 39	5 29	23 28	2 5	3 42	3 17	1 47
24 Su	14 47	5 55	25 2	2 9	4 43	3 43	1 47
25 M	20 50	6 17	26 37	2 13	5 43	4 9	1 47
26 Tu	26 45	6 34	28 12	2 17	6 43	4 36	1 47
27 W	2♌33	6 47	29 47	2 21	7 44	5 2	1 47
28 Th	8♌12	6N55	1♒22	2S25	8♍44	5♍28	1N46

DAY	♃ LONG	♃ LAT	♄ LONG	♄ LAT	♅ LONG	♅ LAT	♆ LONG	♆ LAT	♇ LONG	♇ LAT
	° '	° '	° '	° '	° '	° '	° '	° '	° '	° '
1 Tu	23♐23.4	0N22	7♑29.7	0N40	13♐ 2.2	0N 0	27♊55.2	1S13	16♊44.9	9S21
6 Su	23 47.7	0 21	7 38.7	0 39	13 5.8	0 0	27 57.0	1 12	16 45.7	9 20
11 F	24 12.0	0 21	7 47.7	0 39	13 9.4	0 0	27 58.8	1 12	16 46.5	9 20
16 W	24 36.2	0 20	7 56.8	0 38	13 13.0	0 0	28 0.6	1 12	16 47.3	9 20
21 M	25 0.5	0 20	8 5.8	0 38	13 16.6	0 0	28 2.5	1 12	16 48.1	9 20
26 S	25 24.8	0 19	8 14.8	0 38	13 20.2	0 0	28 4.3	1 12	16 48.9	9 20
31 Th	25 49.2	0 19	8 23.8	0 37	13 23.7	0 0	28 6.1	1 12	16 49.8	9 19
5 Tu	26 13.5	0 18	8 32.9	0 37	13 27.3	0 0	28 7.9	1 12	16 50.6	9 19
10 Su	26 37.9	0 17	8 41.9	0 36	13 30.9	0 0	28 9.8	1 12	16 51.4	9 19
15 F	27 2.2	0 17	8 50.9	0 36	13 34.5	0S 0	28 11.6	1 12	16 52.2	9 19
20 W	27 26.6	0 16	8 59.9	0 36	13 38.1	0 0	28 13.4	1 12	16 53.0	9 19
25 M	27 51.0	0 16	9 9.0	0 35	13 41.6	0 0	28 15.2	1 12	16 53.8	9 18

☿a.462679	☿p.382759
♀ .722330	♀ .726364
⊕p.983202	⊕ .985418
♂ 1.65078	♂a 1.66289
♃ 5.27421	♃ 5.26337
♄ 10.0673	♄ 10.0663
♅ 19.0596	♅ 19.0652
♆ 29.8771	♆ 29.8777
♇ 46.8228	♇ 46.8110
☊	Perihelia
☿ 17°♉ 10	☿ 15°♊ 52
♀ 15 ♊ 48	♀ 10 ♌ 23
⊕	⊕ 11 ♋ 14
♂ 18 ♉ 48	♂ 4 ♓ 18
♃ 9 ♋ 27	♃ 12 ♈ 16
♄ 22 ♋ 49	♄ 1 ♋ 33
♅ 13 ♊ 34	♅ 26 ♍ 18
♆ 10 ♌ 43	♆ 13 ♈ 7
♇ 18 ♋ 52	♇ 13 ♏ 30

1	⊕⚺♂	3am14
T	♀ ♏	12pm14
2	♀⚼♇	2pm25
W	⊕ P	8 14
3	☿⚺♄	9am27
4	⊕⚻♅	2am30
F	☿△♂	9pm44
5	☿☌♅	9am41
6	⊕⚻☿	3am54
Su	♀⚹♄	6 43
	☿ A	8 52
	☿☍♇	5pm49
7	♀∠♃	1am 5
M	♂∠♆	4pm42
	⊕⚺♇	5 27
8	♂△♅	1am27
9	☿☌♃	9am31
W	♀⚼♆	2pm25
	♀⚺♅	4 58
10	♀□♂	7am40
Th	☿☍♆	7pm20
11	☿⚼♂	9am12
F	☿ ♑	12pm43
	♀⚻♇	11 32
12	☿∠♀	9am41
14	☿☌♄	7am40
15	⊕⚻♃	8am53
T	♀∠♄	8pm10
16	☿⚺♅	3am47
W	♂⚹♇	8 40
	♀⚺♃	10pm19
17	☿⚻♇	8am52
Th	☿⚻♂	1pm 2
18	⊕⚺♆	6pm45
19	⊕⚼♅	0am 3
S	♀⚻♆	0 45
	⊕△♀	11 17
20	☿⚺♃	1am13
Su	♀ ♐	6 26
	⊕ ♌	5pm15
21	☿⚻♆	1am 4
M	☿∠♅	2 52
	☿ ♒	3pm52
22	⊕☍☿	2am24
T	☿⚼♇	5 22
	⊕∠♇	11 50
23	☿⚹♀	0am14
24	☿⚺♄	3am54
Th	☿∠♃	6pm58
25	♀⚺♄	10am35
F	☿⚼♆	2pm10
	☿⚹♅	3 59
26	☿△♇	3pm44
28	☿☍♂	1am37
M	☿∠♄	10 34
	♀☌♅	4pm13
	⊕⚻♄	9 57
29	☿⚹♃	1am30
T	☿△♆	4pm46
30	☿ ♓	4am32
W	♀0S	4 55
	♀☍♇	8pm33
31	⊕⚼♃	9am27
Th	♂⚼♄	10 8
1	☿⚹♄	6am46
2	⊕⚻☿	7am37
S	☿□♅	11 6
	⊕∠♆	3pm 4
	⊕△♅	10 29
3	☿□♇	5am54
5	☿□♀	1am37
T	☿⚻♂	3 38
	☿□♃	7 34
	♀△♂	9 2
	☿□♆	5pm 9
	♀☌♃	7 49
6	☿ ♈	2am30
W	⊕⚹♇	7 22
	⊕⚼☿	12pm47
	♀☍♆	11 53
7	♂△♃	6am30
Th	☿□♄	8pm27
8	♀ ♑	4am 1
F	☿⚼♂	11 58
	☿△♅	7pm 9
9	☿⚹♇	10am26
10	⊕△☿	3am50
11	☿△♃	5am57
M	♂⚹♆	7 7
	☿⚹♆	12pm 7
	☿△♂	12 32
	☿⚼♅	1 39
	☿ ♉	7 53
12	☿∠♇	3am44
13	⊕⚼♄	4am10
W	☿△♀	5 9
	☿△♄	8 29
	♀☌♄	5pm38
	☿⚼♃	9 16
14	☿∠♆	2am17
Th	☿⚻♅	3 48
	⊕⚼♀	4pm44
	☿⚺♇	5 0
	♅0S	6 3
	☿ON	6 11
15	♂ ♍	11am34
F	☿⚼♄	8pm37
16	⊕□☿	8am52
S	☿⚻♃	9 22
	⊕△♃	12pm 9
	☿⚺♆	1 26
	☿⚼♀	1 50
	♀⚺♅	6 15
	☿ ♊	8 23
	☿□♂	10 51
17	⊕⚹♆	1pm 6
18	☿⚻♄	6am40
M	♀⚼♂	11 26
	♀⚻♇	8pm 7
19	☿☍♅	0am27
T	⊕ ♍	7 43
	☿ P	8 29
	☿☌♇	12pm50
	☿⚻♀	6 23
21	☿☍♃	5am21
Th	☿☌♆	7 59
	☿ ♋	2pm44
22	⊕⚹☿	1am17
F	☿⚹♂	1 46
	⊕☌♂	6 15
23	☿☍♄	1am44
S	☿⚻♅	7pm39
24	☿⚺♇	8am19
Su	☿∠♂	4pm47
	⊕∠☿	11 28
25	♂ A	7am27
M	♀⚺♃	7pm41
26	♀⚻♆	0am53
T	☿⚻♃	4 54
	☿⚺♆	6 11
	♀∠♅	7 43
	☿⚼♅	8 2
	☿☍♀	8 9
	☿ ♌	1pm22
	☿∠♇	9 18
27	♀ ♒	3am18
W	☿⚺♂	11 21
28	⊕⚺☿	2am50
Th	☿⚻♄	4 32
	♀⚼♇	8 14
	⊕△♄	12pm32
	☿⚼♃	9 42
	☿∠♆	10 11

Ephemeris & Nautical Almanac (renamed *The Astronomical Ephemeris* in 1981). This ephemeris, issued annually by the U.S. Naval Observatory, is relatively expensive, and extremely hard to locate for back years, large university or urban libraries often being the only source. For a time in the 1960s, Ebertin Verlag of West Germany issued annual heliocentric ephemerides which were inexpensive and relatively accessible; but there remained the problem of back and future years, and they are no longer in print.

More recently, Michael Erlewine, who has done considerable ground-breaking work in heliocentric astrology, has published a book titled *The Sun is Shining*, by means of which an astrologer can calculate heliocentric positions with the aid of a small calculator. Yet, while useful, it is not as convenient to use as a true ephemeris.

A few years ago, various groups including Astro-Graphics Services, Phenomena Publications and Matrix began to explore the possibilities of producing a full heliocentric ephemeris for the 20th century. After negotiations and fiscal adjustments, A.G.S. inherited the now scaled-down project and published a small edition of a ten-year helio ephemeris for the 1980s. This, unfortunately, was the limit of what the original planners could provide for the present.

With the increasing cry from astrologers for a more extensive helio ephemeris—a cry arising primarily from the publication of T. Patrick Davis' work on helio astrology, described below—I told Neil Michelsen in the fall of 1981 that if Astro Computing Services had the resources, interest and energy to produce a full heliocentric ephemeris, they should do so. The result is this present volume.

Use of Heliocentric Astrology

It should be said at the outset that heliocentric astrology is neither more nor less scientific than geocentric astrology. We should not use heliocentric astrology simply because it is based on a "more scientific" view of the Solar System. The fact that "standard" astrology has always been done from the geocentric perspective has always been one of the criticisms leveled at astrology by its critics; however, this is a completely specious argument. What concerns astrology is the experience of effects *upon the Earth*. It is therefore logical to look at the heavens from an Earth-centered perspective.

Based upon this point of view, one would be justified in asking why we should look at heliocentric astrology at all. In fact many astrologers have dismissed heliocentric astrology's effectiveness. But the answer to this challenge is simple: The Sun affects us more than any other celestial body, and we are, in fact, within the limits of the Sun's atmosphere, or *corona*. It's accurate, then, to say that while we are on the surface of the Earth, we are also within the direct sphere of influence of the Sun. (Compare this to an airplane in the upper reaches of the Earth's atmosphere. Wouldn't traditional, geocentric astrology consider it within the Earth's sphere of influence?)

One of the most powerful of the Sun's influences, outside of the daily radiation that heats the Earth, is the *solar wind*, a stream of particles coming from the surface of the Sun toward the Earth and other planets. These particles cause tremendous disturbances of the Earth's ionosphere. There are indications that they in turn are connected with particularly disturbed periods in Earth's history.

What should we use heliocentric astrology for? Many feel that it is most useful for mundane astrology and studying mass behavior, having little usefulness in individual natal astrology. But those of us who have studied the matter more extensively do not agree. Heliocentric positions are apparently useful for both mundane and personal astrology. A purely heliocentric astrology lacks some of the major factors that are found in geocentric astrology, such as the Moon, all of the houses, and the Lunar Nodes; and there are fewer differences among the heliocentric charts of individuals born on the same day than among the geocentric ones. But this does not alter the fact that heliocentric astrology is useful for the study of individuals.

We aren't suggesting that heliocentric charts be used *instead of* geocentric charts. The two systems of charting should be used together, at least for individual natal astrology. However, as we shall see, even though there are some factors of geocentric astrology that are missing in heliocentric astrology, there are also some factors which are unique to heliocentric astrology.

For example, in heliocentric astrology the planets Mercury and Venus are no longer tied to the position of the Sun (or Earth as it actually would be in heliocentric astrology). That is, Mercury is no longer restricted to a zone 28° either side of the Sun, nor Venus to a 48° elongation. Also, Mercury in particular moves very rapidly, more than 6° per day at times. And, while there are no house cusps or lunar nodes, there are planetary nodes and the Perihelia of the planets (points where the planets come closest to the Sun). Planetary nodes have been used geocentrically as well, but there are problems with their use in geocentric astrology. These problems are discussed below.

Contrasts of Types

Michael Erlewine has suggested that a personality typology can be derived from the comparison of dominant aspect patterns in the heliocentric chart with those in the geocentric chart. To take a simple example, one can compare the dominance of hard and soft aspects in the two charts. One might have a predominantly hard aspect chart heliocentrically, and a soft aspect chart geocentrically. This would produce a personality type that would be quite different from an individual that had a soft aspect chart heliocentrically and a hard aspect chart geocentrically. The first type (*helio hard/geo soft*) may have a great deal of inner turbulence and experience internal psychological crises, but have a relatively easy time handling the outside world. This could result in a rather energetic individual, though one who might have difficulty attaining inner peace. The second type (*helio soft/geo hard*) may be more tranquil internally, but might experience more difficulty dealing with the exterior world. This could be especially difficult because the lack of inner turbulence can also express itself as a lack of inner energy with which to face challenges from the outer world.

I do not mean to imply that geocentric astrology does not indicate psychological states; but these states are more often projected onto external circumstances than with heliocentric, or have a social dimension even when they are internal. In natal astrology, the heliocentric chart seems to describe the inward nature of the individual *with little reference to the changes brought on by encounters with the environment*. Such encounters, after all, are symbolized by the houses. It might be regarded as what the individual might be like if his or her development were solely the result of inner drives. This is not to say, though, that heliocentric astrology is more spiritual or esoteric than geocentric astrology. It is simply more internal. Nor does that mean less observable. For example, health and other physical problems seem to be shown more clearly and simply in heliocentric charts than in geocentric ones.

Socio-Political Responses

While on an individual basis heliocentric astrology seems to have a tendency to affect inward states most significantly, it also has a very powerful effect on mass behavior and is, therefore, extremely useful in mundane astrology, especially for predicting the likelihood of history-making events which are the result of spontaneous mass behavior rather than planned, intentional activity.

For example, a series of hard aspects between the planets, both inner and outer, seems to correlate with times when groups of individuals are likely to be disturbed. Riots tend to occur at such times and people in groups seem to be more irritable than usual. On the other hand, periods in which soft aspects prevail are times of low energy. People are calm and placid, and may even have difficulty staying awake long enough to get a job done.

Considerable work has been done relating heliocentric planetary aspects to disturbances on the surface of the Sun, most notably solar flares and sunspots. John Nelson, formerly of R.C.A., is particularly known for his work correlating disturbances in the Earth's ionosphere with heliocentric planetary positions. Ionospheric disturbances also are related to both sunspots and geomagnetic storms. Recent work by both Thomas Shanks and Geoffrey Dean has begun to call Nelson's work into question; however, there still seems to be some kind of connection between heliocentric planetary positions and solar events. The correlations may not be exactly the way that Nelson views them, but they appear to be real correlations nevertheless. Dean himself has noted a possible relationship between planetary declination on the solar equator and the formation of sunspots.

In my own work I have noted that periods of revolutionary activity, such as the American and French Revolutions, seem to come at the peaks of solar activity. In accordance with the principle cited above, revolutions seem to be the result of outbreaks of popular outrage, rather than the result of consciously planned activity. In contrast, wars which are usually *planned* by the agressor nations do not correlate with solar activity at all.

Mixing Media:
The Use of Heliocentric with Geocentric Positions

Several advocates of heliocentric astrology recently have begun to recommend the use of heliocentric positions along with geocentric positions in the standard geocentric chart. Premier among these has been T. Patrick Davis in her 1980 book, *Revolutionizing Astrology With Heliocentric*. According to this practice, one should look at the aspects that heliocentric planets form with geocentric planets as well as those formed with other heliocentric positions. House and sign positions of heliocentric positions are treated just as if they were geocentric. No real interpretic distinction is made between the two frameworks, except that there is an Earth as well as a Sun. Transits and progressions are made with both heliocentric and geocentric positions to both heliocentric and geocentric natal positions. The two coordinate systems are mixed in every possible way.

On the face of it, this seems to be an extremely implausible procedure, like adding apples and oranges. Yet there is a possible rationale. Refer to Figure 1. In this figure we have a schematic representation of *Venus heliocentrically* at 0° Aries, with the *geocentric Moon* also at

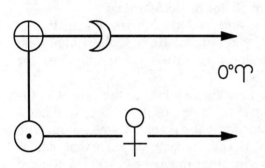

0° Aries. That is, the "line of sight" from the Sun toward Venus, and from the Earth toward the Moon, are both in the direction which we call 0° Aries. Connecting the Sun and Earth, we obtain a base line from which the Earth-Moon and Sun-Venus lines run. Note that the Earth-Moon line is parallel to the Sun-Venus line. Just possibly, it isn't important in astrology that placements or aspects be drawn from a single center. It's possible, perhaps, for there to be more than one center, such that aspects are formed by looking at the angular relationships between lines radiating from each center to the planets in question. This is possible, I say, but we need much more rigorous work than has been done so far in order to reach a sure decision.

However, while it may be plausible to mix two coordinate systems in this manner, I personally don't recommend it. It strikes me as far better to keep the two systems separate, and to discriminate between the two types of charts by finding for each a role that it plays in interpretation better than the other. The problem is that one is nearly doubling the number of factors in a single chart. Thus, it's not surprising that advocates of the mixed-coordinate school claim that their system explains phenomena that were not previously explainable. The more factors that we introduce into a single chart without differentiation, the greater the risk we run that the results are *chance* combinations without meaning. This same logic applies, incidentally to hypothetical planets, asteroids and other devices which increase the content of a chart.

Obviously any new factor or technique should be used if it consistently explains the previously unexplained with great accuracy. However, I am not convinced at this time that this is the case with the mixing of heliocentric and geocentric coordinates.

Having stated my opinion on the matter, I recommend finally that one should explore this matter for oneself and come to one's own conclusions. Davis' book, mentioned above, is the primary sourcebook for this theory of heliocentric astrology.

Some Techniques Peculiar to Heliocentric Astrology

Despite the lack of houses and the Moon, there are some factors which are either peculiar to heliocentric astrology, or are much less ambiguous when used in heliocentric astrology. Among these are *Perihelia* and *planetary nodes*.

Perihelia. Perihelia (plural of *Perihelion*) are the points in the orbits of the planets at which they come closest to the Sun. When a planet passes through its Perihelion it also reaches its maximum orbital speed. In John Nelson's work there is some evidence that planets have their maximum effects when they move the fastest. High speed enables the planet to make the maximum number of aspects in the minimum time. This idea is somewhat contradictory to conventional (geocentric) astrological methods in which a slow-moving planet is given more emphasis than a fast-moving one; yet, if a manifest phenomenon is the result of several critical energy points being reached in the shortest possible time (i.e., several hard aspects occurring in a short period), then the Nelson hypothesis makes sense. It's interesting to note that mundane astrologers in the 19th Century (as well as in modern times) have regarded approaches of the outer planets to their Perihelia to be very important, usually signifying crises in the offing.

Planetary Nodes. Most astrologers do not think of planetary nodes as being solely of relevance to heliocentric astrology. They are being used geocentrically by several astrologers, at least experimentally (see *The Node Book* by Zipporah Dobyns). But there are ambiguities in the use of planetary nodes geocentrically that one does not encounter in heliocentric astrology.

A geocentric node of a planet is normally defined as the geocentric position of the *point* in the planetary orbit where the planet crosses the plane of the Earth's orbit. For purposes of the helio-geo conversion, the nodal point is implicitly defined, therefore, as having the same distance from the Sun that the planet would have were it occupying that position in its orbit. From a strictly astronomical point of view this idea makes sense; but from an astrological point of view it can at least be questioned, in two ways.

First of all, one can take the position of Charles A. Jayne and Carl Payne Tobey that the nodes are not to be treated as points in an orbit with a definite distance from the Sun, but as *linear axes* formed by the intersection of the two orbital planes. It is a basic principle of geometry that two planes intersecting form *an infinite line of intersection*. If a node is in fact an axis, then it is an infinite line and, therefore, its geocentric and heliocentric longitudes are identical. Fixed star longitudes are an example of this phenomenon in that, except for a minute parallax correction, the geocentric and heliocentric longitudes are identical. This is because the distances of the fixed stars from our Solar System are so great that they can be treated *as if* they were infinite.

I personally do not know whether this redefinition of the planetary nodes is correct or not. I do know that persons who have investigated the matter have claimed that the heliocentric longitudes of the nodes work as well in the geocentric chart as in the heliocentric chart. It is obviously not a cut-and-dried issue.

A second problem in the use of geocentric planetary nodes I consider to be more serious. Looking at the planetary nodes from the point of view of the original definitions outlined above (i.e., as the geocentric positions of the nodal point on the planet's orbit), the node is apparently intended to be a place where there is an exchange of energy between the planet and the Earth. After all, the node is defined as a place where the planet crosses the Earth's orbit. If an interchange of energy is real, then this notion is not so much incorrect as incomplete. If a planetary orbit exchanges energy with the Earth by crossing the plane of the Earth's orbit, then there must also be an exchange of energy whenever the Earth crosses the plane of another planet's orbit. Heliocentrically, the planet's node upon the Earth's orbit and the Earth's node upon the planet's orbit line up exactly, so that there is no discrepancy. However, geocentrically there can be a tremendous difference between the two nodes, depending upon how far the Earth is in its orbit from its node upon the planet's orbital plane. Of course, when the Earth is on this node, the two nodes line up exactly. In my own chart, for instance, the Sun-Earth is on the nodes of Uranus such that the Uranus-on-Earth nodes perfectly coincide with the Earth-on-Uranus nodes. If we are going to continue to use geocentric nodes as originally defined above, we are then obliged, in my opinion, to double the number of nodes being considered so that we have not only the planet-Earth geocentric nodes, but also the Earth-planet geocentric nodes.

My main point, however, is that *all of these problems disappear when one uses heliocentric coordinates*. The nodes as defined conventionally line up with the Jayne/Tobey-defined nodes so that there is no discrepancy. The planet-Earth nodes and the Earth-planet nodes also line up so that there is only one set of planetary nodes for all occasions. Heliocentric astrology simplifies these matters completely.

Conclusions

Obviously in a short introduction such as this, one can only touch on a few of the issues that pertain to heliocentric astrology. I would like to conclude by making a plea. Geocentric astrological techniques are not so reliable that they should be taken as the paradigm for the study of heliocentric astrology. We are dealing here with something that is new and different, and should not be afraid to develop new methods to view it or work with it. We can use the old ideas from geocentric astrology as a guide, but no more than that.

Given this orientation, the greater emergence of heliocentric astrology at the present time can be the occasion for a rebirth of astrology as a whole, because the new insights that we get from it should feed back and affect the way in which we approach all of astrology.

Bibliography

Best, Simon, & Nick Kollerstrom, *Planting by the Moon 1982* (San Diego: Astro Computing Services, 1981).

Davis, T. Patrick, *Revolutionizing Astrology With Heliocentric* (Windemere, FL: Davis Research Reports, 1980).

Dean, Geoffrey, & Arthur Mather, *Recent Advances in Natal Astrology* (Subiaco, W. Australia: Analogic, 1977).

Erlewine, Michael & Margaret, and David Wilson, *Interface: Planetary Nodes* (Ann Arbor, MI: Heart Center/Circle Books Inc., 1976).

Landscheidt, Theodor, *Cosmic Cybernetics* (Aalen, Germany: Ebertin-Verlag, 1973).

Nelson, John H., *Cosmic Patterns* (Washington, DC: American Federation of Astrologers, 1974).

Nelson, John H., *The Propagation Wizard's Handbook* (Peterborough, NH: A 73 Publication, 1978).

Appendix D

Heliocentric Neptune's Perihelion Pattern, 1980-2000

Note: This is a visual representation of Neptune's rapid perihelion variance. Do not use this graph to figure Neptune's exact perihelion except at points given (for January 1st of each year). Perihelion positions for the "time" between the dots will not necessarily lie along the drawn curve. The purpose of this connect-the-dots rendering of a planetary phenomenon is for conceptual clarity only.

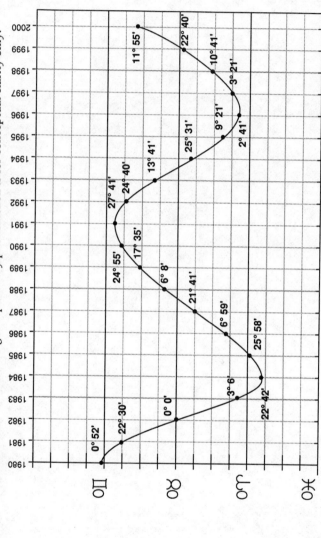

Appendix E

Frequency of Conjunctions:
Synodic Periods of Planetary Pairs

	☿	♀	⊕	♂	♃	♄	⚷	♅	♆
♀	144.65d								
⊕	115.88d	587.92d							
♂	100.93d	333.92d	779.94d						
♃	89.82d	236.99d	398.55d	816.44d					
♄	88.73d	229.49d	378.09d	733.86d	19.86y				
⚷	88.42d	227.47d	372.66d	714.71d	15.49y	70.50y			
♅	88.25d	226.36d	369.99d	708.74d	13.81y	45.36y	127.23y		
♆	88.13d	225.54d	367.49d	694.94d	12.91y	35.87y	73.02y	171.40y	
♇	88.08d	225.26d	366.73d	693.20d	12.46d	33.42y	63.54y	126.94y	489.42y

d = days
y = years
Calculations based upon mean orbital periods.

Bibliography

The Astro-Graphics Heliocentric Ephemeris 1981-1990. Astro-Graphics Services Inc., Box 28, Orleans, MA 02653, 1981.

Avertt, Eugene H., ed. *Frontiers of Astrophysics.* Smithsonian Institute Astrophysical Observatory, 1976.

Dean, Geoffrey. *Recent Advances in Natal Astrology, A Critical Review, 1900-1976.* Copyright, 1976, Geoffrey Dean.

Erlewine, Michael & Margaret. *Astrophysical Directions.* The Heart School of Astrology, Ann Arbor, MI, 1977. (Available from Matrix, 315 Marion, Big Rapids, MI.)

Erlewine, Michael & Margaret; Wilson, David. *Interface: Planetary Nodes.* Heart Center, Ann Arbor, MI, 1976.

Erlewine, Michael & Margaret. *The Sun Is Shining, Heliocentric Ephemerides, 1653-2050.* Heart Center, Ann Arbor, MI, 1975.

Heath, Sir Thomas. *Aristarchus of Samos, The Ancient Copernicus.* Dover Publications, Inc., New York, 1981.

Inglis, Stuart J. *Planets, Stars and Galaxies.* John Wiley & Sons, New York, 1972.

Kaufmann, William J. III. *Planets and Moons.* W. H. Freeman, San Francisco, CA, 1979.

Kuhn, Thomas S. *The Copernican Revolution, Planetary Astronomy in the Development of Western Thought.* Harvard University Press, Cambridge, MA, 1977.

Kuhn, Thomas S. *The Structure of Scientific Revolutions.* The University of Chicago Press, Chicago, IL, 1970.

Michelsen, Neil F. *The American Heliocentric Ephemeris of the 20th Century.* Astro Computing Services, San Diego, CA, 1982.

Nelson, John H. *Cosmic Patterns: Their Influences on Man and His Communication.* American Federation of Astrologers, Tempe, AZ, 1974.

Pannekock, A. *A History of Astronomy.* George Allen and Unwin, Ltd., London, 1961.

Ptolemy's Tetrabiblos. Symbols & Signs, North Hollywood, CA, 1976.

Rudhyar, Dane. *The Sun Is Also A Star.* E. P . Dutton and Co., Inc., New York, 1975.

Sanford, P. W. and Culhane, J. L. *X-Ray Astronomy.* Faber and Faber, Ltd., London, 1981.

Shanks, Thomas. *Terrestrial Cycles and Planetary Motion.* "Journal of Geocosmic Research," 2:1, NCGR, New York, 1976.

Shu, Frank L. *The Physical Universe, An Introduction to Astronomy.* University Science Books, Mill Valley, CA, 1982.

Sleeper, H. P., Jr. *Planetary Resonances, Bi-Stable Oscillations Modes, and Solar Activity Cycles.* National Aeronautics and Space Administration, NASA CR-2035, Washington, DC, 1972.

STAY IN TOUCH

On the following pages you will find listed, with their current prices, some of the books and tapes now available on related subjects. Your book dealer stocks most of these, and will stock new titles in the Llewellyn series as they become available. We urge your patronage.

However, to obtain our full catalog, to keep informed of new titles as they are released and to benefit from informative articles and helpful news, you are invited to write for our bi-monthly news magazine/catalog. A sample copy is free, and it will continue coming to you at no cost as long as you are an active mail customer. Or you may keep it coming for a full year with a donation of just $2.00 in U.S.A. ($7.00 for Canada & Mexico, $20.00 overseas, first class mail). Many bookstores also have *The Llewellyn New Times* available to their customers. Ask for it.

Stay in touch! In *The Llewellyn New Times'* pages you will find news and reviews of new books, tapes and services, announcements of meetings and seminars, articles helpful to our readers, news of authors, advertising of products and services, special money-making opportunities, and much more.

The Llewellyn New Times
P.O. Box 64383-Dept. 738, St. Paul, MN 55164-0383, U.S.A.

• • •

TO ORDER BOOKS AND TAPES

If your book dealer does not have the books and tapes described on the following pages readily available, you may order them direct from the publisher by sending full price in U.S. funds, plus $2.00 for postage and handling for the first book, and 50¢ for each additional book. There are no postage and handling charges for orders over $50. UPS Delivery: We ship UPS whenever possible. Delivery guaranteed. Provide your street address as UPS does not deliver to P.O. Boxes. UPS to Canada requires a $50 minimum order. Allow 4-6 weeks for delivery. Orders outside the U.S.A and Canada: Airmail—add retail price of book; add $5 for each non-book item (tapes, etc.); add $1 per item for surface mail.

FOR GROUP STUDY AND PURCHASE

Because there is a great deal of interest in group discussion and study of the subject matter of this book, we feel that we should encourage the adoption and use of this particular book by such groups by offering a special "quantity" price to group leaders or "agents."

Our Special Quantity Price for a minimum order of five copies of *The Sun at the Center* is $38.85 cash-with-order. This price includes postage and handling within the United States. Minnesota residents must add 6% sales tax. For additional quantities, please order in multiples of five. For Canadian and foreign orders, add postage and handling charges as above. Credit card (VISA, Master Card, American Express) orders are accepted. Charge card orders only may be phoned free ($15.00 minimum order) within the U.S.A. or Canada by dialing 1-800-THE MOON. Customer service calls dial 1-612-291-1970. Mail Orders to:

LLEWELLYN PUBLICATIONS
P.O. Box 64383-Dept. 738 / St. Paul, MN 55164-0383, U.S.A.

Do You Know Where Your Heliocentric Planets Are?

CHIRON
by Barbara Hand Clow

This new astrology book is about the most recently discovered planet, Chiron. This little-known planet was first sighted in 1977. It has an eccentric orbit, on a 50-51 year cycle between Saturn and Uranus. It brought farsightedness into astrology because Chiron is the *bridge to the outer planets*, Neptune and Pluto, from the inner ones.

The small but influential planet of Chiron reveals *how* the New Age Initiation will affect each one of us. Chiron is an Initiator, an Alchemist, a Healer, and a Spiritual Guide. For those who are astrologers, *Chiron* has more information than any other book about this planet.

Learn *why* Chiron rules Virgo and the Sixth House. Have the necessary information about Chiron in each house, in each sign, and how the aspects affect each person's chart.

Chiron is sure to become a best-selling, albeit controvesial, book in the astrological world. The influences of Chiron are an important new factor in understanding capabilities and potentials which we all have. Chiron rules: Healing with the hands, Healing with crystals, Initiation and Alchemy and Alteration of the body by Mind and Spirit. Chiron also rules Cartomancy and the Tarot reader. As such it is an especially vital resource for everyone who uses the Tarot.

0-87542-094-X, 320 pgs., 6 x 9, charts,softcover   **$9.95**

SPIRITUAL, METAPHYSICAL & NEW TRENDS IN MODERN ASTROLOGY
Edited by Joan McEvers

This is the first book in a new series offered by Llewellyn called the *New World Astrology Series*. Edited by well-known astrologer, lecturer and writer Joan McEvers, this book pulls together the latest thoughts by the best astrologers in the field of Spiritual Astrology.

She has put together this outstanding group with these informative and exciting topics.

- Gray Keen: Perspective: The Ethereal Conclusion.
- Marion D. March: Some Insights Into Esoteric Astrology.
- Kimberly McSherry: The Feminine Element of Astrology: Reframing the Darkness.
- Kathleen Burt: The Spiritual Rulers and Their Role in the Transformation.
- Shirley Lyons Meier: The Secrets Behind Carl Payne Tobey's Secondary Chart.
- Jeff Jawer: Astrodrama.
- Donna Van Toen: Alice Bailey Revisited.
- Philip Sedgwick: Galactic Studies.
- Myrna Lofthus: The Spiritual Programming Within a Natal Chart.
- Angel Thompson: Transformational Astrology.

0-87542-380-9, 288 pages, 5¼ x 8, softcover   **$9.95**

THE LLEWELLYN ANNUALS

Llewellyn's MOON SIGN BOOK: Approximately 400 pages of valuable information on gardening, fishing, weather, stock market forecasts, personal horoscopes, good planting dates, and general instructions for finding the best date to do just about anything! Articles by prominent forecasters and writers in the fields of gardening, astrology, politics, economics and cycles. This special almanac, different from any other, has been published annually since 1906. It's fun, informative and has been a great help to millions in their daily planning. **State year $4.95**

Llewellyn's SUN SIGN BOOK: Your personal horoscope for the entire year! All 12 signs are included in one handy book. Also included are forecasts, special feature articles, and an action guide for each sign. Monthly horoscopes are written by Gloria Star, author of *Optimum Child*, for your personal Sun Sign. Articles on a variety of subjects written by well-known astrologers from around the country. Much more than just a horoscope guide! Entertaining and fun the year round.

State year $4.95

Llewellyn's DAILY PLANETARY GUIDE and ASTROLOGER'S DATEBOOK: Includes all of the major daily aspects plus their exact times in Eastern and Pacific time zones, lunar phases, signs and voids plus their times, planetary motion, a monthly ephemeris, sunrise and sunset tables, special articles on the planets, signs, aspects, a business guide, planetary hours, rulerships, and much more. Large 5¼ × 8 format for more writing space, spiral bound to lay flat, address and phone listings, time zone conversion chart and blank horoscope chart. **State year $6.95**

Llewellyn's ASTROLOGICAL CALENDAR: Large wall calendar of 52 pages. Beautiful full color cover and color inside. Includes special feature articles by famous astrologers, introductory information on astrology. Lunar Gardening Guide, celestial phenomena for the year, a blank horoscope chart for your own chart data, and monthly date pages which include aspects, lunar information, planetary motion, ephemeris, personal forecasts, lucky dates, planting and fishing dates, and more. 10 x 13 size. Set in Central time, with conversion table for other time zones worldwide.

State year $8.95

Llewellyn's MAGICKAL ALMANAC
Edited by Ray Buckland
The Magickal Almanac examines some of the many forms that Magick can take, allowing the reader a peek behind a veil of secrecy into Egyptian, Shamanic, Wiccan and other traditions. The almanac pages for each month provide information important in the many aspects of working Magick: sunrise and sunset, phases and signs of the Moon, and festival dates, as well as the tarot card, herb, incense, color, and ingresses of the Sun and Moon associated with the particular day.

Articles addressing one form of Magick, with rituals the reader can easily follow, appear each month. An indispensable guide for all interested in the Magickal arts, *The Magickal Almanac* features writing by some of the most prominent authors in the field.

State year $9.95

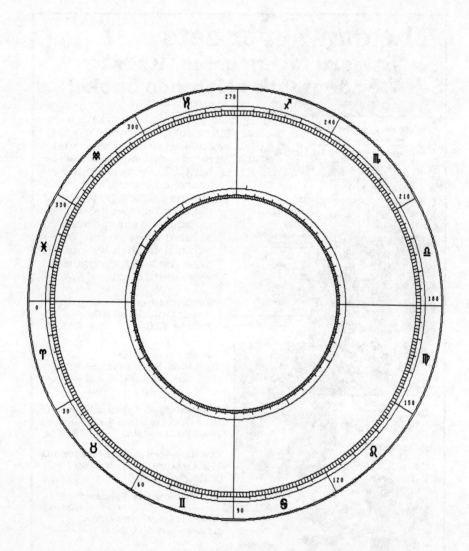